Returning to Sacred World

A Spiritual Toolkit for the Emerging Reality

First published by O-Books, 2010
O Books is an imprint of John Hunt Publishing Ltd., The Bothy, Deershot Lodge, Park Lane, Ropley,
Hants, SO24 0BE, UK
office1@o-books.net
www.o-books.net

Distribution in:	South Africa
	Stephan Phillips (pty) Ltd
UK and Europe	Email: orders@stephanphillips.com
Orca Book Services Ltd	Tel: 27 21 4489839 Telefax: 27 21 4479879
Home trade orders	
tradeorders@orcabookservices.co.uk	Text copyright Stephen Gray 2009
Tel: 01235 465521	
Fax: 01235 465555	ISBN: 978 1 84694 390 4
Export orders	
exportorders@orcabookservices.co.uk	
Tel: 01235 465516 or 01235 465517	
Fax: 01235 465555	
USA and Canada	Design: Tom Davies
NBN	
custserv@nbnbooks.com	All rights reserved. Except for brief quotations
Tel: 1 800 462 6420 Fax: 1 800 338 4550	in critical articles or reviews, no part of this
	book may be reproduced in any manner without
Australia and New Zealand	prior written permission from the publishers.
Brumby Books	
sales@brumbybooks.com.au	The rights of Stephen Gray as author have been
Tel: 61 3 9761 5535 Fax: 61 3 9761 7095	asserted in accordance with the Copyright,
	Designs and Patents Act 1988.
Far East (offices in Singapore, Thailand,	
Hong Kong, Taiwan)	A CIP catalogue record for this book is available
Pansing Distribution Pte Ltd	from the British Library.
kemal@pansing.com	
Tel: 65 6319 9939 Fax: 65 6462 5761	Printed by Digital Book Print

O Books operates a distinctive and ethical publishing philosophy in
all areas of its business, from its global network of authors to
production and worldwide distribution.

Returning to Sacred World

A Spiritual Toolkit for the Emerging Reality

Stephen Gray

BOOKS

Winchester, UK
Washington, USA

CONTENTS

Introduction

A delicate light had begun to filter through the canvas walls of the tipi. Another long and intense night of praying, singing and straight talk in the company of Grandfather Peyote was now easing almost imperceptibly into the early hours of a new day. There was a break in the proceedings while we sat silently around a nourishing fire. Faces were relaxed and glowing as a rare and exquisite stillness infused the atmosphere. In those few moments I felt the unmistakable presence of the peace that heals, the peace that opens the channels for love to flow through, and it struck me with great clarity that this is the primordial reality available to all us struggling souls. Beneath the complexity and confusion of human thinking, this is the spiritual home all hearts are crying out for.

To say the least, this is an unsettling time. Old ground is giving way almost by the day. There are sharp rifts in the encompassing and protecting membrane that holds consensual reality together. Many sensitives, mystics, and others for whom the barrier between the visible and the unseen is less than solid are feeling this movement intensely. Many are noticing how events have begun to tumble in upon one another more and more rapidly. Many of us are also seeing an increase in odd coincidences and synchronicities in our lives. Perhaps you who are reading these words now are finding your values and priorities shifting as old certainties come unanchored. You may even be in a new place you don't yet recognize. Many others don't want to acknowledge these changes at all and only hope that things will return to the way they were.

If you've been drawn to pick up this book, I suspect you know it only too well: we find ourselves not in the middle of an era, but standing at a unique and extremely challenging moment in the intersection where something old is passing away—some would say hastening to a fiery crash—and something new is not yet born. These "somethings" are more complex and vast than at any time in the known history of human existence, not least because over six billion of us have become linked in ways previously unimaginable. Times like these can look like chaos. Many have become discouraged or cynical and see no light ahead. We need hope. We need a vision that resonates with our deepest innate intelligence. These are times that call us to dig deep within ourselves, to rouse our greatest capacity to understand and manifest, to believe, as Bishop Desmond Tutu has said, in "the possibility of possibility."

According to Yogi Berra, baseball's accidental philosopher, "If you don't know where you're going, you might wind up somewhere else." If there was ever a need to know who we are and where we envision going, this is the time. The purpose of this book is to draw together powerful teachings and tools for awakening, to gather stories, quotes and anecdotes, ancient indigenous prophecies, and brilliant visions into a holistic, integrated view of our circumstances and possibilities at this momentous juncture on our dearly beloved and beleaguered planet.

Part 1 of *Returning to Sacred World* lays out the conceptual landscape for these ideas. Here's a brief summary of the basic principles under discussion. I take it as a starting point that humans dwell mostly in the continuing state of what Buddhists would call *samsara*: the egoic state of mind in which, on the most essential level, one doesn't know who one is and clings to the illusion of a separate self in a mute and inanimate universe. Following from that foundation, it's helpful to understand that there's been a historical development of that mindstate, most crucially among what are sometimes called the "dominator" cultures that have often determined the fate of much of the world. This historical condition of spiritual disconnection has led to a crisis, a nexus point where an increasingly rapid transformation process akin to a death/rebirth experience is unfolding on the planet. In these "far from equilibrium" conditions, the spiritual awakening of as many people as possible may be necessary to the survival of the human enterprise.

If the premise outlined above describes our predicament with any degree of accuracy, it's essential to understand that, as the wise ones keep reminding us, awakened heart is our unconditioned, natural state and is thus accessible, probably to a much greater extent than ever before. As well, there's a powerful vision afoot that this must be a time of great openness to information about the means to uncover this awakening, a time for dissolving fixed conceptual boundaries and limitations and feeling our way toward a new understanding.

There's a term (and idea) on the loose these days; "syncretism" or "syncretic," meaning to combine different religions, cultures and ways of thinking. If there is anything unique about the approach of this book in the marketplace of ideas, it's an attunement to syncretic perception, an intuition of a gathering and urgently needed synthesis of knowledge and practice from around the world. It looks like all those willing to keep their eyes open are now being drawn into a collective awakening journey. The message is that we are interconnected at levels much deeper than most of us have suspected.

One of the most significant pre-Columbian prophecies from the "New World" — reportedly known throughout the Andes of South America — is sometimes referred to as the prophecy of the Eagle and the Condor. It indicates that after a protracted period of wandering in the wilderness, disrespected and disregarded, wisdom carriers from the "four directions" of the planet are now rising up in clear purpose and determination to help heal the wounds and give birth to a new, sane stewardship of planet Earth.

Building on the foundation laid down in Part 1, Part 11 will move into a discussion of highly applicable teachings and concepts that I have winnowed from forty years of this syncretic spiritual journey of practice, study, and teaching. Buddhist teachings, with their brilliant understanding of the obstacles and possibilities in the human mind, will play a large role in this section of the book. These insights will be complemented in particular by what I've learned from years of active participation in indigenous spiritual work, especially through the peyote medicine prayer ceremonies of the Native American Church.

With regard to the means to uncover our naturally existing awakened hearts and clarify our vision, there exist many time-tested and powerful practices for healing, such as meditation and prayer. I've had extensive experience with those two practices in particular and I discuss them at length at the beginning of Part 111. However, at this crucial moment we may also need extremely direct medicines. There is a field of investigation that has been severely undervalued, wildly misrepresented, and largely hidden from public view. This "hidden" story is that mind-manifesting, spirit-infused plant teachers/healers/ medicines have played a significant role in the healing and awakening of a great many individuals and communities stretching from the earliest beginnings of human existence to the present moment. These gifts are here as allies in spiritual work for the courageous and the committed and as healing agents that ultimately should be much more available than they are in our current environment of ignorance and control.

Leonard Cohen, ancient bard and Zen monk of Boogie Street, wrote in his song *The Future* that, "the blizzard of the world has crossed the threshold, and it's overturned the order of the soul." My thesis on the provocative topic of plant wisdom is—and I'm far from alone in this view—first, that these are indeed extraordinary times calling for extraordinary measures and medicines; second, that these substances have been neglected and vilified for the same core reasons that indigenous wisdom, women's wisdom, Earth wisdom, and the authentic voice of living Spirit altogether have been suppressed, ignored and drowned out by the noise of the ego-encased mentality; and third, that we have offered to us a remarkable and severely underutilized set of tools that, if approached with knowledge, experience and care, and if combined with disciplined spiritual practice and right intention, have the potential to greatly deepen the awakening journey and reconnect many of us to the wisdom of the Earth- and Spirit-matrix in which we are embedded. The final five chapters of the book will explore in depth some of the most important and useful of these medicines.

Of course, these topics are not exactly the common currency of casual chat around the office cooler and a reader might wonder where this author gets off claiming authority on such ambitious subject matter. Please allow me to briefly introduce myself then. I'll confess right off the bat that as far as I know, I'm not enlightened (my wife would likely confirm that assessment.) Neither am I a leading authority in any one particular area of study or practice. My position is that of lifelong student, teacher, artist, hunter and gatherer, messenger and storyteller. My talent is in cultivating, harvesting and sifting good ideas from multiple sources, absorbing their nourishment wholeheartedly, and forming them into a holistic perspective. I move between worlds. I've traveled spiritual and healing pathways both deep and wide for the past forty years and *Returning to Sacred World* explores and clarifies important aspects of a number of them. I've followed my nose and by some combination of predilection and karma my path seems to have traversed somewhere clear of slavish, uncritical adherence to one particular method or "ism" on the one hand, and what my old Buddhist teacher called "spiritual shopping"—where no commitment is made—on the other hand. As well as all that, such authority as I may rightfully claim in writing about spiritual paths also comes from my credentials as a bona fide member of the "Mishap" and "Worst Horse is the Best Horse" lineages, (more on those in Chapter 12). Like many of us, I've duly noted and learned from seasons spent stumbling through the dark woods.

I've also been very fortunate to have encountered brilliant teachers of deep wisdom, both in person and through written works. Though in a weak moment I might confess I've been a hard nut to crack, I've listened well, read copiously, taken to heart teachings that made sense, and practiced with diligence and sincerity. I've learned a little about a lot of paths and lot about a few, and this particular route has led me to an intuition that my own syncretic journey parallels in important respects the planetary journey at this time. A gathering confluence of strains, ideas, and energies is building to the understanding that the planet is spiraling in toward connectedness in some complex and mysterious way. Some of the ancient, but still living, indigenous prophecies point to this coalescing, this joining of vision, intention and action from the four directions to heal the wounds of the world and bring about enlightened society.

A clarification or two may be in order. The information in this book is as true and reliable as I have been able to make it. However, a few of the names have been changed to protect privacy. Native American Church members, for example, are right to be very protective of a vision, a way of life, and a set of practices which have often been seriously threatened and which have required great courage and commitment to sustain.

It's also important to stress that in writing about entheogenic substances, some of which are not legally sanctioned in some or many countries, I'm not counseling anyone to break the law. In that regard, each person is responsible for his or her own choices. The purpose of this book is to assist in a shift of perspective toward an understanding of our predicament and a commitment to the healing and wisdom so badly needed now.

My intention and my prayer are that the ideas presented here provide a springboard for stimulating inspiration and passion to explore further. We all have to make our own discoveries and forge our own pathways and it's not my wish to twist anyone's arm into the shape of a dogma. These offerings are presented after long, careful consideration and extensive field testing. I can only hope that you who read this book will approach it with an open mind and heart, and in your particular way of understanding and acting, deepen and further your own awakening and that of our fellow planetary inhabitants. Our future may depend upon it.

Part 1

Darkness and Light
A world in transition

1

In the Time of Crisis and Transformation

Humans constitute the link between all the particles of the universe that crisscross and fill up space. Our ultimate horizon is not bounded by the visible world but dives deep into the sacred universe, into the unity and dynamism of a Great Whole of which only certain parts are visible. There is a submerged part of the iceberg waiting to be discovered and revisited. We are cosmic beings.[1]
Bernadette Rebienot,
Bwiti elder from Gabon

If it were possible, I'd boil the information in this book down to a few crisp reminders, things like: don't turn your head away; be open to all possibilities; learn how to settle your discursive mind; pay attention; keep breathing, keep letting go; and maybe most important of all, have confidence that we're capable of manifesting our best visions on this planet. The state of mind often referred to as *nowness* may be our only refuge during this time. It may also be the gateway to incredible information which puts life into a wholly new perspective. The current configuration is unraveling right before our eyes. The illusory separation of the individual from other humans, from nature, from Spirit, is a dysfunctional modality whose karma appears to have arrived at the nexus. To put it bluntly: the dominant worldview being acted out in the mainstream economic, political, and religious arenas of the world has run its course.

One can quibble about how long we have to take concerted action on radically revisioned priorities to get back into a life-sustaining balance on this planet—five, ten, twenty years . . . maybe—but I think you have to be in extreme denial not to understand that, taken into even the near future without such a paradigm shift, the human enterprise is headed toward a cliff. Even with no understanding of how deeply we've cut ourselves off from our native awakened natures, our "indigenous souls" as Martín Prechtel describes it, a pragmatist would look around and see that our current trajectory is completely unsustainable.

In *Secrets of the Talking Jaguar*—the story of his thirteen years of training and practice as a shaman and village leader in the Mayan town of Santiago Atitlan in the mountains of Guatemala— Prechtel wrote eloquently about how the traditional Maya of that region worked hard to honor, and as they said, give back to or feed those who feed us: the air, the earth, the water, the Creator. This, they said, is how we maintain life.

On these questions of basic survival, a rapidly growing congregation of intelligent, knowledgeable voices is speaking out around the world to draw people's attention to areas of primary concern: wanton greed and irresponsibility in the corporate world, obsessive consumerism, spiritual barrenness, lurking shortages of petroleum energy and of basic necessities like water and food, massive societal upheavals from diseases like AIDS, near exponential rates of species extinction, disruptive and disturbing climate-change probabilities. The list goes on, as anyone reading this book is mostly likely well aware.

So basic intelligence and intuition tell us that a change of vision and a change of heart are essential to our continued existence in any version that doesn't look like some kind of post-apocalyptic nightmare. Beyond that, if you take all these imminent possibilities—the climate changes and the insight that the collective karma of dysfunctional mindsets is coming home to roost—and entertain the possibility that the visions and prophecies of mystics, shamans, and indigenous people from around the world are not just the superstitions or wish-fulfillment fantasies of primitive minds—a different scenario unfolds.

> We have now reached the point where the masks are beginning to fall away and we are discovering that there is an angel within the monkey, struggling to get free. This is what the historical crisis is all about. I am very optimistic. I see it as a necessary chaos that will lead to a new and more attractive order.[2]
>
> *Terence McKenna*

My intention is to support the understanding that all these factors are coming together right now. To some it may seem depressing and frightening, but the basis for this view is actually a faith born of conviction in the potential of human beings to heal the outer and inner damage done, and to create and participate in the beauty that has been laid out for us as our destiny. It's also based on the understanding that when faced with crises, humans gain access to previously untapped, even unknown inner resources. "Necessity is the mother of invention" isn't just an old homily. This view is also based on some degree of confidence that, as Victor Hugo famously remarked "There's nothing more powerful than an idea whose time has come."

There's no dogma being laid down here and we won't be gathering in someone's backyard on a designated evening anticipating the arrival of the spacecraft which will whisk the enraptured believers away to a better world. No one I've ever met or heard about knows all the factors in play. What I'm inviting you to do is to consider the *possibility* that the conjunction of events that has brought us to this precipice is not simply random or accidental, but that perhaps events occur at their appointed hour when conditions have ripened fully.

You might, for example, ask if it's more than coincidence that all the geological and historical energies and events we see coming to a head are converging at the same time. Just as we humans appear to be stressing the carrying capacity of the planet and pushing her to the brink, we're on the cusp of a worldwide web of interconnectedness that can disseminate information and ideas to most of the planet more or less instantaneously. Might we actually be, at this precise moment in history, in the rudimentary stages of a developing oneness, a lifting of the veil that keeps us convinced of our separateness? Perhaps our technological "web" of connectedness is a child's toy, a vehicle with training wheels preparing channels in our minds for a later stage of maturity.

> In the beginner's mind there are many possibilities,
> but in the expert's mind there are few.[3]
> *Shunryu Suzuki Roshi*

Information is bubbling up from underground, from forgotten corners. It behooves us to pay attention, to maintain open minds about where the needed information is coming from and what it will look like. If our minds are fixed, if we already think we know where to look and where not to look, we can easily miss the guidance available. And difficult as it may be to conceive of, we shouldn't underestimate the potential for significant numbers of people to get it very quickly, to awaken to truths that are buried at the core of all of us, as in "Of course! Why didn't I see that before?"

Perhaps the reality of our oneness and interdependence with everything— taught by the Buddha twenty-five hundred years ago and experienced by people throughout history—becomes increasingly apparent, actually felt by more and more people as the realization sinks in that our separateness and its attendant struggles are no longer successful survival strategies and are rapidly destroying the place. Perhaps the letting go, the softening of hearts, the surrendering of aggression, the developing of trust that this requires come to be seen not as abstract concepts and distant ideals but as essential, and accessible, survival qualities. As a Buddhist friend recently put it, "When the going gets tough, the tough let go."

An image or metaphor comes to mind here. We as a species could be likened to an addict. Some addicts get the message and turn around before their lives are completely broken. Others need to have everything ripped away so that the choice truly becomes life or death. We may need to find our world broken before we're shocked into waking up to what's really going on here and come to understand what we need to do to heal ourselves and our planet. The question then of course becomes: Will enough of us make that choice and undertake that journey?

> Each one of us on earth at this time is being called to rebuild the sacred circle in ourselves.[4]
> *Dhyani Ywahoo,*
> *Cherokee*

Convergent Indigenous Prophecies

In what may seem a strange coincidence, there exist convergent prophecies from a significant number of indigenous groups that historically had no contact with each other. A number of these prophecies predicted a five-hundred-year period of materialism and imbalance, a long, dark night of the soul—from the spiritual point of view and especially from the vantage point of many indigenous societies. Those conditions would then begin to break down and open up to a dawning understanding that would have the potential to bring us back to Spirit-connected sanity. What follows is a discussion of some of the prophecies

I've encountered first-hand or via written testimony. Though my familiarity is mostly with those from the Americas, there are many more from around the planet and no doubt many that disappeared as oral cultures lost their continuity with the old stories. An indigenous elder whose life is devoted to the realization of the prayer for planetary healing told me that virtually every indigenous group around the planet that has maintained some continuity with the old stories has similar prophecies about this time.

It's important to note that the carriers of these prophecies generally withheld the information from a world they knew was not ready to receive it and would dismiss and denigrate it. It's only recently, during the past few decades, that the visions contained in these prophecies are being brought forth. There is a conviction and determination arising among healers, elders, visionaries and the "New People" all over the world, supported by the Spirit, to propagate and manifest this beautiful vision.

Before passing on some of this information, I want to briefly address the issue of prophecy itself. The concept is of course derided by rationalists and cynics. How can anyone see through a window into the future? To accept the possibility involves entertaining ideas about time that differ radically from the modern view. There's something mysterious going on and the way that most of us in these modern societies process linear time is seriously open to question.

Take for example the fact that there could never have been a beginning to life altogether, or maybe I should call it Spirit. Buddhist and other teachings speak of unconditioned, indestructible, eternal reality. The same applies to the possibility of an ending to existence. I get chills every time I contemplate it. And similarly with what we label space: if you were to point your finger up into the sky and imagine a straight line extending from it, where would it end? Could our conceptions of time and space be ultimately nothing more than mental constructs that reflect our deeply conditioned beliefs? The reality of the eternal now is an experience, an understanding, and a state of being that is alien to most of us, and yet appears to be the key and the gateway to a mysterious and incomprehensible possibility: that past, present, and future are not what we think they are, that they're elastic and intertwined in some essential way. Just as strange (as will be explored at more length in Chapter 14) from my own experience and from numerous accounts I've heard and read, it is indeed possible to exist, at least temporarily, in a state of timelessness. And then who knows what information, what visions may appear in the depths? Another Buddhist teaching says "Emptiness becomes luminosity."

How is it possible, for example, that Padmasambhava, who is said to have brought Buddhism to the Tibetans from India, could have written these lines in the eighth century?

When the iron bird flies and horses run on wheels,
The Tibetan people will be scattered like ants
across the face of the earth,
And the Dharma will come to the land of the red men.[5]

Strangely coincident and equally hermetic to the modern, rational, linear mind are the following lines attributed to the Hopi prophecies:

When the iron bird flies, the red-robed people of the East
who have lost their land will appear,
and the two brothers from across the great ocean will be reunited.[6]

In his preface to *The Mayan Calendar and the Transformation of Consciousness*, Carl Johan Calleman framed the issue of prophecy by stating that: "The key to understanding that prophecy is indeed possible lies in the recognition that human thinking is not

17

something that takes place "inside" the head of a person in isolation from the rest of the cosmos. Our thinking, and by consequence our actions as well, develop largely through resonance with an evolving cosmic consciousness mediated by the earth, whose various energy shifts are described by the Mayan calendar. Thus, we are all "channelers;" and, frankly, at least until now, we have been able to think for ourselves in only a very limited sense."[7]

Barbara Tedlock, in her book *The Woman in the Shaman's Body*, also had an interesting comment on the ability to foretell events. Her Native American grandmother Nohomis was Tedlock's link to the old teachings during her youth. Nohomis had visions of her granddaughter carrying on this knowledge and would teach her during their visits. "I still remember her explaining that our thoughts and emotions overlap and intermingle, and that this mixing of head and heart connects us to future events hidden in the dark womb of time."[8]

These prophecies have been passed down from generation to generation in indigenous cultures and communities that have been able to keep at least a small flame of their traditions alive. Some have coded the information in such places as wampum belts, carvings and rock paintings; others through the teaching stories that are often told by the grandparents to the grandchildren as is the practice in many North American tribes.

There is a similar prophecy among Native people of North America called the Seven Fires Prophecy. It's said that in the old days when the people lived in peace and fullness, seven prophets came to the Anishnabe people and left them with seven predictions.

In the time of the Seventh Fire, New People will emerge. They will retrace their steps to find what was left by the trail... The task of the New People will not be easy. If the New People will remain strong in their quest, the Water Drum of the

Midewiwin Lodge will again sound its voice. There will be a rebirth of the Anishnabe Nation and a rekindling of old flames. The Sacred Fire will again be lit.

It is this time that the light-skinned race will be given a choice between two roads. If they choose the right road, then the Seventh Fire will light the Eighth and final Fire, an eternal fire of peace, love, brotherhood and sisterhood. If the light-skinned race makes the wrong choice of the roads, then the destruction which they brought with them in coming to this country will come back at them and cause much suffering and death to all the Earth's people.[9]

One might envision this time of the Seventh Fire as the ripening of accumulated karma, the consequences of centuries of uninitiated, soulless behavior, being drawn vortex-like into fires of purification. Elders are saying that we are into this time of fire now and that much is at stake. This is a time when the collapse of apparently solid systems has created openings. There's great possibility in the air right now. And although I don't believe in focusing on worst-case possibilities, it must also be acknowledged that some are also saying that the window of opportunity available to shift priorities away from the material illusion may now be all but closed.

Scientists sometimes use the term "the tipping point" to describe systems that have reached a point of no return. Some have suggested that the tipping point for Earth as a system may not be far in the future, especially if there isn't a radical realignment of priorities in these next few years. In that scenario, elders have said that the only way to view the times coming is for us to get our relationship to Spirit straight, pay attention, and stay present in the face of whatever chaos may unfold.

Another prophecy, the Prophecy of the Eagle and the Condor, originates from the ancient Inca in South America. According to Incan spiritual messenger Willaru Huayta "The Incan prophecies say that now, in this age, when the eagle of the North and the condor of the South fly together, the Earth will awaken."[10]

The prophecy points to the joining of visionary energies from the four directions of the planet, and as I write this, signs of this worldwide confluence are appearing with increasing frequency. There are conferences taking place and associations being formed at meetings between highly regarded wisdom carriers from many different traditions. Shamans from ancient indigenous cultures are gathering with spiritual leaders from major religions to share their versions of this prayer and their teachings for liberation. The Dalai Lama, for example, has attended some of these summits side by side with shamans from places as far-flung as Ecuador and Nepal.

A vision held by some and shared with me by native American spiritual elder and visionary Kanucas, says that the "blizzard of the world"—the juggernaut of the modern machine—and the stability of living conditions in general, will experience a moment when all the neurons seem to have clicked into place and conditions of breakdown will spread more or less suddenly. During the lead-up to this moment, those inspired by and committed to the manifestation of the vision for planetary awakening are working at multiple levels to encourage and build the necessary links. According to this vision, there will be a kind of crossfade where, as the old world falls apart, something inexplicable will occur to manifest the prayer shared by initiated people from the four directions.

The Hopi Prophecy, from the Hopi ("Peaceful People") nation of the Four Corners region of the United States has been both passed down in stories through the generations and recorded in petroglyphs. One of the leading messengers of the Hopi Prophecy was Thomas Banyacya, who, for half a century until his death in 1999 traveled and spoke of these prophetic visions and warnings, including presentations he made to the United Nations in 1992 and 1993. Banyacya considered that opportunity to be a fulfillment of his life's work because the Hopi Prophecy had spoken about that body, calling it "the house of mica."

The Hopi Prophecy predicted, in stark and poetic detail, significant events of the past five hundred years, from the coming of the white-skinned men who "struck their enemies with thunder;" to the movement of "spinning wheels" across the continent; the arrival of a strange beast, resembling a buffalo, that would overrun the land; the land crossed by "snakes of iron" and crisscrossed by a giant spider's web and "rivers of stone;" the "gourd of ashes falling on the earth two times" (Hiroshima and Nagasaki); the sea turning black; and youth wearing long hair coming to learn the wisdom of the tribal nations.[11]

Another significant pointer aimed precisely at this moment comes from the stone-carved codices of the classical Maya from approximately the first millennium CE. There's been much scholarly interest in these codices and the few books that were written after the invasions of the Spanish in the sixteenth century, and this material is available for study in several books, including Carl Johan Calleman's 2004 treatise *The Mayan Calendar and the Transformation of Consciousness*. Greatly simplified, his thesis goes something like this: The Maya had accurate calendars that pre-date historical time. They broke time down into larger and smaller divisions. The Thirteenth Heaven is the last, approximately four-hundred year period of the Long Count which began in 3114 BCE and ends, essentially, on October 28, 2011, with some sort of resonance or wave that carries through to December 21, 2012. According to Calleman, the calendar suggests a sequence of events and shifting energies in the last few years of this Thirteenth Heaven that describes the breakdown of old systems and the beginning of a new era which will be more about telepathy and intuition than technology: "The frame of reference that is now emerging will simply not allow us to deny the existence of a living cosmos. If we do, there will be a backlash of some kind."[12]

Calleman claims that according to his understanding of the calendar, it will be impossible not to be aligned with the awakened energy after that time. He's far from alone in this claim. One version or another of the vision that only harmonious, non-egoic energies will be supportable in the age to come appears in many of the prophecies and teachings. The concept is staggering in its implications and neither you nor I have any solid idea of whether or not this could be true. I pass it along for your consideration, in the hope that it may energize your commitment to wake up without "thinking that there is ample time to do things later" as one Buddhist teaching cautions. As Calleman puts it: "With a dualistic mind, it will not be possible to be in resonance with the new unitary divine reality under one power, the Creator. It would thus seem wise for all of us to prepare ourselves, beginning today, by immersing ourselves in the cosmic flow of time and in all possible ways seeking to transcend the influence of dualist Underworlds (time periods with particular dominant energies) on our thinking, acting, and being."[13]

Ken Carey wrote several books in the late 1980s and early 1990s on this emerging sacred reality. In the preface to his 1985 book *Vision*, Carey explained that although he was well aware of the suspicions accorded people who claim to be channeling the voice of Spirit, and despite his struggle to come to terms with what was happening to him, this did in fact occur to him and he felt the responsibility to pass the information on: "Everything was so still. I felt something. I heard something, a low humming, an energy field, a Presence. When I first heard the voice, I cried."[14]

Carey went on to explain that the voice described itself as "the presence where there is no time but the eternal now," and that the message—consonant with that of the indigenous prophecies—is that our history has led us to this moment when Spirit has come to consciously dwell in us: "The individuals who will form my body on earth and provide the means of my creative action in the age to come are those who choose of their own will to honor the ways of love and to respect the nature of human design. Human beings who use their free will to choose motivations of fear cannot remain conscious in my Presence."[15]

Your job is to breathe

Note that none of these voices suggest we get fearful and cultivate a bunker mentality. That's an aspect of the very mentality that needs to be overcome. The message is clear. It's not about hiding or protecting ourselves. The war on terror will never be won. There's always another crack in the fortress wall. During an encounter with the plant medicine ayahuasca— "mother ayahuasca" as healers in Peru often call her—I was looking for clarification of my direction. In response, I was told "Your job is just to breathe."

So it's about paying attention, about opening into awakened heart at the pace we can handle, developing our intuition and compassion, and dedicating ourselves to whatever we are personally capable of contributing. At the most basic, non-cerebral level it's perhaps like Terence McKenna was told by the plant Spirit when he was shown this meeting with the transcendental object at the end of time. Terence asked this presence what he should do and received the answer "Relax."

Whether or not these predictions and prophecies are accurate with respect to time, there is compelling evidence to suggest that it's crucial we approach these next few years with great alertness, not putting off getting our relationship to life as clear as we can, not thinking there's ample time to do things later. Kanucas told us recently that Spirit told him to pass on to us that time is short and that we need to get our prayers in order, get clear about our highest priorities and values.

Chögyam Trungpa Rinpoché (pronounced rim-po-shay) was

a wild and brilliant Tibetan Buddhist master who planted vigorous seeds of Buddhadharma in the West. The word "Rinpoché" is an honorific that literally means "precious one." Trungpa Rinpoché played an extremely important role in my life and I will refer to him often in this book, usually as Rinpoché. Rinpoché was passionate about the need for the world to wake up in short order. He once suggested we question some of our personal projects and entertainments, things we do that might— in a more settled era—be justifiable indulgences, but may now be opportunities lost to add energy and creativity where and when they're needed most.

In fact this may be, in some respects, the central theme of this current transit; that there may not be any middle ground for much longer; that the fires of purification may burn all that away and leave us standing groundless in the space of reality. Denial would not be possible in this scenario. All of us would have to take responsibility for who we are and what we're doing. In such a scenario you either learn to surrender or you cling to crumbling edifices in increasingly painful and bewildering desperation.

Clearly, that awakening isn't going to be easy for most of us. I know from my own experience. I've been participating regularly in ceremonies of the Native American Church for years now. At every meeting I face the uncompromising reality of the peyote medicine Spirit and I've struggled with the overwhelming power of that Spirit presence. For the past seven years it's been a gradual process of learning to trust the power of the Spirit in the moment, little by little coming out of my head and surrendering my insistence on controlling experience. Kanucas told us that the Spirit wants to meet us, but that it can only meet us where it is and that we have the choice to make that meeting hard or easy. At some point you learn that it's a clear choice.

Buddhist teachings describe the path of awakening as one of gradually losing your ground, of seeing through and allowing to dissolve the familiar illusions by which you coped in the world of confusion. As this ground falls away, the practitioner slowly learns to let be, to "rest in the nature of Alaya." Without any theory like this, any kind of context or support for the breakdown of external and internal protections that the majority of people in the so-called First World have, the predictable reaction to seeing the ground dissolve under oneself is fear and bewilderment.

That, again, is why it may be urgent for those who can hear the message to think of this time as one of extraordinary circumstances requiring focus and commitment. Teachers say we need to heal ourselves and then be available to help others, to be rocks of sanity, to be with people as they fall, to act as midwives, and to provide support and inspiration toward the rebirth that can arise from dying to old structures. In whatever form it can be communicated, the message needs to go out that fear is always an illusion we create in our thoughts, that its logic is extremely seductive, but that there is another way, not a dogma, not an ideology, but a practice and a way of living that's natural and available to us.

Wisdom Carriers and Enlightened Collectives

The only habit you must cultivate, though it may go against the programming and traditions of your society, is to allow your consciousness the relaxed flow of attention that brings you a clear and accurate picture of the phenomenal world and continuous awareness of the Eternal Presence from which it has unfolded. Such a state of consciousness will allow you to enjoy the rushing energy currents and heightened awareness that will sweep through the earth during the expansion of the non-time interval and will maximize the stabilizing influence that radiates from you into your local surroundings.[16]
Ken Carey

If in fact the planet experiences the full impact of a more or less sudden breakdown or shift, through any combination of an ingression of spiritual energy, geological/environmental events, and human created catastrophes like nuclear conflagrations or severe collapse of world economies, the question arises: what might things look like after that time? The discussion of possible scenarios may be equally applicable if change is slower, and although I wouldn't pretend to have the answers, I can report that there is information available which might be helpful in preparing for such outcomes.

In the past twenty or thirty years a body of thought has been building toward this time. The most simplistic versions have come from some of the so-called "new age" spokespeople. These people have sometimes taken ideas from the Native prophecies that tell of a dawning golden age of enlightenment just around the corner, and posited a relatively painless transition. Skeptics and cynics sneer at what they consider the childish naivety of this kind of thinking. Such dismissals, understandable as they are, are complicated by the fact that most people in the privileged "classes"—the materially comfortable—don't want even to think about the possibility of losing what they/we are deeply attached to, especially since in these cultures the felt, experienced sense of anything greater than the separate ego has largely been lost and buried.

As events play out in these years immediately ahead of us, the reality is likely to be much more complex than either the deniers or the more naive have imagined. It may be that much of what occurs in the coming years has been and to some extent still is in our hands. But, disturbing as it is to contemplate, it behooves us to at least consider the most severe possibilities. It may turn out that not enough energy comes forward to shift the trajectory of the material illusion before shattering damage occurs. It may also be that natural disasters, both created by human activity and independent of it, have reached the point where even a sudden, radical, worldwide change of lifestyle will not be able to stem the momentum of processes like global warming and its attendant consequences.

The prophecies, visions and teachings of indigenous spiritual traditions have addressed this possibility. One theme I've come across is that there will be small groups of wisdom carriers who are able to remain off the grid, as it were, sustaining themselves from the land in simple ways for a period of time until conditions become conducive to bringing out the Spirit-guided vision for life-sustaining society. The Hopi Prophecy speaks to that version of events, indicating that the Hopi would keep the flame of awakened understanding alive through a difficult period. Kanucas also told us that part of the vision is that if even one initiated person can keep the flame alive in his or her heart, the seed can be planted again.

According to Alex Polari de Alverga in his book *Forest of Visions*, the Santo Daime church in the heart of the Brazilian Amazon also carries strong images of this time of transformation. Their elders have for years exhorted the members to work hard at aligning themselves with Spirit so that in difficult times they can maintain that knowledge and help to bring about this new era of awakened stewardship. Their vision is very similar to that of the Hopi and others. Groups like themselves, self-reliant and far from the globally interconnected centers of temporal power, would hold the connection to Spirit until such time as conditions allow the gradual dissemination of that understanding back into a wider world. As a kind of side note here, some of the Santo Daime elders say the crunch will come a couple of years later than the 2012 timeline suggested elsewhere.

Enlightened collectives will fulfill an important function in the arising of the new consciousness.[17]
Eckhart Tolle

To summarize and clarify this version of possible short- to medium-term futures, there are people gathering in like-minded spiritual communities of varying kinds. If external conditions become difficult, we might see this gathering process intensify in the next few years. This picture is similar in some respects to the idea that there may be no more middle ground where one can continue on in the denial illusions of the past. Commitments may be increasingly necessary, choosing a path and a sangha to work and maybe even to live with.

The issue of working and living with groups is worth a brief examination at this point. If I were asked to suggest cautions in this regard, I would say pay close attention to the state of mind and the assumptions of people in these groups. As many of us know all too well, group-think can be dangerous. Is there a humorless intensity about convincing people of the superiority of that group's particular version of spiritual truth—a proselytizing attitude that may include denigration of other spiritual paths? Is there evident a collection (often subtle and unspoken) of unquestioned, and unquestionable, assumptions in the group? Any appeal that provokes fear should be rejected unequivocally. Any tendency to proclaim "I have found it," should be examined carefully. Transference of one's natural-born intelligence and empowerment to an authority figure should especially be questioned in oneself and others.

In general, a spiritual community has to have a strong foundation of direct individual connection to Spirit in many of the members and be largely free of dogma, ideology, and reliance on leaders. Effective awakening practices need to be the core of the path. That's also one of the reasons the spirit-plant sacraments can be extremely beneficial for those able to work with them skillfully. Though you always learn from others, you have direct, unmediated access to Spirit and you take full responsibility for your own awakening understanding. I personally would want to be around people who are authentic, whose unconditional humble confidence from their own realization trumps any need to dominate or control, and who manifest a relaxed sense of humor coupled with a big, open heart.

> The Q'ero believe that the doorways between the worlds are opening again. Holes in time that we can step through and beyond, where we can explore our human capabilities.[18]
> Willaru Huayta,
> Peruvian spiritual messenger

There's another tricky slant on this period at "the end of history" we need to look at. My function here is as a student and reporter of ideas and information that I've encountered often enough to strike me as important, even central, to any attempt to paint pictures of possible futures for humanity. It's the issue of time and I'll explore it in more depth later. I mention it here to provide context for understanding this complex and mysterious shift under discussion.

The concept of the end of time can only be understood from the point of view that the ego—the compulsively discursive mind, the mind of illusion—is caught in the chains of linear time, pulled out of the now by thoughts of past and future. As I've heard it described a number of times and experienced in personal glimpses, the state of mind of peace is free of that bondage. It's not an abstract concept, it's a discovery reported by many. The full experience of nowness doesn't feel like moving time in the way that people in our modern, urbanized cultures experience it. Linear time lives in thought. Relaxing into full presence appears to dissolve it. If these many prophecies and pointing fingers prove to be correct about the approaching end of history, I think it has to be understood in this way, as what manifests when the Creator, God, Spirit, enlightened mind, the transcendental object at the end of time—or whatever inadequate name you try to give it—is realized as the ground of being.

Imagination is the real and eternal world of which this vegetable universe is but a faint shadow.[19]
William Blake (1757-1827)

One aspect of the prophecies points out that the ultimate refuge is in that state, where attachment to our "bodies" as the only reality has become irrelevant. The eternal life that Jesus spoke of, the enlightenment that Buddha taught, is in the Spirit that transcends and encompasses all concepts of time and space. The Sanskrit word "bodhisattva" basically means: one who is journeying on the path of awakening and who has vowed to help save all others from illusion. Part of the bodhisattva's prayer of intention goes, "From the stormy waves of birth, old age, sickness, and death, from the ocean of samsara may I free all beings."

The brave explorers of deep visionary states come back to report the lesson that death is a non-issue, nothing to fear because we're all part of the greater eternal reality. When Jesus said that those who believe in him will have eternal life, I believe he meant that those who have awakened to the truth know that they are one with reality always, one with the primordial living intelligence in the eternal now.

So again, the potent implication of that for the near future of humanity is the possibility that in the most dire circumstances a state of openness to Spirit may be the only refuge. The myths, stories, teachings, and prophecies from indigenous traditions around the world contain this possibility. At the first Native American Church meeting I ever attended, I noticed attached to Kanucas' door a small bundle containing several items. When I asked him what it was, he said that one of their old stories says that in the time of purification the Eagle will fly over the land from the east to the west. When it looks down and sees one of these sacred bundles it gathers that soul up. The bundle is, in part, the metaphor for the soul awakened enough to answer the call.

Certainly the only justifiable reason for writing about the more difficult and disturbing potential futures is from the foundation of a prayer that the greatest number of people intuitively grasp the connections and focus their energies on waking up with commitment and faith increasingly strengthened by experience. Only the vision that we are all one and that our potential is glorious makes any sense in this context.

Re-envisioning Community

It may also be beneficial to think about the kinds of values we need to cultivate in life-sustaining communities. For starters, "communities" may be the key word. The culture I live in here in urbanized North America seems to have drifted further and further from any sense of community. Most people function largely in isolation, or within small groups of friends and those with similar interests. The corporate consumer juggernaut exacerbates that isolation, sees us as individual units to be targeted separate from any larger context and disconnected from cultural roots and any self-transcending vision for the future. Everyone has the burden of looking out for number one. If you're part of the mainstream economy you have to build up and hoard what must look to a large proportion of humanity like obscene levels of wealth and property. As long ago as the 1980s, investment gurus were telling people they would need a million dollars to retire comfortably. As Terence McKenna put it, "This is the nightmarish reality that Marshall McLuhan and Wyndham Lewis and others foresaw—the creation of the public as herd. The public has no history and no future, the public lives in a golden moment created by a credit system which binds them ineluctably to a web of illusions that is never critiqued. This is the ultimate consequence of having broken off the symbiotic relationship with the Gaian matrix of the planet."[20]

People from old cultures are sometimes shocked at the way

we disregard each other in this part of the world. In many places it would be unthinkable to abandon aging relatives to impersonal institutional environments. There are still a few communities left on this planet where little or no homelessness exists, where orphans and widows are taken in, where people would be ashamed to put their own pleasure and comfort before the needs of the community around them.

In Chapter 3 I'll discuss in more detail some of the core values associated with the best of traditional indigenous worldviews. The point is not to glorify or romanticize so-called "indigenous" cultures. It's about learning what we can by looking at examples of Earth- and Spirit-connected communities. The more I've studied traditional indigenous cultures, the more frequently I've come across radical differences in values regarding wealth and ownership as contrasted against the modern understanding.

Generosity is often one of the most highly honored values, reflecting the attitude of believing in life and in each other. Anything that causes us to tighten and become fearful is shunned or admonished against.

The aim of the old Dakota economic system and that of the white man are one and the same: security—food, clothing, shelter, and an old age free from want. But the two systems are irreconcilable. One says in effect: "Get, get now: all you can, as you can, for yourself, and so insure security for yourself: If all will do this, then everyone will be safe." And it depends on things, primarily.

The other said: "Give, give, give to others. Let the gifts flow freely out and they will flow freely back to you again. In the universal and endless stream of giving this is bound to be so." And that system depended on human beings—friends, relatives.[21]

Ella Deloria
Yankton Dakota

It's heartbreaking to contemplate how far we've fallen from this ideal, even though people everywhere respect generosity. Many of us have become tight and fearful about our wealth, and frankly, this state of mind is at the core of the world problem right now. Material security and accumulation of wealth have become an addiction and a poor substitute for a joyous faith in life, in "all our relations." Our disconnect from each other and from our devotion to the living planet that feeds us causes the majority to rationalize, or at least accept, the actions of our corporations and political leaders and blinds us to what we're doing to the planet and to the level of suffering and basic material deprivation of large numbers of people around the world.

Contrast that to the Mayan worldview described by Prechtel:

"Mayans don't force the world to be what they want it to be: they are friends with it, they belong to life...you can't sell heaven and modern business practices to a people who think they are in heaven, and who insist on giving everything away in a grandiose way to prove it."[22]

We own. We take from the Earth. We refer to her components as resources. Many indigenous cultures didn't believe anyone could own land. The land was sacred, alive. If people had anything, it was the responsibility to love and care for the land. I've been struck in my readings how often in these traditional cultures it was believed that life is maintained and sustained by our ongoing—daily even—gratitude and honoring of nature and Spirit. Native elders are reminding us that the trouble we're in now has developed because we've forgotten our connection to the planet, we've forgotten to thank the air, the earth, and the water that keep us alive every moment. The Maya that Prechtel lived with in Guatemala exalted eloquence above all and believed it was essential to honor the Gods, the living energies and spirits of life, with their delicious words, with their beauty, by living properly with joy, dignity, love, and generosity. Native Americans talk about how in the old ways one began every day by making contact with life.

Concerned voices are raising the alarm regarding rapid loss of biodiversity in recent years. Along with these disappearances—and maybe most tragic of all—is the loss of knowledge of the natural world. The Amazon jungle is said to contain thirty percent of the world's plant species. It's a massive natural pharmacy and it's at great risk. Again and again I come across stories of peoples who knew their environment intimately in this way. This description of the Maya in the village of Santiago Atitlan, Guatemala, has been a common experience all over the world: "The people all knew every kind of wood, crop, meat, and wild edible plant... which part of which plant was edible, and which part was for rope or burning or weaving, or was poisonous, and what was good for what at what time of year."[23]

Our call may be to return to smaller, local economies and social structures; to attempt to rebuild our connections with each other; to reestablish the extended-family structures that have existed everywhere in the past; to share our labor, support, and wealth with each other without the kind of extreme private ownership mentality that currently rules many modern cultures; and to begin to reacquaint ourselves with that which feeds us, with the wealth and wisdom of nature. For example, I believe one could confidently predict a vigorous renaissance of focus on local food-growing and on traditional methods of farming in the near future. You may recall that prior to the destructive practices of modern agribusiness we did have a good few thousand years of deep knowledge about growing and preserving food.

It may be that we can short-circuit the unreal, spirit-draining, international corporate-dominated onslaught in these ways, becoming more conscious of our relationship to every aspect of the material and spiritual worlds. It may in fact be that we're going to be forced by circumstances to live in these simplified ways, whether or not we develop the spiritual connection to the living world. I'll expand on this general topic from a somewhat different angle in Chapter 6, "At Play in the Fields of the Lord: *Awakened Economy 101.*"

There are some interesting movements and developments arising aimed at re-envisioning our notions of how to live in community. Groups like the Eco-Village movement, the Local Food movement, and numerous others are attempts to manifest ways to regain sustainable lifestyles and are growing in popularity around the world. The communication made possible by the internet is stimulating grassroots populism, a growing understanding that people together can develop their own knowledge free from the top-down influence of authorities.

It's interesting that one of the visions that gained significant interest in the late 1960s and early 1970s was the idea of living communally on the land. Unfortunately, naivety and the suddenness of this new concept resulted in a lot of idealistic attempts that didn't have enough grounding in practical knowledge and experience to take the steps required to create stable, lasting communities. Groups of mainly young people— often without the guidance of elders or anyone who had grown up with those traditional ways—attempted to bootstrap themselves more or less overnight from an individualistic, secular, urbanized culture into a radically different mode of communal existence. The most common result was a breakup of the community within a few years.

Now, with more maturity in the cultural knowledge base, the benefits of learning from these past failures—and the greater urgency of affairs in general— there are groups springing up all over the place that are giving serious consideration to bringing about a new vision of community that is realistic and workable for moderns. People are envisioning structures that could take us from where we are and shift us gently toward communities that reflect our best ideas of how we see the future unfolding in ways that are life-enhancing over the long term.

Perhaps the most optimistic view of our current circumstances is that as the karma of our spiritually disconnected activity in the world is coming rapidly home to roost, there really is a growing determination arising in people scattered around the globe, born of this sense of urgency and the increasing clarity of under-standing how destructive and unsustainable the engine of modernity has been. The signs are there if you look for them. There may never have been a more conducive time for the serious consideration of ideas that may once—even recently—have seemed radical or impractically idealistic. Basic living conditions are becoming increasingly problematic, likely to get worse before they get better, and people are opening to new possibilities in response.

However events unfold, however humans approach the challenges ahead, whatever particular visions people have, at this point it almost goes without saying that the most urgent call for all of us is to somehow find a way to come back to the awareness of Spirit by whatever name you call it, to "dispel outer, inner and secret obstacles," surrender the tension of our isolated struggle, and relax into the awakened state. The elders tell us that if we can get our busy, restless minds quiet enough to listen, if we can become humble and simple, if we can learn how and remember to honor and respect all of life, Spirit will enter into us, will speak to us, help us, guide us, point us to the best ideas.

When you wear that power it will beautify your mind and spirit. You become beautiful. Everything that Tunkashila creates is beautiful.[24]
Wallace Black Elk

2

When the Grandmothers Speak...
Reclaiming the feminine principle in human affairs

We have to understand collectively as men and women, that
we need to balance the dynamic of the sexes and truly
empower women. We need to work towards a consciousness
shift, to include the female sensibility in all of our appara-
tuses. That is the prerequisite to solving all of these crises
we're faced with.[1]
Ani DiFranco

There are a number of very astute women in my life. When I
showed an early draft of this chapter to a couple of them, they
cautioned me that a lot of women are sensitive to the appearance
of a man speaking on their behalf, and particularly to indications
of unconscious patronizing. So I want to preface this chapter by
clarifying my intention, which is to add my voice to a still incom-
pletely healed wound and to shine a light on an issue which is
absolutely central to the "turning" addressed throughout this
book. The spiritual and emotional disconnect that has brought
our planet to the brink of expanding ecological, political and
economic disasters is the same disconnect that has resulted in the
massive destruction of indigenous wisdom and knowledge
around the world. It's also the same mindset which has so often

resulted in the oppression of women in societies throughout history.

There's a powerful way of understanding the problem using the term "dominator." The dominator mode is that of ego, the illusion of an entity separate from everything else. That mode is inherently conflictual, competitive, and at the core, insecure. The dominator mentality projects this basic insecurity outward onto the world and attempts to control it, attempts to dominate it.

The concept of the dominator mentality was employed as a central element in the thesis of Riane Eisler in her book *The Chalice and the Blade*. The title refers to the choice between the life-giving offering of the chalice and the life-taking symbol of the sword. Eisler tells a story something like this: There is a natural, unforced kind of social organization—what you might call a "natural hierarchy"—in which, without struggle or domination, people in community find and manifest their own natural abilities, predilections and niches, and these are all honored in the appropriate way. It's the Watercourse Way of the Tao. The sun, the air, the earth, and the water are the life-givers and are praised, honored and fed with love and devotion. In the human realm, women are the most direct source of life creation and are naturally honored in that way. In this kind of societal organization, the complex and potent connection between the life-giving power of the Great Mother Earth and that of women is not seen by men as a humiliation or denigration of their roles in creation and in the life of the community.

> We indigenous women have a principal value, we protect our territory, our lands, our birds, our trees, our rivers, because we are like Mother Earth.[2]
> *Dalia Herminia Yanes,*
> *Warao – Venezuela*

This way of living appears to have been embodied in the

Paleolithic and Neolithic eras up until about 5000 years ago in the region we sometimes refer to as the cradle of civilization. As a prime example, Eisler describes a major archaeological find at the city of Çatalhöyük in Anatolia, now modern Turkey. It's the world's largest archaeological discovery from that era. The city was unearthed with walls, floor plans and even objects in rooms well-preserved. From that information and from depictions on pottery, it's evident that the woman's room was the largest room in the house and that the culture was matrilineal. This is not the same as calling it matriarchal, which means rule by women. Many statues and figurines have been discovered and while there are some figures of male deities, those of female deities are far more common. According to James Mellaart, the original excavator of the site in the 1960s, after Level VI (of the eighteen levels identified) the male deity appears not to be represented at all.[3]

The implication is that there was no male-dominated, nuclear-family structure in this culture, nor was there any glorification of weaponry, conquest, or military heroism evident on the pottery, (in stark contrast to the imagery of later pottery once male domination was firmly in place). All indications suggest that at that time the region was populated by peaceful, egalitarian, agrarian societies with a highly developed artistic sense, advanced knowledge of edible and medicinal plants, and a deep understanding of their relationship to the planet and to Spirit. Again, the point is not to romanticize these cultures in a naive wish to return to an imagined, idealized past, but to learn something useful from them and many other more recent indigenous cultures from around the world.

A matrilineal structure seems to be a natural configuration and it can be found in societies all over the planet wherever the dominator hand of religion and imperialism had not reached. Though I haven't made any kind of exhaustive study of this, I've come across evidence from a large enough sampling of the literature of indigenous peoples as well as the work of anthropologists and archaeologists to make a good guess at the extent of the matrilineal mode. It was definitely widespread throughout North America where the Native people were still living in their traditional ways. Here's a typical testimonial, from Ohiyesa, a Santee Sioux (also Wahpeton Dakota) from Minnesota who was raised in the traditional nomadic life of his people in the middle of the nineteenth century. "It has been said that the position of woman is the test of civilization, and that of our women was secure. In them was vested our standard of morals and the purity of our blood. The wife did not take the name of her husband nor enter his clan, and the children belonged to the clan of the mother. All of the family property was held by her, descent was traced in the maternal line, and the honor of the house was in her hands."[4]

In her book, Eisler used the term "partnership" societies to describe cultures like these, and opposed it to that of dominator cultures. The partnership mode of human society is one where this natural hierarchy is allowed to flourish. As the Maya said, "things flourish by themselves." What naturally flourishes is compassion, happiness, relaxed, openhearted sensitivity to others and to all aspects of life. The Earth and everything on it are understood as interconnected, sacred, and to be cared for. As the Maya say: honored and fed with our delicious words, our beauty, our dignity.

The archaeological records show that beginning around 5000 years ago, male-dominated warrior tribes from the European Steppes swept into the region and conquered these preexisting and clearly more sophisticated, but undefended, non-warlike societies. Some readers may question the assertion that these partnership societies were more sophisticated than those of the invaders. The evidence for this is in the archeological digs in the region. Experts in that field tell us that the pottery in particular was a good indication of the level of cultural and artistic development, and that evidence shows a marked decline in the skill and knowledge of arts, crafts, medicine, spiritual life etcetera after the conquests. The pottery records also show the demotion over time of the exalted placement of the Goddess figure to; first, one of sharing that honor with a male deity; then becoming subservient to him; and finally, in many places throughout the middle-east over the next couple of thousand years, disappearing altogether.

> Everything 'feminine' (earth, nature, body, matter) underwent
> a profound depreciation with the onset of our aeon...[5]
> *Edward Edinger*

I'm not suggesting of course that this has been the only thing going on for that period of time. In Buddhist terms our natural, primordial state is one of awakened heart and unconditional goodness. That goodness, along with great intelligence and creativity, has obviously been a stream moving throughout human history, more or less strongly in one place or another, arising in the natural kindness of the human heart and the brilliant creativity of the human mind. The opening to Spirit is always available and even the history we know about is populated with great mystics and great creators. The key fact is that governance has in these cultures almost always been in the hands of men, and not just men but men for the most part firmly entrenched in the dominator mentality.

Much of our history then is cast in the shadow of these stories of conquest and domination, of conflict between different empires, religions, and customs, and most significantly, cast in the shadow of the denigration and suppression—often violent— of deeper, wiser understandings, many of which have been the root qualities inherent in our awakened natures.

One could even make the case that this in fact is "The Fall" that is spoken about in the Bible. The real fall from grace has been our lost connection to our awakened nature and to the sources of life, to the feminine principle, to the Mother Earth. An ancient root of the word "sin" is "to miss the mark." If there is any sin in this fall that must be it: the unhappy disconnect from a joyful, harmonious state of mind and way of life.

Here's what's so interesting, not to mention tragic, about this picture. The dominator mentality simply cannot grasp the meaning of partnership or equality. There *is* no equality in the dominator mind. To the ego, life is a constant struggle to maintain and enhance the individual's survival position. Ego sees everything from that perspective. If you're not in charge, in control, on top, then you're subservient, defeated, weak, on the bottom.

I've mentioned elsewhere a handy Buddhist teaching for viewing the behavior of the ego-centered mind, the mind lost in confusion. According to these teachings we habitually see the world through the filter of the Three Poisons. The first of these is passion: attempting to grasp, consume, own, hoard everything that is seen as desirable, as capable of filling the hole. The second is aggression: fear, anger, and violence directed toward everything seen as threatening, as other, as enemy. The third of the Three Poisons is ignorance: denying, ignoring and denigrating everything interpreted as having no relevance to ego's struggle. This template could well be laid across the historical landscape of the dominator cultures.

As with much of today's corporate mentality, there's no still point, no place of rest. Ego is constantly trying to repair leaks and control the flow of events. There is no "all things flourish by themselves" under the rule of ego. To stop is to allow the specter of death to come into view. The now is never enough. It's evident by observing the behavior of corporations. The mantra is "expand or die." If the economy isn't growing, we're supposed to worry, but how much can the economy grow before it consumes everything and chokes on its own waste?

There's no future for that worldview. It's the "setting sun" mentality that has no faith in life and so is hell-bent on getting everything as fast as possible without any perspective on the whole. There will be no fine-tuning of the ever-expanding economy. The only way we'll be able to create sustainable existence will be to come back to ourselves, to come back into balance in ourselves, to still ourselves enough to feel the world, to feel our heart's connection to everything. Then we might learn to live far more simply and sensitively, walking lightly on the earth.

> The hardhearted commercial cupidity, myopic dynastic political and religious stupidity, and the Earth- and people-hating spiritual amnesia sold to us as a forward-moving vision, by which we find ourselves barraged today, are nothing new at all, but a disregard for the female principle of life which has been with us for a long, long while, an anathema that needs to be composted into something out of which we can finally grow real cultures of grief, beauty, and peace.[6]
> *Martín Prechtel*

One of history's most dramatic demonstrations of the insanity of the dominator mindset—the mindset alienated from and afraid of the feminine principle—was the witch-hunts of central Europe that took place roughly between 1450 and 1750 CE. Church and secular authorities cooperated in the trial, torture, and execution of tens of thousands of victims, the great majority of whom were women. The alienation that possessed these men led them to associate women with evil, with everything negative and destructive of Christian society.

The classic evocation of this deranged misogyny is the *Malleus maleficarum* (The Hammer of Witches), published by Catholic inquisition authorities in 1485-86. "All wickedness," wrote the authors, "is but little to the wickedness of a woman. ...

What else is woman but a foe to friendship, an inescapable punishment, a necessary evil, a natural temptation, a desirable calamity, domestic danger, a delectable detriment, an evil nature, painted with fair colors. ... Women are by nature instruments of Satan—they are by nature carnal, a structural defect rooted in the original creation."[7]

The healing abilities, the knowledge of medicinal and visionary plants, and above all the fact that the witches appeared to have their own power unmediated by the authority of the Church, were perceived as a direct threat to the male hierarchy of the day. I could well imagine the authorities solidifying their hold over the populace in the same way political leaders do today with scare stories about crime, drugs, communists, terrorists, etcetera. It's also no surprise that this women-hating mentality lumps sexuality into the Satanic category. Sex invites humanity, humility, surrender, openness, love, pleasure, ecstasy, and transcendence. The self-hating, anti-life minds of the religious authorities couldn't bear that concept. If people were able to freely experience the beauty and pleasure of life in the sacred garden they wouldn't have needed these distorted souls to tell them they'd been kicked out of the garden for their wickedness and needed to be led to some fictional salvation in a nonexistent future. It's been reported that the difference between that view and the understanding of many, perhaps most, of the indigenous cultures, was that those cultures never saw themselves as being expelled from the garden. This very life is the garden, they reported, to be appreciated fully in the here and now.

The Women emerging are the hearts of the nations.[8]
Megisi, Turtle Mountain Ojibway

And now we are in urgent need of recovering this lost understanding. We men need to listen to, respect and learn from the wisdom qualities of women like never before. I'm speaking deliberately about the wisdom aspect. The conditioning in dominator cultures has been so intense and thorough that women, although they've been "allowed" the qualities rejected by men for having no value and importance in governance, have lost much of their own wisdom and power. It's not that men are supposed to try to erase or deny who we are or try to be like women. It's that we need to unearth and embody the qualities we've repressed in ourselves. From women we need to learn how to let ourselves feel more. We need to trust our intuition. We need to develop our tenderness and our nurturing and healing abilities. We need to deepen our understanding of the value of community and cooperative decision-making. We need to feel the silent rhythms of life on many levels and honor those whose sensitivities are sources of guidance.

With the serenity of the Mother Earth, that is the tool that I work with that is pure.[9]
Julietta Casimiro,
Mazatec – Mexico

I want to make it really clear to men reading this that it's not supposed to be about men feeling wrong: defensive, guilty, belittled, or emasculated. Those feelings are elements of the dominator mentality so deeply ingrained in us. Those are the kinds of programs we have to bring out from the unconscious and into the light of awareness which wears them away. Women simply have to be given all possible support—from both genders—to lead in the ways they are naturally stronger, clearer, and more connected, without men feeling diminished by that.

A lot of us men have a lot of inner work to do to get to that level of maturity, that level of unconditional confidence in ourselves where we don't feel threatened by the authentic power of others. When asked how he knew that he had arrived at enlightenment, the Buddha is supposed to have put his palm on the ground and said, "This solid earth is my witness." Women's wisdom—if a man such as myself dare claim that level of understanding—is like that; intuitive, direct, of the Earth, felt in the blood.

I'll share a simple example. I'm sure there are a million and one. There was a tragic mass-shooting at a college in Montreal some time ago. The only child of my friend Maria went to a school next door to that one and I called her here on the west coast, 5000 kilometres from Montreal, when I heard the news stories that day. I wanted to make sure her son was okay. Maria hadn't heard or seen any of the news when I called, but she told me that Julian was safe because she always knows when something isn't right with him. She said she has an unerring connection to her son in that way and that whenever he's in difficulty she feels it in her chest. It doesn't matter how far away he is in physical distance.

It's been suggested that that is at least partly the explanation for the basic insecurity of men in the cosmos. Everybody knows at the core that we don't really know anything about what we're doing here: cast into this wild, chaotic sea of life in a boundless universe. We know how infinitesimally small we are in the face of that and we struggle desperately for meaning, for security, for a sense of importance, for some power to hold onto. But women at least have this non-intellectualized connection to the womb of the Earth, the blood of life, that men so often lack. As a female friend pointed out, it's not that men in general completely lack that connection. It's also because we have, to a great degree, forgotten how to read and communicate with the world in those ways.

It's time to work through the deadly serious, competitive, aggressive aspects of ourselves. It's time to unravel the chains around our vulnerability, around our hearts. There's a Buddhist slogan that goes, "All gain and victory to others, all loss and defeat to oneself." I'm sure that sounds outrageous to some and I have to say I've been wrapping my mind around the concept for close to thirty years. This teaching asks us to "exchange self for others" and is similar in intent to the Christian teaching of the Golden Mean, which asks us to "do unto others as we would have them do unto us."

This idea of offering victory to others is meant to be a practice, a discipline, an antidote to grasping, to competitiveness, to aggression. It asks us to observe our tightness, to observe this aggression, and when we catch it to release it, to breathe, relax, send our attention and if possible our hearts out to others. We're counseled to have a laugh at ourselves. A friend of mine once asked, "Would you rather be right or would you rather enjoy yourself?" Next week will you give a damn whether or not you were right about some minor point of information, or whether the tennis serve was in or out? In working with women, our partners for example, can you observe the defensiveness that arises when you're criticized? Did the wound in you get poked? Did it provoke anger? Violence? Can you remain present? Can you breathe and soften your heart in that very moment? Can you see the absurdity of the situation, the grief in the situation, the humor in the situation?

In Gabon, when the Grandmothers speak the President listens.[10]
Bernadette Rebienot,
Bwiti elder (and grandmother of 23)

Visions coming through to the indigenous elders these days are suggesting that we, both men and women, need now to think seriously about encouraging women to take the lead in society in increasingly influential roles. The evidence speaks for itself; men with decision-making power have largely failed in their responsibility to take care of the planet and sustain life for the generations to come. Men need to be open to it and encourage it and women need to take the power, not over men or over anything else, but out of a learned or remembered confidence in themselves as holders of essential keys to our survival. My friend Deanna, who has known and worked with a lot of abused women, also reminds me of how important it is to create conditions for women to feel safe to develop their inherent power.

Maybe we could try some experiments for awhile. Isn't that what life is about anyway: exploration, experimentation, discovery, learning? We come from the great tradition of the mishap lineage, children of illusion. I went to a Native American Church meeting a while ago and for the first time, possibly in the history of the Church throughout The United States, the main "officers" of the meeting were women. A woman carried the drum for the night, a woman looked after and fed the sacred fire, a woman took care of the doorway, a woman took care of the cedar blessings for the night. Since that night I've attended several other NAC ceremonies where women have taken some of the officer roles traditionally assigned to men.

This implies of course that the new leadership mode needs to arise from a different place from the ways men have governed, and not from women becoming more like men have been in positions of power. In my country of Canada, for example, there are currently a lot of women in the federal government, but the rules of engagement are still firmly in the domain of male competitiveness, aggression, intellectualizing, and disconnection from heart wisdom. In the current environment, in North America at least, it's much more difficult for a woman to find her own way in the corridors of power than it is for men. Hillary Clinton's campaign for leadership of the Democratic Party in 2008 provided a clear example of that challenge. Many people expected her to be strong but not too hard or aggressive, and human but not too emotional or weak.

Our people predicted through oral teachings, and as we say in Central America, it was written in stone; the gliffs were made, they were carved, left for the generations to come, and we were told that exactly at this particular time, the women would lead the nations.[11]

Flordemayo,

Mayan - Highlands of Central America

We may be close to a tipping point where a widespread awakening to this understanding makes a sudden leap forward. There are signs all over the place, almost always under the radar of the mainstream media, that women are beginning to act from the strong conviction that there's no more time to waste, that they can't sit idly by, waiting for men to get it and stop the destruction of this planet. These movements are coming from the peripheries, from the fringes, from those ignored and suppressed in the past, from the indigenous soul, bubbling up from the ground, rising up from this solid Earth.

The ground is now fertile, ready to receive the message of the grandmothers.[12]

In October of 2004, thirteen Indigenous Grandmothers from around the world came together with seven highly-regarded women elders from the Western societies to honor and act upon ancient prophecies which told of this time, and in fact told them of the role they needed to play in revisioning global priorities. As Mayan elder/healer/curandera Flordemayo said at the conference, "We must do what we have been asked to do...We are standing in the vibration of a sacred prophecy. The prophecy tells us that consciousness is preparing the spirit of the feminine, the spirit of the grandmothers. In the prophecy, we shall walk into the light united from the four directions."[13]

The grandmothers say that the hour is late but not too late and that they are determined to grow this movement of rediscovering the sacred ways of indigenous people, reverence for the

Earth and for all life. Here's their mission statement:

> We, The International Council of Thirteen Indigenous
> Grandmothers, represent a global alliance of prayer,
> education, and healing for our Mother Earth, all Her inhabi-
> tants, all the children, and for the next seven generations to
> come. We are deeply concerned with the unprecedented
> destruction of our Mother Earth and the destruction of
> indigenous ways of life. We believe the teachings of our
> ancestors will light our way through an uncertain future. We
> look to further our vision through the realization of projects
> that protect our diverse cultures: lands, medicines, language
> and ceremonial ways of prayer and through projects that
> educate and nurture our children.[14]

As direct channels of new life and all the blood and bone intelligence that brings with it, many women understand the
connection in ways mysterious to men. This is the way forward,
this is the missing half, the missing link. Listening to these elders
we can begin to repair the damage done. As I pointed out at the
beginning of this chapter, it's all connected. The healing and
rebalancing of the feminine principle is an essential aspect of the
awakening of the intelligence that enters into reconciliation with
life altogether.

One last point on this subject. No doubt you've noticed that
many of the women referred to and quoted in this chapter have
been indigenous, tribal people, from cultures sometimes called
the "Earth people." This is not a coincidence. In the next chapter
we'll explore some of the core understandings that put the
wisdom of the Earth people at the very center of the vision and
prayer for planetary transformation.

3

We Speak on the Basis of Our Visions
Learning from Indigenous Wisdom

So I pray for you that you obtain the same power I have. You and I are no different. It's just that understanding. You just drifted away from it, just walked away from it for thousands and thousands of years. That's how come you have lost contact. So now you're trying to find your roots. They are still here.[1]

Wallace Black Elk

Though key differences between traditional, indigenous cultures in general and the modern, materialistic/capitalist cultures are suggested throughout this book, I want to focus in here on some of the significant contrasts between them, because a lot of people now sense that the way forward points toward what indigenous wisdom has to show us about living in harmony with Earth and Spirit. Chapter 2 explored the issue of the partnership societies of antiquity and how they were overthrown by the dominator societies that built the framework for the historical period of the past 5000 years. That discussion included the issue of essential lost wisdom that resulted from the denigration of women and the solidification of ego in these cultures and it was pointed out that the parts of ourselves that were being suppressed and ignored are the aspects of the feminine principle that we need to recover for our survival at this crucial juncture. In the words of Katsi Cook, an elder of the Mohawk Nation, "These indigenous teachings are not there just to make us ooh and ah and think, 'isn't that pretty?' They're there for our very survival."[2]

There are people who understand that there's a different way in which humans have lived in communities throughout history and prehistory. The basis of that way, as I understand it at this point of my unfolding spiritual journey, is the central principle that there is a living, eternal intelligence of some kind, the great mystery behind all of creation. It isn't merely a theory or a belief system but has been experienced directly by many people. Wisdom teachings remind us that humans beings—if allowed to develop freely and naturally—are fully capable of waking up to that truth, waking up to the realization that the living heart of the Great Spirit is the same awakened heart that beats within us. Coming to that realization, we begin to harmonize with the patterns of life and to understand in our marrow the meaning of the phrase "all my relations."

In the same way that a recognition and honoring of the feminine principle is called for, the lessons and models of many of the world's indigenous societies can be examined as embodying values that are needed to reestablish balance, harmony, peace, and long-term sustainability across this increasingly small, connected planet. Another qualifier might be in order before going further. Obviously there have been problems, imbalances, conflicts, and spiritual cul-de-sacs all over the place. No one is suggesting that just because a culture is indigenous it was enlightened or ideal. We're not talking about the romantic conception of the "Noble Savage" or of primitive, simple-minded nature dwellers. However, we live in a strange and unique time when the last threads of traditional values and Earth- and Spirit-knowledge have almost disappeared, at the same time that people of vision from within and without those cultures are attempting to recoup, maintain, and communicate these values before they're lost altogether.

We speak on the basis of our visions, whereas scientists do not believe in visions.[3]
Akushti Butuna Karijuna

Many people now—elders, shamans, visionaries, activists, living carriers of the ancient spiritual understandings and representatives of cultures from around the world—are speaking up in urgent pleas. They're asking us to examine our priorities and understand how the dominating mindsets of our political/economic machinery are pushing the planet to the brink of disaster. Prechtel described how the Maya saw the entrance of a newborn into life as an event that triggered an inevitable forgetting of its real self within the shrouds of matter. They understood that the responsibility of the community is to guide the newly arrived soul toward a remembering of its true nature. He called the work and journey of that process "initiation" and said that the Maya can see whether or not a person is initiated. Their experiences with non-native people from North America and Europe led them to label these places "the land of the dead," as they saw and felt no spark of the divine, no authentic, empowered deportment in these people.

We are reminded that nothing will ever feel right out there until it feels right inside, until we surrender to the awakened-heart state of peace. In words attributed to the Buddha, "The hunger of desire pollutes the world." We who are not at peace within never feel at home and are constantly and restlessly searching for something in the world to ease that dissatisfaction. The Buddha also taught The Four Noble Truths, the first two of which describe this predicament: the truth of dissatisfaction or suffering that pervades our lives in the confused, egoic state of mind; and the truth that this suffering is caused by attachment—craving and clinging to the idea of a separate self, to the hope of satisfaction and salvation in the material, the transient, the external.

This *is* the Garden

Having lost contact with our natural, awakened state, the uninitiated of the world are willing to believe we have been expelled from the garden. We feel alienated and uncomfortable in the world. In initiated cultures it never occurred to people that they had been banished from the garden. They knew they lived in it. They felt their connection to the world around them, felt the security of their place in the cosmos. When people have a deep experience of spiritual awakening, they often return to report that they experienced the feeling of "coming home."

Stories from the indigenous peoples' first encounters with the Europeans often had a common theme. The natives were frequently disturbed and confused by the energy of the explorers, by the unsettled looks in their eyes and the furrows in their brows. They were sometimes described as ghosts, not fully present. Some had a haunted quality, as though pursued by unknown demons, thinking that they were moving toward something while in reality running from something. Buddhist teachings call this the twin demons of hope and fear.

The explorers were often driven by tales of gold, an abstract "treasure" they believed would quench their thirst. Some of the Indians in those early days were actually able to rid themselves of the Spanish interlopers by telling them fabricated stories of gold awaiting farther inland.

This experience of nowness—the awareness of and trust in the guidance of Spirit, the absence of the need to keep moving, to acquire, to hoard—is one of the essential differences between the uninitiated peoples and the ancient cultures of garden-dwelling indigenous people. Stories are told again and again by people from these cultures, from the high plateaus of Tibet to the forest communities of the Amazon, that they see how the Europeans are unable to stop their busy minds. In the movie *The Journals of Knud Rasmussen*, taken from the journals kept in the early 1920s of the explorer and anthropologist's travels across the Arctic, the visitor asked the last great shaman of an Inuit community what his traditional beliefs were. The shaman replied simply, "Our spirits are offended if we think too much."

The idea of progress so central to the thinking of the European cultures seemed strange to the indigenous soul. The implication was that there was something flawed about the present, a lack that had to be filled. That attitude expressed a state of mind that in general was anathema to the Earth people. In Prechtel's description, the Maya of Santiago Atitlán functioned from the conviction that the world didn't need improving by humans. It was already designed perfectly by great creators. The people's job is to celebrate it, praise it, and care for it. An anecdote from Ronald Wright's book *Stolen Continents* pointedly exposed these juxtaposed mindsets. In 1887, Henry Dawes, an influential American Senator, "praised" Cherokee values while justifying his (successful) bill, The Dawes Severalty Act, whose purpose was to divide Indian lands into private plots—160 acres per family—notably leaving much unclaimed land in their territory available for whites.

> There is not a pauper in that nation, and the nation does not owe a dollar. It built its own capitol...its schools and hospitals. Yet the defect of the system was apparent. They have got as far as they can go, because they hold their land in common...There is no selfishness, which is at the bottom of civilization.[4]

They "hold their land in common." How foreign that concept is to our cultures. Apparently, when you feel at home, when you truly have faith in life, in the generosity of the Creator, there's no need to insure yourself against adversity by struggling to accumulate and hoard wealth in a competitive, individualistic modus operandi. Most of us have never experienced that way of living and are understandably afraid of being overly generous, of giving away too much in a culture that isn't showing great signs of reciprocal giving. Who's going to go first? And yet it seems so often the poorest peoples are the most generous. There have been studies done with questions for people in countries around the world to subjectively rate their happiness level. In one such study the people of Bangladesh came first. It was suggested by one of the study's authors that with about a fifty percent chance of losing their homes and belongings to flooding every couple of years, Bangladeshis generally saw no point in worrying about accumulating wealth and material security. In the University of Michigan's World Values Survey of 2004, Nigeria—another poverty-stricken country—was at the top of the list. The United States, the wealthiest country on the planet, doesn't make it into the top fifteen on any of the surveys I came across. Researchers for World Values Survey described the desire for material goods as a "happiness suppressant." In an interesting twist on this theme, a recent study claimed to demonstrate that money can indeed buy happiness . . . but only if you give it away.

Chapter 18 will explore the importance of mindfulness/awareness meditation in the personal and planetary awakening journey. I'll mention briefly at this point that a practice that helps us stare down, outlast, and gradually release tension-maintaining fears is strongly indicated for us busy-minded, restless Westerners. We're stuck in samsara, the endless ocean of dissatisfaction, as long as we're clinging to ideas, concepts, and wealth we're convinced we need to feel secure, to protect us against disaster, against annihilation. Our dependence on things seem to have replaced our connection to each other and to the living world that keeps us alive. One of our Buddhist blessing chants included the phrase, "To this meditator who is not attached to food and wealth..."

There's a wonderful story about the great Tibetan saint Milarepa. He had been meditating in a cave for years. His only possession was the robe he was wearing. As time passed, the robe became increasingly threadbare until eventually it consisted of only a few sorry shreds of cloth hanging from his bony frame. The story says that Milarepa's final realization of complete enlightenment came when one day he stepped outside of the cave into a strong wind which scooped up his tattered robe and whisked it away into the irretrievable distance. That was the metaphor for him, the "aha" experience. Nothing to cling to.

It's also evident that the language we use to talk about our lives plays a huge role in conditioning our worldview. I've come across a few telling examples of indigenous languages that form the basis for a very different understanding of the world from our modern outlook in the dominant cultures. One example in particular that struck me is that of Runasimi, the ancient and still active language of the Inca of Peru. According to Ronald Wright in his 1984 book *Cut Stones and Crossroads*, Runasimi has no verb "to have." In order to say that you have a house, you need to say "Wasiyoq kani," which translates as "I am with a house." Imagine for a moment, if you will, the implications of a living your life with a language that has no concept for "to have." To view your connection as one of being *with* something points at a radically different, reciprocal relationship with the "things" of this world. Not coincidentally I'm sure, the Incan Empire was also a moneyless society and dealt with the exchange of goods and labor in ways much different from our mercantile cultures.

Another essential life-sustaining understanding we of the modern societies can learn from indigenous people is our relationship to Gaia, the living Earth. Wallace Black Elk referred to himself and people like him as Earth People, who know that the Earth is alive and that you can communicate with many different elements of it. Contemporary use of the word "nature" often implies our separation from it.

The forest, the plants, in Africa are our parents. We know how to say good morning to them, we respect them. We speak with them, especially when we have to cure.[5]

Bernadette Rebeniot,

Omyene - Gabon, Africa

Stories from indigenous people all over the world describe their intimate relationship with and their embeddedness in the living Gaian web. The Earth people tell us that the Earth is not an inert, dead substance. They tell us the Earth is a being, or perhaps a family of beings. They tell us there is intelligence and communication in nature, in the plants, the creatures, the elements. They tell us the trees will communicate with us if we will learn to listen. They tell us the creatures of the air, the earth, and the water can communicate to us, can tell us their stories, teach us their wisdom, help us with our prayers, direct our healing work.

The Crying of the People

Imagine how our political and educational priorities, our business and consumer practices, our visions for sustaining life into the future would shift if many of us could open to these understandings. If we saw the world as ourselves, if we felt our living connection to everything in the Gaian matrix, there's no doubt that our behavior would change. It comes back to the teachings about opening our hearts, letting ourselves be touched by the sacred world in all its variegated and brilliant wonder. Elders of the old ways tell us we have forgotten to thank the elements and this is leading to our downfall. Those who haven't forgotten to praise, honor, celebrate, and pray to and for the health and well-being of all aspects of the world believe it's essential to think and feel and act this way to sustain life altogether. The historical conditioning that brought us to our modern worldview saw us at the top of the chain of life, with dominion over all, with the right to use the riches of the planet as we see fit. We have taken the Earth and the living intelligence that creates and supports life for granted, and now we see that our failure to feed and care for the world has ruptured the cycle.

At the Global Women's Gathering of 2004, Hopi elder Mona Polacca shared a legend from the Kiowa people that in brief summary goes as follows: There was a time when all the two-leggeds, the four-leggeds, the winged, the creeping crawlers, and the water dwellers of the earth could communicate with each other and were able to live around and among all the others harmoniously. However, at some point a darkness began to inhabit them and they started bumping into each other, hurting each other as they did so. A climate of conflict overtook the dwellers of the Earth. At a certain point the spirit-being Saynday got tired of seeing all this suffering and disharmony. He prayed fervently to the creator and in time the harmonious, interdependent dance of life reasserted itself.

Stories and testimonials are coming from all corners to communicate that this is what's happening now. There is a dawning understanding among wisdom carriers that enough is enough, that this destructive pattern cannot continue any longer. Perhaps we even needed to reach this critical condition for enough of those who can intuitively sense this coalescing picture to grasp the depths of the power of determined, sincere intention and prayer, and to discover the confidence that anything is possible in alignment with the Great Spirit. Many of those who say they're on speaking terms with the Creator are saying that it is indeed possible, that we can bring back the lost harmony which will allow the continuance of our world. And this ties in again with the vision of alliances being formed, of joining energies from the four directions, gaining strength from the like-minded.

We feel the crying of the people to connect with life again. It is time now.[6]
Grandmother Sarah Smith, Mohawk Nation.

4

Come Together

The older I get, the more I am aware of the fact that we are not just one family here on this planet, but one organism.[1]
Ani DiFranco

A few years ago my friend Daniel made a couple of visits to a remote Inuit community on Baffin Island in the Canadian Arctic. He reported that in their native tongue the local inhabitants had only the number "one" and nothing for two or more. The concept of keeping track, of tabulating individual possessions, didn't seem to enter into their thinking. They remembered harsh years when food sources were scarce and many died of starvation. But they went hungry together. You didn't see one overfed guy in his huge home on the hill with a plentiful stash of frozen seals while the emaciated masses down below scrambled for scraps. Anthropologists and other explorers have come across numerous isolated cultures around the planet whose worldview is similar.

In the dominator cultures we count things. I don't mean to diminish the remarkable generosity that does exist on this planet. There are abundant examples of support and generosity among family, friends, communities, and even situations where a great number of people contribute supplies, funds, and labor to help poverty stricken regions, victims of natural disasters, and the like. But for the most part, when it's business as usual, as most of you reading this are no doubt aware, we're on our own.

The lost connection to the Gaian mind, to our oneness with each other, to our awakened hearts, produced a Darwinian survival-of-the-fittest mentality. Competition is held to be the order of things. People often claim these attitudes are permanently encoded in our minds as human nature. Seeing life in such terms results, as we know, in some people accumulating extreme wealth, so far beyond real need it's absurd. The majority of the rest of us in the rich countries save, hoard, and worry about our money—or lack thereof. Our financial gurus tell us we're going to need vast sums to protect us from a nightmarish old-age of poverty and deprivation.

> Almost every problem we have can be ascribed to the fact that human beings are utterly beguiled by their feelings of separateness.[2]
> *Sam Harris*

The inner experience of lack that motivates us—referring in particular now to the top dogs in the material enterprise—has hastened crises in the environment, supported cruel tyrants who protect the interests of the wealthy nations while helping themselves, and destroyed the traditional local economies of so-called developing countries in favor of monocrop agricultures. Whole countries survive on the basis of their production of coffee, sugar, bananas etcetera and the financial well-being of their citizens rises or falls with the price manipulations of the heavy hitters in London and New York and the squeeze put on suppliers by mega-corporations.

The dominance of fear and ego pits nation against nation, tribe against tribe, religion against religion. Wars are fought (among other reasons of course) because of personal pain and confusion projected onto enemies, onto other. Because we don't experience our "non-dual interdependence" with each other and with all elements of our planet, we stand idly by as others suffer.

Contrast this to the attitude of the traditional Maya, as one of numerous examples among indigenous peoples with connections to their ancient roots.

> The Maya have long used a special expression for greeting others: *In Lak'ech*, which means "I am another you." A whole philosophy has been developed around these beautiful words of recognition, which are applied not only to human beings but also to animals, flowers, stones, and spirits. It means that we are not separate; we are all part of the same web; and if any part of this web is hurt, the rest will suffer.[3]
> *Carl Johan Calleman*

I'm deliberately painting a stark portrait of the dominant illusion to make the point distinct, but as discussed in Chapter 1, there's a coalescing vision for our future which sees, not separateness, competition, and aggression, not scrambling to reach the top or struggling desperately to keep ourselves from being trampled — but cooperation, coming together, relaxing of armored boundaries. In this vision, these attitudes and understandings are seen as the necessary and inevitable tools for life-sustaining, life-enhancing, awakened existence on this planet.

For starters, we need to understand what we've been doing to ourselves, and consequently, as Calleman pointed out, to the rest of the web. There's a Buddhist teaching that says we're afraid of external phenomena, which are actually our own projections. Or put another way, believing is seeing. We're prisoners of our concepts. In general, because we don't trust life, we create a massive mess of compensatory behaviors and structures, many of which appear to be ultimately unnecessary. But we don't know any other way. We don't know what non-dual interdependence is because those who taught and conditioned us didn't know it either.

In the softening, we begin to dissolve the boundaries. With

quieter, more spacious minds we see how tight we've been, how fearful of external phenomena we are. As we stare down the attacks and the compelling stories of Fear we begin to see through it, we begin to realize it was a paper tiger, granted power only by our ignorance, and we gradually learn to relax into nowness. Little by little (for most of us I suspect), we let down those barriers that separate us.

> The Buddhist solution to this delusion of self is to realize our interpenetrating non-duality with the world, which is wisdom, and actualize it in the way we live, which is love.[4]
> *David R. Loy*

What might our world, our communities look like if large numbers of us are able to open up our boundaries like this and get connected to the free-flowing energy available? It's safe to say it would probably have radical implications for the ways that we work and share our lives with each other. Currently there's a kind of vertical integration still conditioning a significant segment of the populace. It starts from the political, religious, and economic power structures, influence pedlars, and information disseminators at the top, and connects straight down to the individual. Despite the humanization and liberalization of laws that's been occurring this past half-century or so in this part of the world, there is still an underlying patriarchy at work. For examples look no further than the prohibition against cognitive freedom that claims the authority to disallow people from choosing to alter their consciousness through plants and other substances. Taking one particular example, I know what cannabis is and what it does, both from my own generally sparing and respectful use and from studying the research and the historic use of the plant around the world. No authority figure has the right to tell me I may not make use of that plant.

A telling symbol of patterns of relating in contemporary

technologized societies is the television. Apart from the content itself—remember, as long ago as the early 1960s we used to call it "the boob tube" and "the idiot box"—television does something strange to the flow of energy in a room. If you're alone with it it's almost totally one-way communication. You may have your responses but of course the TV's not listening. If several people are together watching it, the natural tendency to form a circle—a mandala—is broken and straightened out into a line, with all the attention focused on one inanimate point. I don't mean to imply there's anything dysfunctional about directing attention to a particular point in general. But when the TV has a central placement in the home and is on for hours every day . . .

Images of Interconnectivity

Most of us have certainly experienced the circle in action and the way it can connect people. Think of gathering around a fire with friends. For me, the all-night prayer meetings of the Native American Church have provided a wonderful example of how that configuration enhances our connection and empowers each participant as a valued human before the Spirit.

It's not for nothing that the circle is universal in human experience and the natural formation for gathering to communicate. The circle isn't linear like much of modern thinking—it has no beginning and no end. Everyone more or less faces everyone else. There's no one position in a circle inherently more important than any other, so it symbolizes and facilitates equality. The circle models a beautiful vision for our relationship to the whole, that we are both individuals and unified in this configuration.

Another beautiful image or metaphor to describe our connectedness is *Indra's Net*. This image is said to have originated in ancient Buddhism and Hinduism. *Indra* refers to the god Indra. According to one brief summary; "In the heaven of Indra, a vast net or web of silken strands spans across space infinitely in every direction. Every intersection of gossamer thread hosts a shining luminous pearl or multifaceted jewel. The surface of every jewel completely reflects every other, and the net as a whole. Likewise, each reflected jewel in itself reflects every other, that reflects every other, that reflects every other, without end, as mirrors to infinity."[5]

Each jewel represents an individual unit of consciousness. Any movement or change in one jewel is reflected, however minutely, in every other jewel. This reflecting light and the gossamer thread connect each to each and to all. There is no hierarchy, no above or below. As Thaddeus Golas said in his charmingly titled little book *The Lazy Man's Guide to Enlightenment*, "We are equal beings and the universe is our relations with each other." [6]

A hopeful development in our dawning recognition of the spiritual impoverishment from which we're attempting to recover is the archetype of the web. (Ironic as these events so often are, the internet was first developed for military use.) There's something uncanny about the adoption of the term "web" to describe the network of connectivity created by the internet. It's probably wise to look ahead, to see this development as a stage or step toward increasingly sophisticated methods of human communication. It's as though we're preparing new channels in the mind so that later developments are more readily met and assimilated.

This we know: All things are connected
Like the blood that unites one family.[7]
Chief Seattle,
c.1786-1866

Our world-wide-web could be understood as a rudimentary development toward a rebirth of an ancient and innate ability, the ability to communicate at deeper, more subtle levels with each other. We may be evolving toward direct mind transmission of information, unrestricted by the limits of time and space and free of the convolutions and obfuscations commonly found in normal verbal communication. Anyone who's been paying attention and isn't deeply blocked by his rationalistic/mechanistic conditioning is aware by now that instant communication between people at a physical distance is a natural occurrence, even if most of us moderns haven't learned how to recognize and utilize that ability. There are many reports—from intelligent, sensible people—of information being transmitted and received in this way, especially when the stakes are high. The famous psychologist Carl Jung, in his book of memoirs, *Memories, Dreams, Reflections*, told a number of stories about synchronicities he experienced, often in dreams. This one is typical: One night Jung "dreamed that my wife's bed was a deep pit with stone walls. It was a grave, and somehow had a suggestion of classical antiquity about it. Then I heard a deep sigh, as if someone were giving up the ghost. A figure that resembled my wife sat up in the pit and floated upward. It wore a white gown into which curious black symbols were woven. I awoke, roused my wife, and checked the time. It was three o'clock in the morning. The dream was so curious that I thought at once that it might signal a death. At seven o'clock came the news that a cousin of my wife had died at three o'clock in the morning."[8]

Jung labeled this type of phenomenon "synchronicity," described by Richard Tarnas as "observed coincidences in which two or more independent events having no apparent causal connection nevertheless seem to form a meaningful pattern...The events give the distinct impression of having been precisely arranged, invisibly orchestrated."[9]

Jung is a role model in the way he lived his life alert to these unexpected conjunctions. He said that they often manifest to inform important situations and can be utilized to guide and clarify such challenges. Many of us experience synchronicities frequently. They suggest a level of active interdependence or interpenetration with the world that reminds us of the living intelligence of this ocean of life in which we all swim and the potential for a much more effective, attuned way to move through our days.

The Tibetan people, through their Buddhist practices, had ancient techniques for divination, for connecting with information from other physical locations. In his autobiography *Born In Tibet,* about his childhood and youth in Eastern Tibet, where he was being trained to be the Supreme Abbot of a group of seven monasteries, Rinpoché described the way he and his companions survived and eventually escaped arrest during the rapidly changing, traumatic invasion by the Chinese in the 1950s. Using these techniques for divination, like one he called "tagpa," they would seek information and receive consistently reliable answers on the safety of a particular escape route, on the whereabouts of the Chinese troops, and on the situation of other groups.

There are countless stories like these. I suspect that in the generations ahead, we will rediscover these abilities and learn to use them. It's a combination of conditioning over long centuries and an accompanying fear of information out of our rational control and knowledge that holds these abilities back. It's no great revelation to point out how people who appear to have contact with information unseen by the rest of us have often been considered flakey, deluded, or worse.

Many people also fear a loss of individuality and free will. I feel confident in saying, based on both research and personal experience, that that is not the vision being presented. Free will and native intelligence are enshrined as among the highest values of awakened, empowered communities. The problem is the ego, the need for personal power and recognition in unskillful ways. We all understand this on some level. We all, except perhaps some of those most guilty of it, know what we mean when we talk about a person as having a big ego. We know how much space those people take up. We bristle in the presence of puffed-up arrogance. Hopefully we're conscious enough to observe what happens when we ourselves succumb to the temptations of self-aggrandizement.

It should also be noted for some who might be confused about the basic notion of ego, that its power doesn't by any means always manifest as the outward expression of "big ego." Ego—in Buddhist descriptions for example—is portrayed as struggle, resistance, denial, fear, numbness, the false belief in and commitment to the reality of a separate self. It all lives in the virtual world of thought. The ego illusion is often just as strong in those of us who don't look like we're taking up a lot of space or throwing our weight around.

Co-creative Potential

A beautiful analogy for or example of the way we can enter deeper levels of oneness and still retain, even enhance our uniqueness, is in making music with other people. All group music has this potential to some degree. Orchestral musicians, rock musicians, choral singers, all need to attune to the feeling, the shifting dynamics, the pulse of the music, the moment by moment movement of the energy of those around them. The more spontaneous, the more improvisatory the music, the more each individual is challenged to temporarily dissolve all thoughts of self and enter into a shared group space. If you don't empty your mind, relax, and listen, you can't enter that space. Improvisational ensemble jazz and some of the more skilled "jamming" style rock bands provide excellent examples of this. I've often heard jazz musicians refer to their band as a listening band. It's a matter of letting go, getting out of your head, and into the creative confluence of focused minds. At the same time, each individual still has to bring her own heart and soul, total attention, spontaneous intelligence, musical feel, and passion to the moment. It can be a truly delicious, transporting, even healing experience. A new entity, just for that purpose, for that moment, can arise from the cumulative attention of the individuals. At its heights, this shared-space mind can take on a life of its own, leading without a leader into new territory created in the now moment. In the Native American Church prayer meetings, it's been reported that sometimes "the song sings the singers."

Buddhist teachings encourage us to give up privacy, relax the barriers that make us less accessible to others, allow ourselves to be tender and openhearted, to meet each other honestly, with authentic presence. Terence McKenna has a lovely image on this topic. He proffered the octopus as the totemic animal image for neo-human communication:

> The octopus becomes its own linguistic intent. Octopi have a large repertoire of color changes, dots, blushes, and traveling bars that move across their surfaces...The mind and body of the octopus are the same and hence equally visible; the octopus wears its language like a second skin. Octopi can hardly not communicate. Indeed, their use of "ink" clouds to conceal themselves may indicate that this is the only way that they can have anything like a private thought.[10]

Though the concept is frightening to a lot of us, it's also encouraging to contemplate living in such a way that one would have nothing to hide. Rinpoché taught that renunciation in the Buddhist/Shambhala path means renouncing or relaxing out of anything that makes you less accessible to others. If you live your life like that it's the ultimate statement of unconditional confidence in yourself and in life, that you aren't trying to protect anything. It may also be the most honorable and respectful way you can treat others as well as yourself. By being open and honest with people, I'm encouraging the development of that ability I want to see in the world, that people learn to recognize and trust the intuitive mind, the telepathic mind. If you sense something is going on with me and I deny it, either directly or indirectly via body language, lack of responsiveness and so on, I'm not confirming that kind of intelligence in you. Some call it "crazy making." Knowing this, we might find ourselves taking greater responsibility for our thoughts, our words, and our actions.

It's reasonable to suggest that we've barely begun to tap the co-creative potential that opens up when the walls come down. The uniqueness of individuals working in harmony with other minds toward new discoveries and a larger vision has possibilities that beggar the imagination. Of course, this has always gone on among us and in this remarkable time, with our sophisticated world-wide communication networks, the possibilities for collaboration—for building upon and adding to the insights and understandings of others—are almost unlimited.

> Sacred Mind is the only mind in town. To awaken in any part of it is to begin to feel its presence in every part.[11]
> *Christopher M. Bache, Ph.D*

Further, without the assistance of our machines, there's powerful support for the truth of our connectivity from many sources of wisdom throughout the ages as well as increasingly compelling evidence from modern researchers and explorers of deep and vast realms of consciousness. Take a look for example at the work of the English scientist Rupert Sheldrake on morphic resonance, which, simply speaking, points at how information and learning move within the "species mind" beyond the brain. Another author with much of value to add to the dialogue on our connectedness is Christopher M. Bache, a professor of religion at the State University of Ohio in Youngstown. Using techniques of what he terms "psychedelic therapy," Bache has made a remarkable lifetime exploration of realities beyond the boundaries of the ego. His book *Dark Night, Early Dawn* is a potent and visionary examination of these frontiers of interconnectivity. In the context of "the great turning" the existence of this forgotten information and the possibilities for information and learning to move rapidly throughout the species mind may prove to be very encouraging as conditions come into increasingly stark focus in the coming years.

Here's a hopeful vision, a possible scenario for where we might be going. In this scenario, many of the changes discussed in Chapter 1 actually come about, as numerous pre-Columbian prophecies have predicted. Due to a combination of conjoining factors—not the least of which is the inventiveness which is provoked by urgent necessity—a large number of people get the message, use the tools available, open up quickly in these next years and become aligned with Spirit. The ideas whose time has come begin to make increasing sense to those others at first less supple in this period of transformation. It becomes more and more obvious to more and more people at all levels of influence and activity in the human community, that we were on a suicidal path created by our own misunderstanding, the way you look back at an abusive relationship and shake your head at how you allowed it to happen, how you were so blind to the obvious and how much you suffered for it. Fear begins to be seen for what it really is—a dysfunctional illusion. Aligning with and allowing the natural flow of unobstructed energy begins to be understood as a radically superior mode of living, in fact the only way to live that makes sense. As a result of this urgently provoked proliferation of sanity and commitment, the world is able to pull back from the brink and skirt the worst-case scenarios of wars over scarce resources, severe environmental degradation, and a number of other dark possibilities.

As this new understanding sinks in, we come to see that we

the people have the power to create our best visions and that bad behavior on the part of religious, political, and corporate power-brokers had only been allowed to happen because of our self-imposed disempowerment. We come to embody and live the view that what affects any part of the web affects the whole, and decision-making comes to stem from that kind of basic sanity and skillfulness. We see the walls of division around the world—religious, racial, economic—collapsing from lack of maintenance. The complementary sharing of ideas and information that's already on the loose takes off exponentially. The whole planet gradually wakes up to reality, the reality of eternal life in the Spirit. We begin to understand that enlightenment is not a final destination—the perfect retirement home in the clouds—but that it's actually the beginning of the journey of co-creation with that unnameable eternal intelligence of which we are living parts, jewels in the net of Indra. The joy of living in love and creative imagination that has always been our potential and our birthright finally settles across the landscape. Life in its largest, universal sense is seen to be a creative adventure with unlimited possibilities. May the dreamers of good visions unite.

Don't let it bring you down,
it's only castles burning,
so find someone who's turning,
and you may come around.[12]
Neil Young

5

Putting the Art Pedal to the Metal

True art evolves us—opens our arms and weakens our prejudices so that the ever-present seeds of healing and renewal
can take root in our soul and sinew.[1]
Daniel Ladinsky

Just my opinion, (and a few others much wiser than I): all true art
is spiritual in the sense that it comes through from elsewhere,
however we choose to define that. It comes from the muse, from
Spirit, from a higher, purer voice than the rational, ego-
controlled information that most of us—artists included—are
receiving and generating in our ordinary daily experience.
Artistic inspiration and intention seem to enter through a gap in
the thinking mind. Rinpoché called it "first thought, best
thought"—the lightning-fast insights we receive in that gap
before our categorizing, conceptualizing minds have kicked in.

Artistic inspiration often requires courage, a letting go of
control over what we're willing to see. What the muse is bringing
through, what Spirit wants to say, just might not fit into the
programs we've established to keep ourselves stable and
comfortable. Art has real power and can challenge and shake
foundations. It's beholden to a higher law. You could say that art
is truth, spiritual in its ability to bypass the usual filters and fly
straight to our intuition, to our feelings, to our dreams, to the
places in us that are crying out for healing, that are crying out for

beauty in this world.

> Genuine spirituality, like art, is open and dynamic...both are the hope of a world so badly in need of transformation.[2]
> *Sister Veronica Brady*

There's a wonderful book called *Songwriters on Songwriting* by Paul Zollo; it's a collection of interviews on the creative process with many of the best songwriters of the past fifty years or so in the English-speaking world. A common thread among these artists is the gentleness, the devotion, and the mental silence they say is necessary to open the channels that allow the muse to speak and be heard. Like the voice of Spirit, creative inspiration is often hidden in the corners of our vision, and easily smothered and silenced by the speed and aggression of the mind and the cacophony of modern environments. Songwriter and singer Rickie Lee Jones spoke of song ideas as spirit beings that are coming through. In her words: "Your logic will tell you, 'I want this to be this way', but you mustn't interfere with the spirit that's writing...And you have to be really quiet and careful with it when it's first being born, and you can't tell it it's wrong, 'cause it will just die."[3]

I've heard similar cautions from Kanucas and other elders in the NAC about the shyness and fragility of spirits that have been invoked and invited in for teaching and healing assistance. These people tell us we need to be very settled, quiet in our minds, and focused and sincere in our attention and intention. Some of the elders talk about how different things are when you get a group of well-processed elders together in a meeting who can sit still in mind and body. It's not hard to see why this kind of spirit presence has been missed in the dominator cultures; too much assumption, judgment, restlessness, ambition, arrogance, dogma, too much self, too much expert's mind and not enough "beginner's mind," to use Zen teacher Shunryu Suzuki's term.

To Honor the Muse

Our connection to the spirit of art is our connection to truths beyond the known territories, beyond the already ploughed ground of our mindstuff. Art can be the expression of our longing to honor life, to give voice to our deepest devotion to this miracle. Not all artists like to think in these "spiritual" terms, and many will say that the ideas come from themselves. This may often be just another way of describing the same phenomenon. If the Spirit—God, Buddha mind, the Muse—is both within and outside of us, then the distinction may be irrelevant. Whatever the muse is and from whatever source it originates, I believe most true artists understand it as a fundamentally different kind of information and recognize when it's present, both in their own work and in that of others. Songwriter Bruce Springsteen once said he knew he had something real when he felt a tingling down his spine. A Buddhist friend of mine realized there was something other than himself present during his intensive practice sessions of chant and visualization when a unique kind of warmth came over him in moments of deep presence.

> There are moments of silent depth in which you look upon the world-order fully present. Then in its very flight the note will be heard.[4]
> *Martin Buber*

In that way, art is expression which is closer if not identical to awakened spiritual practice and presence. Artists will often say that the discursive mind has to step aside—has to quiet down— for artistic inspiration to appear. Bob Dylan said, "You have to be able to get the thoughts out of your head. You must get rid of all that baggage."[5] Songwriter David Crosby liked to quip that the magic happens when "the elves have taken over the workshop."[6]

In the interview with Paul Zollo he talked about how he was never able to force this inspiration, how it could come at any time, sometimes in the most unlikely or inconvenient situations, and his part was to be available, to be open to receiving.

Artists can be guiding lights for the rest of us. They let us know that we can go far deeper than we've been going, that pulling aside the veil of the busy mind and outwitting the guards can open us up to levels of experience we never knew existed. In another interview, Dylan said that the world of his imagination was more real than the so-called real world of most people. Messengers returning from deep mystical experiences, meditation breakthroughs, and medicine-provoked explorations often report similar news—that they've encountered realms felt in the marrow as real beyond anything experienced in consensual reality.

Here's another lovely anecdote from the Paul Zollo book, by Louis Perez, a songwriter with the American band Los Lobos. "I find that if you let it take you, it's usually the right direction...I had a friend who told me he would write himself a little note that he would keep by the bed and when he woke up he would look at it. And it said, 'Dear Paul, I won't be needing your help today. Signed, God.' "[7]

We don't know what this mysterious muse is, but we can train ourselves to connect with it, not only for the purposes of creating a work of art as we might typically define that, but also as an enlightened way to live. Rinpoché taught a concept he called the principle of "Heaven, Earth, and Man" as a way to understand and work with the process of creating. He said that this principle comes from the Chinese and Japanese traditions and is sometimes evident in the art and architecture of Asia.

In the simplest terms, Heaven is vision, non-thought, the source of inspiration, the empty canvas, the blank page. It's the "don't know" mindstate that allows space for an idea to come in, for the openness that allows the unknown to appear. The implication is that it may require courage to feel the fear or insecurity of that space and meet it without closing down or falling into habitual patterns. It needs to be met with a spacious, unhesitating mind, free of obscuring thought. Control is certainly its nemesis.

The Earth principle enters when the artist brings down an idea from Heaven. This is where "first thought best thought" meets form, technique, knowledge, experience. You connect with the medium and bring the inspiration to earth, which is watered by heaven and yields to your effort. When heaven and earth are properly joined in this way, earth cooperates with and grounds the vision, allowing the idea to manifest in some realized form, which is the Man principle, the realization of an idea in the world. The joining of heaven and earth produces good fruit—inspired art, healing, sacred world activity.

A favorite story on this topic comes from Gary Snyder, one of the great beat poets who came out of the 1950s and a lifelong Buddhist. Snyder said that he lived his life in service to the muse. He described how he was always ready to take down an idea, a phrase, or a few lines. For example, when he was lecturing at university he would sometimes briefly excuse himself in the middle of a class to step out of the room so he could jot down something that had just appeared.

Other artists talk about keeping recording devices, pencil and paper, etcetera beside their beds during the night, or just being willing to live with an interrupted night's sleep to get up and record ideas that wake them. This openness and sensitivity to the kind of information that artists wait for, court, and strive for is very similar to those qualities of attention and focus required for people in general to invite awakening: slowing down the speed of mind, learning to open the heart, developing courage and perseverance to remain present and open to experience—inner and outer—without conceptual boxes, without judgment.

The Art of Everyday Living

Everybody has the tendency toward intrinsic beauty and intrinsic goodness, and talent comes along with that automatically....When your visual and auditory world is properly synchronized and you have a sense of humor, you are able to perceive the phenomenal world fully and truly. That is talent. Talent comes from the appreciation of basic beauty and basic goodness arising from the fundamental peace and coolness of dharma.[8]

Chögyam Trungpa

The connection between these qualities or attributes we're uncovering in ourselves in the awakening journey and the notion of art, is one that moves into the center of the lives of us all. In this respect it's not so much about those who seem to have the great artistic talent as it is about living daily life in an unhurried, attentive, dignified, and elegant way. From that point of view, from the moment we wake up in the morning until we drift off to sleep at night we could be living as artists. The artist's path is a path of nowness, a path of paying attention. If we can develop or uncover this naturally existing attitude in ourselves and see what's around us as we move through the day, many of the apparently insignificant details of our lives can be uplifted.

There's no question that this way of being presents a daunting challenge for most of us and requires discipline and perseverance—watching our minds drift into carelessness and numbness, into obsession with what we think is important—while ignoring the moment-to-moment world we're passing through breath by breath. I'm sure all of us have often caught ourselves and observed those around us racing through our days from one thing to the next as if only the destination was important. Maybe we'd like to walk, relax, take the time to look around and appreciate the color of our surroundings, or for that matter tune in to the "little" things that might be calling for our attention in the immediate or the larger picture. But we find the demands of our schedule force us to compromise any such vision and be completely efficient about driving on through the to-do list.

The awakened approach to the art of everyday living—we are reminded—is one of doing things with full, relaxed attention and presence, including washing the dishes, brushing our teeth, and cleaning out the cat litter box, with our minds and bodies on the same page as it were. Another favorite old story comes to mind about Lao Tzu, the famous Chinese sage of antiquity, reported to be the author of the Tao Te Ching and the founder of Taoism. He is quoted as saying, "A good traveler has no fixed plans, and is not intent on arriving." In this story Lao Tzu is making a long, arduous, and sometimes dangerous journey on horseback— accompanied by his assistant—to a great holy city he had wanted to visit for many years. One day the two travelers rounded a bend in the road which brought them out of the woods into a clearing, where they suddenly saw the fabled city on the horizon ahead. Without a further thought, the assistant galloped off excitedly toward the city. After some distance, he glanced over his shoulder expecting to find Lao Tzu beside him. Seeing nothing but the dust-cloud kicked up by his own horse, the assistant stopped and looked back to see his master about where he had left him at the edge of the woods. The surprised assistant then rode back and said, "Master, Master, are you not excited to get to the great city we've dreamed about so often and come so far to visit?" "Yes, of course," replied Lao Tzu with a smile, "but here is good too."

Nations are Destroy'd or Flourish in proportion as
Their Painting Poetry and Music are Destroy'd or Flourish.[9]
William Blake

There's a strong case to be made that art understood in this way will—in fact must—play a central role in our recuperation, in the healing of the planet, in the renaissance of life as it could be here. Art, dharma art if you will, is to be an essential ingredient in the rebirth of wonder and beauty and sanity. We embrace and honor life, living deeply in the now, giving ourselves over to something bigger, doing things wholeheartedly, for their own sake, for joy, for gratitude—letting them take us where they want us to go. Writers often talk about how they have no idea where the plot of their novel is going, they just enter the characters completely and follow the naturally unfolding information as it presents itself to them when their minds are absorbed in that space.

Art is about recreating spontaneity and play in the fields of the Lord, listening to and acting on the information coming from the phenomenal world, and celebrating this unique canvas of our brilliantly designed planetary environment of sight, sound, smell, taste, touch, feeling, and physical movement in earth's particular configuration of material density. It's about learning to move through our days regarding everything as sacred, as worthy of our devotion, worthy of our prayers, worthy of our love. Art is about reconnecting to the web of life, and it's about giving back to the Creator in gratitude and praise.

Devotion to Beauty

There are countless examples of this kind of devotion and single-minded commitment to a vision. Some people spend their whole lives bringing an idea to fruition. I once visited the Stiftsbibliothek—the Abbey Library at the Cloister in San Gallen in eastern Switzerland—parts of which have been there for over twelve hundred years. The library is famous for its stunningly beautiful interior and the antiquity of its books, many of which are handwritten originals, five hundred of them more than a thousand years old. It was designed and built in the eighteenth century by a man who spent most of his life working on it and passed the responsibility on to his son to finish after he had gone. I don't consider myself supersensitive to the unseen, but I began to weep when I entered the library—its power was that palpable. There was hardly a straight line anywhere. Even the bookshelves were built in curved, flowing configurations. I could feel the love and devotion that were behind this work.

There's something intangible, even magical, about how mental energy—intention—can inhabit a work of art, can actually seem to reside in the work, available to the eyes, the ears, the hearts, the minds of those who come to appreciate it, even hundreds or thousands of years later. You could listen to the same piece of music performed on two different occasions or two different recordings. If one of the performances was produced with passionate and sensitive feeling and the other in a perhaps technically superior but colder, more academic manner, most people—regardless of training—can feel the difference.

I recently spent a day in the Musée d'Orsay in Paris, which houses many of the best works from the great painters of the French Impressionist, Post-Impressionist, and Neo-Impressionist periods of the mid- to late nineteenth century. I was stunned at the living energy emanating from these works: landscapes and portraits by painters like Renoir, Cézanne, Pisarro, Monet, Degas, Van Gogh and others that send shivers down the spine and bring tears to the eyes. Some of the images felt as though they must be at least as real and alive as the sources from which they were drawn.

This attitude of commitment and devotion toward the muse and toward one's work has a lot to teach many of us about our relationship to time as well. Again, it's an issue of surrendering to the reality that things have their own time. You do what you do fully and completely, in an unhurried manner, until it's done, until it lets you go. There is freedom in that kind of activity and that way of life, release from the tightly-wound and relentless pulse of mechanical time. There's also a delightfully radical impracticality from the point of view of the mindset that proclaims "time is money." I love to hear these stories of artists who go to incredible lengths of time and expense to create some sort of installation with no apparent purpose other than to be appreciated for what it is—like the man who strung miles of colored fabric in billowing sails across the rolling hills of the midwest, presumably just to demonstrate and honor the beauty of it.

Another remarkable example of sacred art—of devotion in the moment to creating beauty and releasing it—is the Tibetan Buddhist practice of creating sand mandalas. Several monks will create a sand mandala for purposes such as a special religious event, a festival, or an honoring celebration for a highly regarded teacher. These beautiful mandalas, or cosmograms, are said to be for the purpose of reconsecrating the Earth and its inhabitants.

The ritual typically begins with a ceremony of chants, music, and mantra recitation to prepare the environment and invoke spiritual energies. The sand comes from white stones ground and dyed various colors. The monks use a type of funnel to form highly detailed designs based on ancient symbols. The mandalas are usually from a little over one meter (a yard) to several meters in diameter, and may take anywhere from a few days to a few weeks to finish. When they're completed, another ceremony is conducted and the mandala is erased, the sand gathered up and distributed, half to the audience and half to be taken to a nearby body of water, from there to be carried to the ocean and around the world for planetary healing. There's no attachment to the final result, no attempt to capture and preserve it, and obviously no profit to be made from it.

At the risk of being filed under "flake," I have to address the crop circle issue. It's just too bizarre and mysterious to walk past. Most people have by now heard of these crop formations, and most are happy to put the story down to some eccentric folks having a good one on the rest of us. But here's what's fascinating about the phenomenon. As much a brain-shock as it is to the modern conceptual framework, the fact is that if one takes even a relatively cursory look at the information available, it's very difficult for people with a corner of openness in their minds to fit the facts neatly into a box labeled "Made on the sly by human hands." There may turn out to be some stunning rational explanation for these formations, but it hasn't appeared yet—not by a long shot—and none of the so-called hoaxers have demonstrated that they can create anything remotely like the genuine article.

Why do I bring this up in an essay on art and its relationship to a vision for enlightened society? For starters, the formations are often very beautiful when seen as aerial photographs. Many are complex and sophisticated in concept. Formations are populated with little-known symbols and obscure theorems based on Euclidian geometry. There have been large, accurate representations of complex mathematical configurations and fractal formulations like the Mandelbrot Set and the Julia Set. Five new mathematical theorems have been seen so far.

But beyond all that, there's the distinct possibility that we're being shown something remarkable here, something we're meant to learn from. Like the sand mandalas, the crop formations are created with no hope of permanency, celebrity, career advancement, or remuneration. They come in the night when the crop is developed to just the right height and are erased by the farmer's combine within days or weeks. Perhaps they're saying to us: "Look friends, here's something lovely for you, something symbolic and maybe even information-laden, and you can't explain it. We're showing you in a playful fashion that what's going on around here requires you to open up your reality framework. You need to wake up and see that the world is alive with information far more vast than you have allowed yourselves and each other to contemplate. The momentum of your misunderstanding has brought you to a precipice and now you need this information, you need to let down your guard and pay attention without prejudice. The future of the planet depends upon it."

Without turning this into a book on crop formations it would be impossible to do full justice to the complete picture. But perhaps I can tease you with a few facts that may lead you to question the quick dismissal of claims regarding the non-conventional genesis of these creations. There are numerous books, movies, websites and other sources of information created by people who have made a serious study of the phenomenon. What follows is a brief summary of some of the key facts involved.

The patterns are as large as 1,000 feet (about 300 meters) across. They are made with great precision and often with incredible detail. Even the circles themselves are often slightly elliptical, a shape that is said to be much more difficult than an exact circle to measure and produce accurately. Just looking at some of the crop formation photos online would demonstrate their grandeur and precision far better than if I attempted to describe any of them here. One of the most telling pieces of evidence is that typically the plant stalks are not broken or crushed as would be the result of any kind of roller or vehicle moving over the field. According to one of the researchers, the stalks "appear to be subjected to a short and intense burst of heat which softens the stems to drop just above the ground at 90°, where they harden into their new and very permanent position without damage. Plant biologists are baffled by this feature..."[10]

Farmers have often seen steam rising from the laid-out stalks. Significant quantities of surface and subsurface water are found to have evaporated under the "floor." Researchers have found distinct changes in temperature, composition, and crystalline structure in the soil and the crops within the formations. Close-up photos reveal elaborate swirling patterns in the laid-out stalks matching the fundamental vortex pattern found often in nature—

for example with shells, sunflowers, and even galaxies. The swirled patterns have up to five interwoven layers of stalk within a radius of just a few feet.

A whole range of unusual events and phenomena have been associated with the formations. They alter the local electromagnetic field and result in the malfunction of a variety of equipment, including cellphones and cameras. Car batteries have been drained. Compasses are bewildered and can't locate north. Odd lights have been seen by many night-watchers shortly before the patterns are discovered. There are frequent reports of headaches and other unusual pleasant and unpleasant physical and mental anomalies. The list goes on.

One of the features of crop formation creation most difficult for rationalists to explain away is the ways and means of their actual construction. Nothing is trampled. No one has ever been seen creating one that fits the profile of "genuine." No equipment or other evidence has ever been inadvertently left behind. Many have camped around fields with a history of formations—video cameras and sound equipment trained on the field—but have found nothing and seen nobody, even when a new formation is discovered in the morning. The formations are usually created in the hours between 2 and 4 a.m. and a number of reports have shown that they are done very quickly. One well-known example is that of a pilot who flew directly over the Stonehenge monument at dawn and spotted nothing whatsoever out of the ordinary. Fifteen minutes later another pilot flew the same route and clearly observed a massive pattern some 900 feet in diameter with a 149 individual circles.

A highly skilled and prepared team just might be able to replicate the general surface appearance of some of the formations—after many hours of exhaustive measurement and meticulous labor in broad daylight. But such activity has never been observed. And then they would be extremely hard-pressed to recreate the technique by which the stalks are bent without being broken or crushed, and would find it nearly as difficult—and immensely time-consuming—to interweave the stalks in these complex and precisely layered configurations. I challenge you to find the people who could and would design and create these elaborate and often very beautiful formations year after year in multiple locations without ever being caught or claiming authorship. It's an unsolved mystery at this point, and again, perhaps a jolt to our attachment to the rational, material conditioning so predominant in the modern world.

All art constantly aspires towards the condition of music.[11]
Walter Pater, 1839-1894

You'll recall a brief discussion in Chapter 4 regarding music as a model for understanding the mechanics of oneness. It's an amazing treasure we've been gifted with, is it not? And not just a thing of beauty, but also a straight and true path, and in that way also a great teacher. Nowness—the total presence in the moment we keep hearing about—is the key that opens the door into its kingdom. When you're making music, only total, openhearted surrender works, and if you're paying attention you can feel whether you've entered or not and you won't be satisfied when you're outside. That's okay sometimes I guess, like levels or degrees of reality and depth, but when you get down to it, it don't mean a thing if it ain't got that . . .

Of course these days we try to freeze moments like that and listen to recordings of the same captured performance over and over. I can't complain about recorded music, knowing how rich the listening experience has been over the years. Yet there's often something irreplaceable about the physical space of live performance—the energies that move around that space between performers and audience. A lot of musicians will say that having the skill, the focus, and the courage to step out into that space, and then doing it, alone or with like-minded souls, is the musical experience nonpareil.

And if there's an audience, all the better. They too can enter with the same mindstate. A great way to share space for a little while. Music invites us to leave ourselves at the door and then it has its own wonderfully unique way with us, like holy speech, ideas forming and dissolving into space second by second, tumbling and dancing over and with each other, poetry in motion, come and gone like the imprint of a bird in the sky.

I want to share with you one further intuition about music. This point no doubt applies to other art forms as well, but as a musician, that's the medium through which I sense it most directly. I've long felt that much of the most powerful, soulful music has come from peoples who have experienced a great deal of deprivation and oppression. As one of several striking examples, the music of African Americans that is at the root of so much of contemporary music arguably fits that pattern. It's very possible that, as the upheaval and transformation process deepens, music will become more important, more needed, and greater depths of its uplifting and healing potential will become apparent to many more people. We may come to see what truly nourishes us and what has only deceived us with false promise.

Freeing the Awakened Art

I am perpetually awaiting a rebirth of wonder.[12]
Lawrence Ferlinghetti

Many of our modern cultures have become so driven and controlled by the imperative of the bottom-line that art has been denigrated and demoted by the mainstream opinion leaders— including the political and economic decision makers—to the status of a commonplace commodity. Art is often viewed as a mere product, a nice but unnecessary luxury for purposes of escapist entertainment and adornment. We see that mindset controlling the education system for example. There used to be a big poster gracing the walls of music and art teachers in the city where I taught music for many years, "The arts are the soul of education." In North America they're widely treated as a frill, sometimes squeezed in around the so-called core subjects, oftentimes cut altogether. As a sweeping generalization, I'd say that the biggest weakness of the education system is still its lack of understanding and nourishment of creativity, of the artist mind.

The tight scheduling of the school day is in itself an obstacle to the free flow of inspiration. I don't know how it's to be done, but we need to find ways to build in room for the unknown, for chaos, for the unexpected, for the organic movement of time and inspiration. For a lot of kids you can't just say, "Now it's time for art," you can't just shuffle them from box to box on command. Adults need to learn to trust the natural intelligence of children, to trust their way of feeling and movement, to give them time and space to become completely absorbed in what they're doing, without fear or self-consciousness. The adults need to learn to trust that the deepest nature of human beings is ultimately good. Rinpoché used the simple term "basic goodness" to describe the understanding of the awakened heart/mind. When we're awake, when we're at peace with ourselves, relaxed in the now, we're not in danger of wreaking havoc, (except maybe basically good havoc). Our long historical conditioning is to believe in basic badness. If left uncontrolled, we fear, humans will create evil, "an idle mind is the devil's playground."

In societies pervaded by that kind of conditioning, art is often going to be at odds with the culture. It's going to be the black sheep, the explorer of the hard truths and dark sides feared by the authorities. We've all seen how artists have so often been punished for drawing people's attention to the truth. The controllers make laws about what can and cannot be said, and offending works and their creators are banned and destroyed. In fact, it's probably accurate to suggest that the failure to understand and encourage creative freedom in the young is responsible for much of the negative, antisocial, violent elements that appear and gain an audience in modern cultures. The authorities in this culture have, to a meaningful degree, abandoned their rightful role as mentors worthy of veneration for their courage, openness, and wisdom. Thus the young are often left to seek inspiration and influence from outsiders and outlaws who seem to have some spark—however misguided, self-absorbed, or even abusive that energy may be.

> We are beginning to become a mirror of our deepest aspirations. The question then becomes, "What are our deepest aspirations? What will the future be?" Will it be some kind of Mephistophelian nightmare?... Or will we choose the element of care and control, the aesthetic element, the wish to escape into a universe that is, in fact, art?[13]
> *Terence McKenna*

There is a vision afoot regarding the renaissance of sanity and the respiritualization of life that the wisdom carriers are telling us may be our only hope for survival on the bejeweled planet. The vision holds that there will be a rapprochement between art and the conduct of affairs in the larger society, an integration of artistic vision with the dreams and plans of the culture, a renewal of loving care toward the web of life in its totality, no part forgotten or discarded. This goes far beyond the concept of particular specialists creating great art for the rest of us, although we hope to see more of that of course. It's a way of living, a way of seeing available to all of us. All of our daily activities, even the most apparently mundane, are potentially expressions of art, works of art. In that sense there is no separation between art and life. The grounding principle is the dawning of the awakened heart in each of us that brings openness, genuineness, humbleness, gentleness, courage, delight, and spontaneity into all elements of our lives.

The Whole Business of Man is The Arts, & All Things Common.[14]
William Blake

Can you imagine living in a world where art—the joining of heaven and earth, the attitude of creating beauty in all activities—becomes the guiding principle? Can you imagine living in towns and cities that reflect the visions of awakened-mind art over the bottom-line worldview of profit-obsessed commerce, where decisions that affect the community are made with these values held highest? Can you envision environments where people are awake and attentive to the details of life, relating with full presence and creativity to all aspects of this physical reality? Can you entertain the possibility of possibility; that the best idea, the most intelligent vision, could be recognized and manifested; that it's possible for the largely untapped brilliance of natural mind to be elevated to its rightful place in the center of the mandala; that it's possible to create decent, dignified, elegant, enlightened societies? As he was a brilliant master of Dharma Art, I'm going to give Rinpoché the last word on this topic: "There has to be the basic integrity of maintaining our human society in a state of sanity. That is and should be the only way to work with art. The purpose of a work of art is bodhisattva action...geared toward waking people up from their neurosis."[15]

At Play in the Fields of the Lord
Awakened Economy 101

Another vision: It's long bothered me when I think about how many people on this planet spend their working lives engaged in grueling, unfulfilling, and often grossly underpaid work. Of course, humans have a remarkable capacity for making the best of things, and simple, repetitive tasks of themselves are not necessarily demeaning or soul-destroying. Still, I've often felt sad, and just as often outraged, to think of the way countless numbers have been and still are forced to spend their precious and all-too-brief time on Earth. I use the word "forced" deliberately and for obvious reasons, namely: man's inhumanity to man.

Many have written about the political/economic injustices that have birthed and maintained such forms. The psychological/spiritual foundations of exploitive behavior by the powerful have also been analyzed and deconstructed from various angles. In this book I've repeatedly returned to the theme of the spiritual disconnect that allows such heartless lack of respect for others. You don't, for example, need reminders from this source about the pervasiveness of slavery through much of human history.

Though, for the most part of course, legally sanctioned slavery has been expunged from civilized society as a blight, it's easily argued that great numbers of people still find themselves with few options other than working in environments where there is no underpinning vision for fulfillment. The corporate machinery still objectifies and dehumanizes workers as little more than robots churning out endless product for the financial benefit of the owners and shareholders.

In fact, those who would abuse the labor of others for their own enrichment adapted extremely well to the abolition of slavery. It's been pointed out that the post-slavery reality in countries such as England and the United States allowed the owners to continue to have access to cheap labor without the extra responsibility of feeding, housing, and caring for the health of their workers.

At the Fourth Annual Amazonian Shamanism Conference held in Iquitos, Peru in July 2008, Dr. Dennis McKenna—brother of Terence—delivered a brilliant, off-the-cuff talk on the opening evening of presentations. Dr. McKenna cut sharply to the core issue. He distinguished between what he labeled "the death culture" and "the life culture." The death culture describes that fixed mind caught in the compassionless, denying mindstate driven by the compulsive need for control, power, and self-protection—essentially what Buddhists call ego. McKenna described the life culture as that amorphous yet growing worldwide community of people who do get it, or are at the very least learning to get "it," and who are attempting to do something about the crisis before it's too late.

Dr. McKenna told us that, as he sees it, the final battle of our time between these opposed worldviews is in full sway right now. He used the term "tipping point" to describe systems, at any level of organization, that reach a point of no return, and he reported that a growing body of scientific thought is suggesting that the tipping point for the Earth as a system may be as little as ten years away—if a large number of people do not engage in a radical awakening and reprioritizing in the immediate future.

Interactive Co-Creation

A key element of the vision of the life culture is that every human being is sacred, every life is honored. The primary human rights manifesto declares that all people should be able to experience conditions allowing them to live a "rich" life in this brilliant artwork of the gods we call Earth. So a big part of the planetary healing process will inevitably involve a reclamation of the dignity of labor. Though conditions are of course still grim for many millions, I have a strong feeling that that there are small, tender shoots sprouting up all over the place which very well may eventually break through that hard ground.

Though you might not see many obvious indications of change in this regard at the moment, there are actually visible signs of this new economy in its very earliest stages of manifestation. Many people are gradually becoming more astute and skeptical about the way they are treated by the forces that shape their external worlds. If—as many of us now suspect and intuit may happen—the global economic machinery breaks down to any great degree, people will find themselves increasingly turning to each other in local economies. This transformation, of course, points us back toward more simple, direct, and harmonious ways of relating to each other and to the Earth. However, we're also now seeing the stirrings of a new beast in the shape of the worldwide information-sharing networks that are growing so rapidly and wildly.

It looks like a new version of populism is being born through these imperfect machine nodes linking us. It's as though all those participating are autonomous cells in one mind—or a number of minds—but far vaster than each individual mind. Ideas are being born in public. These loosely configured and often spontaneously generated, ad-hoc group minds are able to lubricate or ignore an idea, an offering, a work of art. And of course its a generational shift—as all good shifts should be I suppose. The old mindset gradually dies off with the passing of the old guard and people come of age who've grown up in an environment of communicating freely through the web of information-sharing technologies. Many of the young have now learned something about bypassing the manipulating corporations to choose culture and products. They've seen real democracy at play in these spheres of activity—a kind of leveling or equalizing democracy where the best, or at least the most attractive idea gets the most support and receives encouragement.

This linking mechanism has the potential to provoke an extravaganza of interactive creation. Cynics will look around and question the sophistication of much of what has arisen so far in some of these interactive media. I see current developments as baby steps in the right direction. Of course there's a lot of drivel around. Nonetheless, the principle of the larger perspective still holds. There's a lot to be learned and a lot to be unlearned as we heal from the tsunami of banality that has washed over much of the mainstream cultural landscape. From the vantage point of "the possibility of possibility" it makes great sense—and fits with the wisest spiritual teachings—that we're learning about oneness. There's immense power and potential contained in that seed.

With so many people communicating, it's less likely that particular individuals will stand out completely, and so it morphs into an environment where people simply put their offerings out there for others to connect to or not, sometimes with the hope of monetary reward, but often with the full understanding that it's about ideas and participation.

Terence McKenna had some lovely ideas on that subject that have always stuck with me. He spoke of how language creates. (When I filter the word "language" through my own receptors, it translates as "thought," and that can be expressed in numerous forms.) McKenna talked of language being made visible. An image arises of a group of people creating a "sculpture" together. Each one puts a thought out into the visible space for others to build upon, examine, rearrange etcetera. We've seen rudimentary attempts through the internet at this kind of inter-active creation and I suspect the level of sophistication we'll see in the years ahead will be nearly unlimited, whether or not we continue to have the assistance of our machines.

So then there's hope for a loosening of the heavy noose of the mercantile principle, a renewal of direct, respectful economic relations with one's own community. I can imagine a scenario where, with the birthing of minds that get it about being real, being in love, we begin to see a softening of the financial imper-ative. We learn the vastly superior benefits of looking after each other, of generosity, of creative play in the fields of the Lord, so that we can get our priorities straightened out and devote more energy to healing and beautification.

The Dance of Work and Play

Perhaps we could also jettison our conditioned responses to the words "work" and "play." Do they need to be divided so distinctly? Those who enjoy their occupations the most have often said that, even though they indeed may have worked their asses off to do it right, they never really saw it as work. Some of the most outstanding people in their fields of endeavor have said that their life's work was a natural extension of a childhood passion. They just followed that curiosity and enthusiasm all the way through to their adult careers. Some of our great singers have said that the voice we hear from them now is the voice they had as a child, that unlike others they never lost that connection. Artists of all variations, scientists, mathematicians, athletes and many others have said similar things.

There appear to be signs of a shift in this direction in the workplace. Educated young people of today have been more exposed to that philosophy than previous generations, at least in my part of the world, and often have higher expectations for job satisfaction. Given the amount of time most people spend at their jobs, it makes no sense for those environments to be intensely stress-inducing or spirit-deadening.

I want to stress here also that the vision for reclaiming the dignity of labor need not be considered an elitist view aimed only at the well-educated, the intellectuals, the artists among us. With awakened heart as the foundation, the human creative imagination will find plenty of ways to create satisfying work environments. As a little "teaser," I'll share with you one of a great many examples of how to get big jobs done without excessively abusing the labor of others. The Inca (or Runa as they called themselves) of pre-conquest Peru built some of the most remarkable stone structures the world has ever seen. One of these, just outside the city of Cusco, is reported to have taken 20,000 people sixty years to build. As opposed to having the labor done by the same people, citizens from all over the empire were conscripted for short periods of time, in the manner of a community co-op where everyone pitches in to complete a project. In that way, a great many people were able to make a personal connection with the seat of the empire and claim a degree of ownership over one of its most sacred monuments. And the difficult physical labor required to build such a massive undertaking didn't result in people being used as beasts of burden and thrown away, as have so many millions of workers over the course of history. Oh, and the Runa apparently sang a lot while they worked.

I believe the vision for the "new order" is that work resemble play as much as possible and that mission statements contain words like joy, creativity, and service as their defining principles. Idealistic as this vision may appear to some, it harmonizes with the central thesis under consideration in this book: that the karmic momentum of the human enterprise is hitting the wall; that all existing programs about how to run the show are up for grabs and all dysfunctional, destructive structures must be open for reconfiguration; and that ultimately we have the power to collectively manifest our best ideas. If enough of us can see a better way and can act on our inspiration while holding that prayer firmly in our hearts and following our intuition—or as some would say, following the guidance of Spirit—the vision claims that it is indeed possible to create awakened societies that nurture authentic presence in life-enhancing environments of work and play.

7

The Universe is Alive...and Calling to Us

Above all, we must awaken to and overcome the great hidden anthropocentric projection that has virtually defined the modern mind: *the pervasive projection of soullessness onto the cosmos by the self's own will to power.*[1]
Richard Tarnas

I've been present more than once when Native American Church elders have admonished those present to try not to let their minds or their feet wander during the long night of a peyote medicine prayer ceremony. They say that when the minds in the tipi come together as one and pray hard, the Spirit responds and comes into the space. They also say that this happened much more frequently in the days when most or all of those assembled were experienced and understood this.

One morning, Alex—a roadman (ceremony leader) who was raised in that church and whose lineage of practitioners goes back to its beginnings in the United States—told us in his gentle manner that we need to keep ourselves in the tipi because the fire and the coals give rise to various visions and entities. He told us that if we pay close attention we can meet these spirits and that they're there to teach us and to help us.

It's not revealing any great secret to point out that our modern cultures have, for a long time, been increasingly squeezed into a barren space where no elements of nature, of the Earth, or of the universe altogether, are experienced as alive and minded. Few of us believe or have experienced that the flora and fauna of the planet can communicate with us at more than an extremely rudimentary, instinctual level. It's considered by most to be seriously beyond the pale to claim that non-human entities of any kind—plant, animal, unseen spirit—could engage us in sophisticated communication and function as medical consultants, healers, allies, guides, and teachers. Even the Tibetan Buddhism I was involved with for many years—though it hinted at mysteries and magic—didn't prepare me for the education I've been receiving from the indigenous world.

Buddhism is supposed to be a non-theistic religion. Western students, in general, have a tendency to unconsciously slot that concept into pre-existing, culturally conditioned synapses. We knew that the depiction of God we'd been sold in our own traditions was highly suspect, and most of us in the Buddhist community that I knew tended to think of the many deities and demons described in the Buddhist texts and teachings as archetypes, as metaphors, as qualities, but not necessarily as real, self-existing entities. In large part, this is because most of us have never had any direct, personal experiences with disincarnate entities and of course no support for the possibility—it's hard to recognize things that no one around you acknowledges to be real.

Apparently there is a great discovery or insight which our culture is deliberately designed to suppress, distort, and ignore. That is that Nature is some kind of minded entity.[2]
Terence McKenna

Awakening to the living, communicating intelligences existing in non-human realms is absolutely central to the transformation of consciousness required of us at this crucial moment. I'm far from alone in saying that we need a radical paradigm shift on this as quickly as possible. Large numbers of us need to learn to dissolve that false boundary that causes us to see nature as mute and soulless and humans as owners of a planet that exists solely for our enrichment and our pleasure. We're ignoring sources of information and guidance that may actually make the difference between continuing as a planet on the road to self-destruction, or finding our way back onto a sane, sustainable path.

Glimpses Through the Veil

The Tibetan Buddhist community I was involved with for years was founded and guided by a man who lived in a state of mind where the boundaries between this world and other worlds were very thin. When I was at the three-month program called Seminary, I heard a number of stories from his closest associates about Rinpoché seeing the ghosts of Japanese people who had apparently been imprisoned in the old hotel we were using when it was an internment camp during World War II. During some sections of the program, Rinpoché gave talks in the evening in the main shrine room, a huge ballroom with a very high ceiling and about 400 of us students sitting on meditation cushions facing in the general direction of his raised podium. At the end of the talk and question period we did the closing chants, which took about fifteen minutes. Often, while all but a few had their heads buried in the chant booklets, I cheated and kept my eyes on Rinpoché. More often than not during these chants I saw him looking up in the direction of the center of the room near the ceiling, smiling and clearly engaged in communication with something or someone.

Jeremy Hayward was one of Trungpa Rinpoché's closest students. In his biography, *Warrior King of Shambhala*, Hayward tells a story about sitting beside Rinpoché on the edge of the bed during a retreat very near the end of Rinpoché's short life. When Rinpoché began talking to the space in front of him, Jeremy asked what was going on. Rinpoché answered that the dakinis were there and that they were trying to persuade him to come home, indicating he had completed his work here.

I also heard a lovely story about him from a woman named Nina. Her family owned two houses side by side. Rinpoché was doing a retreat of several weeks in one of them. One night Nina's family invited him over for dinner in the other house, the old family house of her grandparents. The dining room was adjacent and open to a living room with an old fireplace. Throughout the dinner, Rinpoché kept taking Nina's hand and looking over toward the fireplace with a smile. Eventually someone asked him about this odd behavior and he told the group that their grand-father was over there scowling at him, presumably because grandfather had some racial prejudices toward Asians. Rinpoché wanted the spirit presence to know that he was a close friend of the family.

We're Not Alone

The reason for passing along these little stories is to point out how it's our cultural conditioning that often prevents us from seeing what else is present in the environment. Of course there are many among us who are sensitive to the normally unseen, but as a gross generalization, I would say that the less contact a people have had with the modern world's cultural and religious influence, the more likely they are to experience nature as minded and see non-human presences. From the point of view of the spirits, we seem to be particularly thickheaded. Rinpoché himself sometimes became frustrated that his students couldn't see these other beings that were so clear and present for him. "That's the problem," he once said.

For people similar to myself, the information has tended to come through as subtle displays, felt presences, silent commu-niqués, inexplicable synchronicities, and coded messages from dreams. The further I've entered into the plant-employing practices of the indigenous, shamanic cultures, the more those occurrences have begun to form patterns of meaning and communication. I've also done a fair bit of research on shamanic cultures and talked to a lot of people who have had direct encounters across the veil.

Susan Littlehawk is one of these. She carries the women's energy for her people—an indigenous lineage of northwestern United States. She sees what we call unseen presences commonly. Susan told me once about how two old men had been living in her home for a while. These fellows weren't just old, they were about a thousand years old, from two competing tribes in that time. They kept getting into arguments in her house, disturbing the environment, banging doors in the night. After patiently accommodating the ancient spirits for some time, Susan finally got tired of the frequent disruptions and sent them away.

One of the most striking accounts I heard from Susan was her vision one night during a meeting, her women ancestors lined up behind her, perhaps hundreds of them from a long lineage bent over her, as though communicating their support and their pleas for her to be strong and keep the ancient Earth wisdom alive. This vision was confirmed by another woman who'd been at the same meeting and looked over at Susan to see the same sight.

Susan also told us that often when she's called upon to speak during a meeting, she has no idea of what she's going to say or even sometimes what is coming out of her. She feels these presences behind her whispering in her ear, sometimes even in the old languages that she has to somehow intuitively translate. I've been there for a number of these speeches. There's a free-flowing, authoritative, straight-from-the-heart quality to them. No umming and awing. The information is direct and powerful and on several occasions has left more than a few of us in tears.

There are many beings aware of you at all times, loving you, ready to make you feel it whenever you are ready to open up to it, taking care to see that you don't get in too deep, encouraging you to love yourself.[3]

Thaddeus Golas

In the community of people I've met in the Native American Church, this kind of encounter and these kinds of stories about spirit contact are common. And it appears to be a nearly universal phenomenon all across the planet with indigenous peoples who have their own cultural and spiritual traditions. These ancient ways and connections have all but disappeared, perhaps just in time for researchers and chroniclers to record and report on these ways and for committed people to work for their regeneration. Hopefully this thin lifeline can be preserved strong and long enough to provide a trail back to that understanding.

The Mayan community described by Martín Prechtel in his books on his life in Guatemala had a deep—and for some at least—direct and palpable experience of the living spirits of the plants, animals, lakes, mountains etcetera. What's really important about this is that we here in our so-called First World cultures are in deep trouble from the neglect of Spirit that has cut us off from ourselves and the living world around us for so long. I'll remind you that the Maya called our cultures "The Land of the Dead" and referred to all people disconnected from this true indigenous soul that resides in everyone as "uninitiated."

Prechtel described how Chiviliu, a highly regarded shaman from the region, took him in as an apprentice, saying that he had put out a call for someone like Martín who could carry this wisdom lineage out into the world. Those Maya knew everything about the environment they lived in, everything that fed and sustained them. Their shamans were trained to petition directly to various spirits from the natural world and beyond for assistance in healing, community problem solving, and visions for the future. They had a firm understanding and conviction that it's only by awakening to that encompassing reality and honoring and feeding those who feed us that we keep the world alive and maintain life. They say we please the gods and sustain life through our beauty: by being real, living with joy, humor, compassion, creative action, elegance, and devotion to life altogether. They say that the lifestyle of acquisition and of attempting to create permanent structures of security is destructive and unsustainable and will come back somehow, sometime to haunt us.

In *Secrets of the Talking Jaguar*, Prechtel told the story of how Chiviliu foresaw a period of terrible destruction in his region in the immediate future which would all but wipe out his tradition and put Martín's life in great danger. The violence he predicted did indeed soon overcome much of Guatemala and in the following passage Prechtel makes it clear, in his passionate and stark manner, just what is at stake: "Maybe this is why Chiviliu sent me away, to sing and speak these peoples' lives back together. After all, he said that the destruction was coming from them. Our world was being killed by people whose naturalness had been disenfranchised a long time ago. The violence they leveled upon us came from their soulless minds and angry, homeless souls, looking for permanence through violent business growth, killing, forgetting, and mocking everything that reminded them of their inadequacies."[4]

"We've Been Expecting You."

It's all of a piece, all connected. In a sense it's one story with variations on a theme. The theme again, in the simplest terms, is that we in the dominator cultures have wandered away from the garden, and that despite centuries and more of denial, the garden and everything in it are—in ways beyond our comprehension— minded. We, the prodigal sons and daughters, unable to see or hear this minded world, are now being called back in the hope that we'll humble ourselves and relearn how to listen, how to harmonize.

In Part 3 of this book I explore courageous means of re-igniting this lost connection through the direct intercession of spirit-invoking plants themselves. Many of those who have undertaken apprenticeship to the courses of instruction offered by the plant teachers have come back to report a similar occurrence, almost an archetypal experience: the spirits of the vegetal realms are aware of us and they're waiting for us to learn how to navigate the dissolution of our imprisoning egos and cross the threshold into realms of information and guidance. I've encountered a number of accounts very much like the following, written in an unpublished manuscript by an apprenticing ayahuasca shaman in the Amazonian jungle of northern Peru. Ayahuasca is a powerful healing and visionary medicine with a long history of indigenous use throughout the Amazon.

A common element to these stories is that it's usually the first time the journeyer has completely broken through to the other side. The apprentice shaman in question, an American named Alan, was participating in a jungle ritual. Ayahuasca is sometimes called a purgative and often provokes vomiting at a certain point in the journey. Those experienced with the medicine say purging is often the trigger to full entrance into the realms beyond our consensual reality. Alan had to go outside the hut to purge at one point and as he slowly straightened himself out again, he thought at first he saw some of the other participants out of the corner of his eye, and wondered if perhaps they had followed him out of concern. But by the time he pulled himself erect, prepared to be embarrassed, he realized he was witnessing an astonishing scene experienced by his senses as completely real with eyes wide open. In Alan's words, "All the jungle plants in the semicircle of my vision had transformed into indigenous sprits and were glowing internally. The very small plants just off to my left appeared as spirits of indigenous children, and in the outside center of this half-circle, the large shrubs were giant 16-feet-tall tribal spirits, resplendent in attire." As Alan attempted to come to terms with this incomprehensible encounter, the whole group of eight spirits began to sing his name in gorgeous multipart harmony. To Alan it was a deeply moving welcoming ceremony and became a touchstone experience that inspired his commitment to a rigorous apprenticeship of seven years before he eventually became an ayahuasquero himself.

> The spirits can talk to you anytime. They can talk to you over the breakfast table or while you are driving down the freeway—and they will, if you are open to them and you ask them for help.[5]
> *Ralph Metzner*

Other versions of this kind of encounter have the spirits saying something like, "Ah there you are. We've been expecting you. Welcome." Other versions still of the meeting of minds across the dimensions involve spirit presences who come to reassure the supplicant, to provide specific guidance, and to assist and empower healing work. Another favorite anecdote was told to me by a woman whose non-native husband Arnold had been participating in Native American Church ceremonies in the northwestern United States with her for two years. At that point of his involvement, Arnold had begun to get depressed about himself in connection to this practice. He had by then heard a wealth of testimonials and stories from other participants about the remarkable encounters they had experienced in the ceremonies and the powerful healing effect this was having in their lives. Arnold felt like he just wasn't getting it and that he was a fraud who didn't belong. For the next few years he refused to attend any ceremonies.

Several years later a very special meeting was called and Arnold's wife implored him to attend just this one. Arnold reluctantly agreed. In the morning, when the ceremony was over, he excitedly told his wife that an osprey had come and sat on his shoulder for much of the night. Ten years later, Arnold has evolved into a committed and sensitive follower of that path and has since reported numerous direct encounters with the spirits of animals and even trees, always in the context of receiving valuable information.

These stories are offered as a few from a huge library of information testifying to the reality of interspecies communication and direct contact with spirit allies. The ones I've shared here are true and come from the mouths of intelligent, sensible people without an axe to grind, without an agenda they're attempting to promote. I know Susan and Arnold personally. I've participated in an ayahuasca ceremony guided by Alan. I've sat up all night praying with Alex in NAC ceremonies. They're remarkable individuals. But the conditioning that has people in cultures like mine convinced that no such thing is possible runs deep and can take a long time to overcome, even when there is a willingness and openness.

But the evidence is abundant; the universe is alive, nature is alive. According to the accounts of a great many sincere and sane people, the information and assistance are accessible with the right attitude and experience, and perhaps even more important, badly needed at this precise moment.

> This larger engagement . . . will demand an initial act of trust in the possible reality of an ensouled cosmos of transformative beauty and purposeful intelligence.[6]
> *Richard Tarnas*

For many of us in cultures conditioned to disregard and dismiss what we call the non-rational, learning to recognize the messages coming from the quiet and hidden places, from Earth, from Spirit, from the Muse, from our own clear minds, is a little like learning a new language. First we have to quiet our minds and slow ourselves down enough for subtle information to enter through the cracks. Then we have to pay close attention without judgment or expectation. Intuitive information is pre-thought. Many of us seekers are imagining dramatic confirmation of Spirit presence and can easily overlook the information in the corners of our vision. Martín Prechtel spoke of how the Mayan shamans he encountered taught him to listen for the voice of Spirit in all different forms—the patterns of the weather, the play of light on the water, odd coincidences, unexpected encounters, casual remarks, flashes that send a slight charge through the system. As with the learning of a language, what seemed at first to be random, unconnected, and incomprehensible may at some point fall into recognizable patterns. What was there all along begins to unscramble and make sense.

> Far from living our lives in a distant corner of an unsentient universe, we are everywhere surrounded by orders of intelligence beyond reckoning.[7]
> *Christopher M. Bache*

8

Ecstatic Marriage of the Sacred and the Profane
A Short Rant

Here's a theory, some food for thought. As has been suggested in various ways throughout this book and as many people well know, real spiritual awakening and understanding has been in short supply around here. There's been a painful scarcity of authentic presence, perhaps most crucially among those who command power and influence in the worlds of government, commerce, and religion. The religious authorities in general—and in their wake the morality pedlars, those who implement the infrastructures of education that form the belief systems of societies—long ago cut half of themselves off, cut off the feminine, the Earth-connected, the sexual and sensual.

We've been taught to be afraid of the dark, afraid of our shadows, afraid of authentic presence—essentially, afraid of our own minds. God's world has been turned into a bleached and sanitized Hallmark version of the Mysterium Tremendum and stuffed inside a fortress where only the "good' is allowed to dwell. In that interpretation of life the earthy, the sexual, the natural urges, have been expelled from the Kingdom and dumped on the Devil, who is always Other, and always a threat. But without access to that other half—without some understanding of the unconditioned goodness of our nature as Spirit beings traveling in material vehicles—our ceremonies are eviscerated and drained of blood, unable to enliven and awaken.

In perpetrating and perpetuating this shrunken vision, these authorities have abandoned their potential and expected role as wise counselors, as initiators into the wisdom of the tribe, as midwives of authentic empowerment. The Dionysian, Bacchanalian, ecstatic elements of religious life have been suppressed right out of legitimate existence. This has left a huge hole in the core needs of the people to experience the full range of our energy, our passion, our creativity. It must be a law of creativity that thought-created limitation is not to stand in the way and draw cloaks over the free and pure flow of information. The Sentinels—along with the rest of us of course—have to lose the arrogant assumption that they know better than the Muse, better than the Creator. We already have awakened mind—as Buddhist teachings keep reminding us—and we're not to be treated like children. It's just like letting go. You'll never know what people are capable of until you trust them to apply their own intelligence.

In abandoning their proper place in the natural hierarchy of a wise society, the secular and religious leaders have opened the door for these powerful, innate drives to be sought outside of the purvey of the elders and outside the gates of the fortress. This results in many of these forbidden and undernourished needs being acted out counter to the expressed and unexpressed values of the mainstream, official culture—without benefit of a lineage of hard-won knowledge and wisdom—and instead held under the auspices or in the environs of the inexperienced and the uninitiated. "Outlaw" implies excitement, freedom from society's boring, bloodless contracts and constraints. Unsanctioned, untutored, dangerous, illegal, "immoral" behavior offers the juice of forbidden fruit and holds great attraction for the young and unformed.

Much of this kind of experience then ends up being banal,

self-indulgent, and superficial. Much of it falls far short of its potential to awaken and free. The way consciousness-altering substances of all kinds are used in contemporary Western societies clearly illustrates this unrealized potential. Very few people have the slightest inkling of the power of some of these teachers and allies and the methodologies and attitudes required to uncover their benefits. Meanwhile, our contemporary commercial cultural offerings through television, movies, popular music and so on have for the most part been stripped of all spiritual power and become no more than disposable products that retread safe, superficial, market-tested concepts, titillate briefly, and then dissipate into the heap of continually churned-out consumables.

In a healthy society—here comes the theory—there is no separation between religious and secular, between the sacred and the so-called profane. Because the innate goodness and intelligence of humans is honored and included and not feared and controlled, art, sensual/sexual, ecstatic/visionary experience are all welcome in empowered cultural life. The mandala is all-inclusive. Relaxing non-judgmentally and courageously into the flow of energy frees these drives from the dark abodes where they attack from behind and allows them to be transmuted into creative, wisdom energies. In that environment, experience is enriched, builds upon itself, and feeds both individuals and the society. There have of course been communities where these needs have been understood, accepted, encouraged, and enshrined in the cosmology of the culture, where cherished values of love, charity, compassion and peace aren't threatened by the full range of human capability and squeezed into a half-life. As Terence McKenna suggested, the "Archaic Revival" points its holy finger toward our future.

So let's get sexuality back into the Church where it belongs. Let's get ecstatic, transcendent encounters back into the churches and temples and mosques and cultural celebrations where they

111

belong just as much as they do in the jungles, in the deserts, in the mountains and the canyons, in the tipis and the huts and the "pagan" village festivals. Let's put the real, Spirit-fired, healing, entheogenic sacraments back into these ceremonies. Let's bless and shake the cathedral walls with extravagant ceremonies of incandescent rock 'n roll, inspired gospel, shamanic drumming, sacred chant, Bach, blues, Handel, and Spirit-pervaded silence. Let's pray and sing and chant and kundalini dance ourselves into trances and holy space like Tibetans and Sufis and Voudouns and Theyyams and Ravers and Sun Dancers until we drop . . . the one-sided, illusory, isolated, enchained self.

Part 2

Your Head Garland of Non-thought
*Good teachings and wise words from
the four directions*

Introduction to Part Two

In the first section I hope I was able to provide an understandable and plausible philosophical/theoretical framework to discuss some of the central issues that have led *to* and will hopefully lead *through* the crisis and transformation nexus in which we now find ourselves inextricably enmeshed. To summarize it in a sentence: those chapters discussed the pervasive effects of a deep and long-standing spiritual disconnect and the urgent need to remake the connection on a number of levels.

Those of us who have undertaken some kind of commitment to waking up, generally understand that without healing ourselves first, we aren't going to be of full utility to others. My Buddhist experience taught me the value of having both view and practice—understanding something about the landscape we're traversing and then actually making the journey step by step, with "the walk of an elephant" as my old teacher described it. Now I want to build on the overview laid out in the first section and shift the focus somewhat toward more directly practical, useable, and inspirational teachings that can be of help in actually bringing about this shift in the journey toward awakened heart that each one of us has to make.

As I outlined in the introduction to this book, I've been around the spiritual block a few times by now and each time around I come upon new information and new encounters that were missed on the previous round. In that introduction I brought in the concept of syncretism: combining different religions, cultures, and ways of thinking. I've mentioned already and will address again later, that in these urgent times it may be extremely helpful for many more of us to combine the wise employment of medicinal, teaching, visionary plants with daily mindfulness/awareness practices drawn from rich spiritual traditions such as Buddhism.

As my own spiritual path has reflected this syncretic approach, in this next section I'll share a number of ideas I've found to be of particular value along the way. These are ideas and teachings I would like someone to tell *me* about if I didn't already have some familiarity with them. They're also reminders we so easily forget even though we've come upon them before.

You'll also notice that Buddhist teachings get significant attention in this section. Despite the remarkable experiences and deep realizations that can come to one with right use of the plant medicines, I still find that Buddhist teachings—especially as explicated so brilliantly and with such loving detail by my old teacher Trungpa Rinpoché—have been unique and unparalleled in their ability to elucidate the most significant obstacles and antidotes of the spiritual journey. I hope that you who read these chapters will also find the information useful. As a Buddhist prayer goes: "May confusion dawn as wisdom."

9

Slipping out of the Chains of Fear

There is no cause that justifies fear, and there is no work motivated by fear that in any way contributes toward a better world.[1]

Ken Carey

"If you don't use your own mind," Kanucas admonished us one night, "somebody else is going to use it for you." I think most reasonably sophisticated people have some grasp of the mechanics of fear, as in the famous saying by Franklin Delano Roosevelt, "The only thing we have to fear is fear itself." But it's worth taking a close look at how fear functions psychologically in the current planetary environment.

Fear and ego are almost interchangeable terms. Like ego, there's no ultimate reality to fear. It lives in the discursive mind, in our thoughts. We know how difficult it is to come to terms with that in daily, real-world experience. We tend to believe that the way we see a situation is the way it is. We believe the stories fear feeds us. The arguments of the controlling ego in our heads can be exceedingly ingenious and convincing. And of course the sheer physical power of fear—the way it grabs hold of our bodies and rattles us—can also be extremely difficult to pacify.

Another old homily, referring to Satan, goes, "The more you talk about him the more he comes around." Ego survives on its constructs, on its concepts of threat, of enemy. We live in the illusion of our separateness, which is always under threat, always in danger of crumbling if we don't maintain it, defend it, and—if we have the strength—expand it. Do you remember that pop song from the 1980s, *Everybody Wants to Rule the World*? We all have that drive to keep our world under control. For some that hegemony extends only to the edge of their skin. Others think big.

As more and more of us develop the conviction that the future of the planet is at stake, we also increasingly understand how linked we are, how small this spacefaring craft is. Though it's always been true, the way people handle their fear during times of upheaval can and probably will have far-reaching consequences in this interconnected world. For example, several polls in recent years have found that people in this part of the world often believe that overall crime rates are going up, when in fact the numbers are going down. That belief no doubt affects the behavior of the people who believe it.

I suspect the explanation for that particular misconception lies at least partly in the often unconscious feeling that "the center cannot hold." We see our comfort zones being rattled. Traditional cultural values are being challenged daily. The biosphere itself threatens to become increasingly destabilized and unreliable. The world economy can turn in an instant, feels like it's held together with a wish and a prayer. The karma of the marketplace is played out in the public eye, such as with the sub-prime mortgage disaster that began to spiral out of control in the U.S. in late 2007—a stinging lesson on our unprecedented degree of inter-connectedness and a telling example of how greed overcame intelligence and responsibility and built a house of cards that came crumbling down, with consequences that reverberated around the world.

The way ego functions in this regard is that when it can convince itself that it's secure—or at least doing a decent job of maintaining a stable situation—it can relax to some extent and have some confidence in its condition of denial, ignorance in Buddhist terms. But it's a highly conditional situation and when conditions appear to worsen, when the sources of that comfort become unreliable or are ripped out from under us, the ego begins to feel it's losing its ground. If you are completely or primarily identified with ego, if you have no larger perspective and no faith, however tenuous, in your oneness with Spirit, with all of life, you're likely to become frightened and confused as things unravel.

> We think fear is a signal to withdraw, when in fact it is a sign
> we are already withdrawing too much.[2]
> *Thaddeus Golas*

We see that happen when events turn against us, when our plans aren't working out, when our relationships break down, when someone close to us dies. Conditions like those shake our previously comforting stories about our situation. We become vulnerable and confused. Those are the times when people seek help, go to therapists, look for a spiritual connection.

The danger is that when we're afraid, we don't think straight, we don't act skillfully, we search for a source of security to grab onto. We're susceptible to bad ideas, our own and others', and maybe most importantly, we're vulnerable to manipulation by people who have something to gain by preying upon our fear. You see that happen in the political arena all the time. Few candidates for the leadership of a country have fared badly by declaring war on crime, war on "Terror," and accusing their opponents of being soft in those areas.

Working with fear at the most basic—even the smallest—level is a key element of spiritual practice. Simply put, with an increasingly stabilized mindfulness/awareness practice we can hope to find ourselves less distracted by discursive thinking and more present in the moment. Our tendency is to be caught by fear and automatically—more or less unconsciously—fall into our habitual patterns of response. In fact, this quick sequence can become so ingrained that we may not even recognize the fear. A chronic, habitual pattern of avoidance of and refusal to acknowledge fear has been described as cowardice.

So we have to pay attention to this fear in the way we move through our moments. We need to see how fear lurks—often beneath our radar—in everything we do. By acknowledging fear in the moment, even at the level of noticing such things as when we start to chew our nails, we start to see how we do in fact constantly attempt to avoid and ignore it. And in seeing this we begin to learn how to work with fear by remaining present, breathing, softening into the feelings and experiences that are underneath the fear, like tenderness, sadness, loneliness, passion, compassion, clarity, authentic presence—soft front, firm back.

If I was asked to pick out one reminder that could be of most use moving through the moments of a day, I'd have to say it's simply the reminder to breathe, to pay just enough attention to one's presence in the body to be aware of the breath going in and out on its own. When we get stressed, when we get caught into a small or large fear, we tend to lose that attention, go into our heads, and tighten. Breath becomes restricted. As Mother Ayahuasca told me that night during a period when I was confused about the direction I wanted to go in my life, "You're job is to breathe."

The mechanism of these encounters with fear is direct and real. It goes something like this: When fear gets hold of us we've succumbed to its power. We think fear is stronger than we are, stronger than our courage and determination. By remaining present when we feel the fear—at whatever level of intensity—by not averting our gaze and falling back into habitual patterns, the fear may collapse, dissolve, and transmute into freed energy as we "hold our seat," breathe, and soften. Courage has been described as an acquired taste, a developing confidence that comes from repeatedly remaining fully present in the midst of fear.

I believe that the message needs to get out as strongly as possible in these next few years that fear isn't real and can be seen through and dissolved with the right kind of understanding and skill. We may find ourselves increasingly susceptible to it if our sense of security is seriously compromised, so we'll need to be vigilant and clear about who is trying to manipulate us, and then we'll need to work hard and courageously to find our ground in groundlessness. Even in the past year or two, several of my friends and I have felt an opening in more minds. I find myself having conversations on these issues that would not have happened even a year ago. It becomes increasingly difficult to ignore the one story we're being pulled into, and it looks more and more like the center may indeed not hold. The most hopeful part of my mind can picture a situation where more people are open to hearing the truth when they find old certainties failing, and that we may turn toward each other as the isolating corporate juggernaut, with its soul-deadening and planet-destroying machinations and hollow promises, becomes increasingly understood for what it's doing and increasingly unable to paper over the rawness of life.

If, as the whispering of signs and portents intimates, we are moving into an environment of upheaval and transformation— of death and rebirth—in these next years, let's hope and pray that adverse circumstances and deprivations that may unfold will not cause a tsunami of panic reactions that actually feed the fear and unconsciously create their own consequences. Let's hope that events that nudge or force us out of our habitual comfort zones will smarten us up and push us to get our priorities straight, in alignment with awakened wisdom. As the saying goes, "When the going gets tough, the tough let go."

10

Worry>Boredom>Silence

The basic obstacle to clear perception is omnipresent anxiety, which does not allow us to relate to ourselves or to the world outside ourselves.[1]
Chögyam Trungpa

I'd only been up for a few minutes. I was sitting in the bathtub. I noticed there was a subtle worry in my mind, a slight furrowing of the brow. It wasn't attached to anything specific that I could identify. Some call it existential angst—the programs the ego keeps running in the background, the old programs that often travel below the waterline and somehow communicate to the whole mind/body system that things aren't alright, that there's reason to worry, that the hammer waits just around the next corner. Although I wasn't thinking of anything in particular at that moment, and certainly not worrying any topic through my brain, I was still in my head.

And then I remembered something elementary that I've forgotten more times than I can count; worry isn't real, it exists only in the virtual world of my mind. At that moment I noticed how I wasn't fully present, not quite attentive to my surroundings: the body I was inhabiting; my breath entering and leaving effortlessly; the water I was sitting in; the room around me; the soft finger-drumming of the morning rain on the roof. There's no solution or antidote to this state of mind in the discursive mind itself, no intellectual argument that will triumph—only to empty into full presence. I'm sure that doesn't sound like any kind of solution to a lot of people, but it's true. I see it over and over again in my own life and spiritual teachers have been speaking and writing about it since around the time the first knotted brow appeared on a human face.

There's an old Gahan Wilson cartoon, sometimes observed on the bulletin boards at dharma centers. Two young novice monks, evidently on their first day at the Buddhist zendo or monastery, are sitting in meditation posture in front of an older monk or teacher, also sitting, on a raised platform. One of the young monks has obviously just asked the master a question because the caption is his response, "*Nothing* happens next."

I also like what Eckhart Tolle said on this issue—that the now is never enough. Many seekers will look anywhere but at the silent gap between thoughts. What Buddhist teachings call emptiness can be highly uncomfortable, bewildering, or flat-out boring, at least while you're getting your sea legs. Rinpoché had some great teachings about boredom. He talked about hot boredom and cool boredom. Hot boredom, for a meditator, is when you try to sit still but your mind won't join you and your body's uncomfortable, you're jumpy and restless and you want to get away from where you are right now. Most of us, to some degree or another, are in that state a lot of the time.

And if left to ponder your situation for awhile, like maybe while you're waiting in a lineup or in traffic, you flood your mind with a continual stream of discomforting or restless thinking about the lack of perfection of the current circumstances, some other thing you could have or place you could be, or just a random parade of thoughts to keep you from having to relate completely with your boredom and the situation in general. Most often, the thinking that drives the restlessness isn't particularly conscious, but actually more of a feeling, from a vague irritation to a highly uncomfortable impatience . . . unless one makes a point of paying attention to these thoughts as they arise, at which point the energy can shift.

> Instead of trying to run away from this sense of emptiness at our core, we need to become more comfortable with it and more aware, in which case it can transform from a sense of lack into the source of our creativity and spontaneity.
> *David R. Loy*

Hot boredom is often the first obstacle people run into when they attempt to engage with their minds through a sitting meditation practice. A lot of people can't see themselves practicing a bare-attention type of meditation at all. These people often know themselves well enough to describe themselves as people who can't sit still, who have to keep moving. They imagine they couldn't possibly sit still and quiet their minds for even a few minutes. But I can testify from personal experience and observation that that's not true. There's a Buddhist teaching called "The Lion's Roar"—the fearless proclamation that any state of mind is workable. The restless speedy mind *is* workable. It can be tamed. It can relax. And it's not a program of squelching the energy, it's giving it room to breathe and settle down. That doesn't mean it's going to be easy, but Buddhist teachings keep telling us that everyone has Buddha mind, the natural awakened state that is there all the time, just obscured by the continuously overlapping noise of the busy discursive mind.

Cool boredom, which really isn't boredom at all in the usual sense, begins to unfold as you ride out the restlessness and speed and gradually relax into that emptiness, that stillness. On the way there it can take a lot of perseverance and discomfort. Even when the discursive mind has chilled out, the background discomfort doesn't necessarily dissipate. I know, I've been there frequently, like, "okay, nothing going on here. This isn't my kind of living. My thoughts are far more pleasurable and entertaining than this uncomfortable tedium."

One has to hang in through those choppy waters. Often, when his students were complaining to him about the state of their minds, their belief that they weren't making progress on their paths, or their confusion over details of the teachings, Rinpoché's answer was simply, "Sit more." It will take time for most of us, but there will likely come a point when it starts to feel good. Our minds gradually become more clear and peaceful. It feels right, it feels real. Buddhist and other teachings tell us that emptiness—meaning empty of a busy head full of concepts—is the gateway. As one teaching goes: "Emptiness becomes luminosity."

Relaxing into that nowness can be really sweet, touching, beautiful. Speaking as one of the great majority who lost that peace a long time ago, I can say that landing on it again after a long absence might be the best feeling in the world, a taste of "the peace that passeth all understanding" we hear tales about. And then we leave it again, caught up in the drama, the struggle of the self. We come and go in the night like stray cats, hungry for love but afraid of the light.

Come, even if you have broken your vow
a thousand times
Come, yet again, come, come.
Jelaluddin Rumi

I've learned the hard way in the NAC meetings what happens when my mind gets going and what happens when I can surrender that up and be fully there without much discursive thinking. The former condition is inevitably painful—the chains of time (more on the subject of time later.) Grandfather peyote doesn't let you off the hook. You've invited him into your life. He is utterly kind and completely uncompromising. There's only one way to be with him. These are long meetings, twelve hours or more in the tipi. Maybe you only get up once, five minutes to go out and take a pee.

Grandpa ups the ante. You don't get to remain in a state of habitual, undisciplined self-absorption. You have to empty, again and again and again, pay attention, keep your mind on the prayer, sending kind thoughts to others. In fact, the partner to this emptying is this discipline of prayer, this practice of focusing your attention on a beneficial thought. I know that's no revelation to a lot of people. I can testify that it can make a huge and immediate difference in how you feel. It's ironic isn't it? You want to feel good, but trying to figure out how to do that keeps you in your head, in the suffering. By forgetting about yourself in that way you start to feel good. As Kanucas has reminded us on more than one occasion, "Relatives, you didn't come here to get comfortable, you came here to get strong."

I've suffered powerfully in some of those meetings as I've slowly learned what works and what doesn't. I've reached points where I thought I couldn't stand another minute of it. In the meetings they tell you you've made a commitment to stay the night, and fortunately I always took that to heart. I'll mention again the words of Kanucas, "If you don't feel good here, it's your own choice, you're own responsibility. This medicine wants to meet you. It's very kind but it can only meet you where it is. You can make that hard or you can make that easy."

It's kind of tragic how so many of us have not been able to fully hear and accept the teaching of simplicity, of emptiness, of silence. We play the game of hide and seek but won't let ourselves find. Or if we do, we fall into recurring bouts of amnesia and continue to seek. I've noticed some people glaze over—the way you know an idea isn't meeting a ready synapse—when I mention silence as the gateway. Students of spirituality can often be the worst offenders in that sense. They've got their fixed ideas about the beautiful and sophisticated teachings they have treasured all these years. Again, as Tolle says, the now is never enough. We have to complicate everything. It's the domination of head over heart and discursive thought over simple, clear presence.

The reminder keeps coming up for me—and I'm often surprised at how I repeatedly forget the simple truth—that I just need to be still and present and trust that way of being, that way of experiencing. Playing music, jamming with friends, improvising on my guitar or with my voice, are excellent reminders. Can't figure it out? Don't worry about it. Am I hitting the "right" notes, does it sound okay, etc. etc? When I find the courage to let it get out of my control, relax into the moment, give up all thoughts of self, listen with all my attention to what's going on— prepared for it to be nothing—then something else usually happens and I suddenly realize, "What was I thinking?" (and "Why was I thinking?")

One teacher I've referred to several times in this book is Shunryu Suzuki. I highly recommend the little book of his teachings called *Zen Mind, Beginner's Mind.* Suzuki Roshi had a wonderfully unique, clear way of describing the simplicity of meditation practice, the no-big-deal aspect of it. He counseled his students to just keep practicing, forever, and warned them about developing what he called "gaining ideas" in their practice which would take them away from the present. He spoke of what we call "I" as just a door swinging back and forth with the breath, no actual self there at all in that moment. "If you continue this simple practice every day you will obtain a wonderful power. Before you attain it, it is something wonderful, but after you obtain it, it is nothing special. It is just you yourself, nothing special."[4]

So let me put it in a nutshell to finish up here. Maybe you start with anxiety, even if you experience it as a subtle energy running in the background. You commit yourself to a simple mindfulness/awareness meditation practice. It might be really irritating and uncomfortable at times, or even most of the time, especially for the first while. But you persevere, let your breath come in and go out like that swinging door, and perhaps the anxiety gradually settles down. Ah, but then it could get boring, just sitting there doing nothing. However, you might remember someone warned you about that trap, so you persevere some more and the hot boredom relaxes and opens up into cool boredom. Along the way you may have your painful upheavals, but the more you continue the more you begin to notice how good it can feel to just be.

If enough of us were to do this, it would be helping to undo the collective head traffic and calm this whole driven world down. That peace might then be able to flow around and create some healing.

11

Without Goal

The point is to serve, to offer, to be the offering. Out of our zazen, our bearing witness, the offering will arise, of itself the fruit is born. We don't have to worry about what to do.[1]
Roshi Bernie Glassman

There's a story about the Buddha. When he first realized he had fully awakened, he felt moved and compelled to teach others that enlightenment is available to all. After attempting to do that for some time, he concluded it wasn't working, it wasn't flowing. At some point he made the decision to step back, to drop any agenda whatsoever and just fall into situations. As the story goes, he began to simply go from one thing to the next, as the Spirit moved him and situations arose, without an agenda or goal, and the opportunities to help people wake up presented themselves effortlessly.

I like to think there's an "auspicious coincidence" to these kinds of meetings. Not to reduce it to a simplistic explanation, just that there's a need—something presenting itself on the energetic level, unseen in the background—that creates these encounters apparently out of the blue. A friend calls about something else and you slide into a raw, honest, personal conversation. You strike up a conversation with a stranger in the bank lineup that develops into a beneficial relationship. Something gets said that hits a waiting synapse and triggers new ideas, new solutions, revised operating procedures. Or you respond to a request for help and it leads you down avenues and opens up opportunities you never envisioned. Or you follow your nose, your passion, and the path keeps opening up new territory and bigger vision.

When we can get the ego out of the way and let go of our insistence on a particular outcome or state of affairs, then hopefully we can see the situation clearly and allow events to develop naturally, in the way of the Tao, you might say. I see this a lot with the issues that my friends and I are working on in our lives, with our dreams, aspirations, desires, relationships. We jump too soon or overthink things and obscure the first-thought wisdom that quietly unfolds when there's space in our minds. It's about trusting life, Spirit—whatever you want to call it.

It's always easier to observe these struggles in others. I watched my friends Sean and Carol—who had split up four years earlier after twenty years of marriage—go through a complicated dance about whether or not to give it another try. There was a lot at stake for them regarding what they had to leave behind and where they saw themselves going, as they spent a few months sharing the old marital house, preparing it for sale. Carol in particular came into the situation with expectations, and within days of Sean's arrival from his current home overseas was pushing him to "pick a lane." For the next two months confusion ruled the roost. They fell back into some of their old push-pull patterns they hoped they'd gone beyond. Carol spent a lot of that time stressed. Sean drank more than usual and worked himself to exhaustion every day to avoid dealing with the situation.

Finally, Carol came to the conclusion she just had to give it up, let things develop as they may. She realized she couldn't force the outcome. As she told me later, as soon as she came to that decision in her mind, things "opened up" for both of them. There are forces at play much bigger and more complex than the programs and desires we come up with in our heads. Difficult as it is for most of us mortals, the more we can step back far enough from the solidity of our demand upon the situation to get a clear view of events, the less life feels like a heavy, confusing burden as we learn to align ourselves with this Tao of energy movement.

For a lot of us, the starting point is simply to s-l-o-w-w-w d-o-w-w-n-n, to walk the walk of an elephant in our daily lives. If you have demands upon your time that don't make it easy to get some sitting meditation into your schedule, you can still practice slowing and stilling in your daily activities. I think we've all seen enough examples of how rushing doesn't get the job done any faster and is just about guaranteed to create unwanted side effects. It's ongoing. Eckhart Tolle encourages us to learn to treat the thinking mind as a tool we can pick up when needed and set down when not required.

The discursive mind contains the autocrat pushing everyone around. Ego is heavy-handed, so insensitive that most of us live our lives without realizing the depths of our innate wisdom and grace. When we can look clearly, worry comes to be seen as non-solid, we begin to see the experience of problem, of heaviness, of discouragement, as ad-hoc, momentary states of mind that can dissolve into space and leave us able to deal with the challenges of our lives from that still center. As David Loy says, "When we can live in this fashion all things flourish by themselves."[2]

There are various ways to describe this way of being in the world. One of Rinpoché's books is called *Journey Without Goal*. The implication in that title of course is that though there is a journey involved, the journey itself is what matters, not a wish we might have for enlightenment, peace of mind, or any other kind of success or dream we carry around that we imagine will free us from ourselves at some time in the future when we realize our dream, when we get what we desire.

Students of spiritual paths might benefit from the reminder that there's nothing holier or more noble about fixation on the goal of enlightenment than there is with the pursuit of any apparently less spiritual goal, such as ambitions directed toward wealth, fame, or temporal power. In fact, spiritual ambition, or spiritual materialism, is the most insidious version of materialism because of the tendency to proclaim the nobility of the pursuit while fooling yourself into thinking you've transcended conventional materialism.

You may recall from the previous chapter how, in referring to meditation practice in particular, Shunryu Suzuki talked about practicing without gaining ideas which take you away from yourself, away from nowness. He counseled students to meditate with no idea of attainment, just pure, simple zazen, forgetting about yourself, letting go of your ideas of accomplishment. Again, if you can get it, that's a great attitude to bring to life in general. It has to do with coming back down out of the head, out of the dream world, and really getting into what's going on here and now. Letting go of gaining ideas, we begin to focus much less on what we think we can get out of a situation and instead put our attention on what we can give to the situation, on how we can enter it, appreciate it, uplift it, and beautify it. This seems to be the meaning of Kanucas' statement "Our life is a prayer."

This respect for nowness also relates to Buddhist teachings on "one taste" or "one flavor." It's a tricky concept to grasp in a practical, applicable way. As I understand it, the realization of that state of mind means that you don't put so much effort and struggle into attempting to control your experience by avoiding some kinds of experiences and chasing after others. At a deeper, more essential level, it's all one flavor, it's all sacred world, every moment can be entered and related to fully, without resistance. If you can get to that place, it definitely frees up a lot of energy and encourages enjoying life moment by moment.

Another one of my favorite stories from the Buddhist years involved T'ai Situ Rinpoché, a leading Tibetan teacher from the same Kagyu lineage as Trungpa Rinpoché. Situ Rinpoché was doing a speaking tour of the U.S. under the care of Trungpa's

Kasung—the group responsible for protecting the teachings and the teachers. This particular moment occurred as the Kasung were about to chauffeur T'ai Situ from a speaking engagement to the airport. As was their practice, they had a three-car convoy ready to go. The teacher would be in the back seat of the middle car. The Kasung, dressed in their blue blazers and gray flannel slacks, were scurrying around eagerly trying to do everything right. Everyone piled into the cars, but the nervous lead driver put his into reverse and backed right into the Rinpoché's vehicle. The three or four Kasung accompanying T'ai Situ all turned in horror to look for the expected outraged response and were completely surprised to see him sitting there with a huge, thoroughly amused grin on his face, followed by the laughing comment, "That was interesting."

I don't mean to be glib or brush over the daunting challenges and difficulties people have to face in the course of a lifetime. It may be helpful to contemplate a Buddhist teaching that describes our time on this planet as the rare and precious gift of a favorable human birth. And the older you get, the more you see how it passes in the blink of an eyelash. We do have the potential to appreciate it, love it, and enjoy it. If I have the opportunity to look back at my life as death approaches, I hope I won't be thinking: "Oh, this *was* the gift and I missed so much of it because I was so often on my way to somewhere else." If our circumstances allow at least enough of the basics required for simple living, it would seem foolish—tragic even—if we're chronically unable to appreciate life and we don't do something about that.

Elders in the Native American Church talk about staying behind the medicine, staying behind the Spirit, staying behind the prayer that arises from compassion, and not getting out there where your willfulness, your demand, your impatience, close off "the still small voice within." Our task, it appears, is to pay close attention to that voice, to the gap in our minds where that inspiration can be seen, felt, and heard—and to keep reminding ourselves to practice trusting in that space.

This simple "nowness" way of approaching our lives is all of a piece with other themes discussed in this book: the artist's attitude of relating unhurriedly, with total attention, to the experiences we encounter moment by moment and the work we do, seeing everyday existence in all its forms as sacred world, coming back to the indigenous soul in us that feels the thread of connectedness and continuity with all that is. Susan Littlehawk once half-jokingly told me that the Indians were the original hippies, living many of the values and philosophies that the counterculture of the 1960s and 1970s aspired to emulate: a simple, honest, generous life with a dearth of acquisitive hunger or ambition to get ahead of one's fellows; an intimate and deeply respectful attitude toward the Earth; a communal existence that was inclusive of everyone; a strong connection to the Creator and the living Spirit in all forms of life: and an independent spirit within an egalitarian, democratic social structure.

Journeying without goal is journeying without demand, without fixation on dogmatic agendas. It means you don't need to force situations. It means clearing the discursive mind of unnecessary clutter so you can pay attention to ear-whispered information, so you can actually see, hear, and listen to what's going on in the space beyond thought. Apparently the world is alive in ways incomprehensible to minds slotted into deep conditioning by generations of people who have only known nature as mute, who have either believed in no God or only in one conceived in the imagination but never met in the world. This is great news. The past is gone. Nowness, "fresh start," is always available.

Know what it is to be a child.
William Blake,
1757-1827

12

The Worst Horse

In the book *Zen Mind, Beginner's Mind*, Shunryu Suzuki discussed an old Zen Buddhist teaching about how the one who has more difficulty learning may in the end learn the best because that person is forced—if she has the will and persistence—to look at the obstacles and work harder to overcome difficulties and apparent limitations. The anecdote uses the metaphor of horses, some of whom respond to and learn quickly from the lightest of commands, and, at the other end of the continuum, those who require painstakingly patient guidance and encouragement.

> When you are determined to practice with the great mind of the Buddha, you will find that the worst horse is the most valuable one. In your very imperfections you will find the basis for your firm, way-seeking mind.[1]

So the "worst horse" refers to the individual who is struggling, as well as to the most difficult tendencies that anyone may have. When you recognize the obstacles—the problems in your attitudes and behavior—these are set in stark contrast to the awakened qualities. You really get to know those behaviors and how they function in your life. That tends to encourage humility, empathy, and determination.

There are many paths on the healing journey and a multitude

of starting places. Some of us—perhaps more cautious by nature, perhaps more protected by support systems through childhood—have a relatively low tolerance for suffering and seek out ways to deal with our dysfunctions before they drive us into the ditch. Others are extreme, sometimes deeply wounded, or fully in the grip of the daemon, sometimes passionate and intense, given to extravagance, driven to push the envelope. Though I'm not in the latter club, I've been around enough who were. What I've seen is people who didn't or couldn't hold back, who messed up totally, and burned just about everything. And when they chose to live, to heal, that decision had depth and power. Things get real at that point. There's no bullshit and nothing left to protect. What was that old song lyric from *Me and Bobby McGee*? "Freedom's just another word for nothin' left to lose." People who have gone to the brink, where the decision was truly life or death, and gotten themselves straightened out, often have a solid, authentic presence. As an old Bob Dylan song lyric goes, "They're not putting on any airs down on Rue Morgue Avenue."

My ongoing task is to acknowledge my sins and weaknesses: the laziness, greed, aggression, competitiveness, arrogance, selfishness, cowardice, insensitivity, envy, self-doubt, self-absorption, impatience, mental speed, dishonesty, clinging, blaming—the list goes on. I recognize that, given the right provocation under certain difficult conditions, I could be capable of any "sin." One of our tasks is to go beyond judgment, to recognize ourselves in others, not to draw anyone outside the circle of our understanding, not to exclude anyone from the circle of our compassion.

As a practicing member of the Worst Horse lineage, I had the good fortune to conclude, as a young adult, that my mental constructs weren't functioning well and that I needed work. The suffering I experienced in those days provoked me onto the healing path, and now I'm deeply grateful to have met the people and the teachings and healing medicines I've encountered on this journey. Now, peering through openings in the thickets of discursive mind, I try to practice this observing mind-protection as often as possible. While trying to avoid overthinking my "issues," I usually have some confidence that I can catch the little transgressions, like, "Ah, there I go feeling like a big shot again" for example. That dispassionate awareness is often enough to dissolve those constructions on the spot—or at the very least to wear them down over time. The demons can't stand too much daylight. Hopefully one doesn't stew about the problem, make it into a big deal, and worry about one's spiritual health. By shining awareness on this mindstuff, those patterns begin to dissipate— or as a Buddhist teaching goes—are cut off at the root.

> You should rather be grateful for the weeds you have in your mind, because eventually they will enrich your practice.[2]
> *Shunryu Suzuki*

A useful reminder to give oneself is that the point is definitely *not* to judge oneself for these faults and limitations. And when you notice that you are judging yourself, to simply observe that as well. The basic practice of meditation involves slowing the busyness of mind down enough to see its workings clearly. The teachers instruct us to avoid either praise or blame for whatever arises in the mind and simply be aware of thoughts as they arise. Buddhist teachings talk about cultivating "unconditional kindness" to ourselves as the necessary first step to transcending suffering, learning to get beyond our cocoons and extend that kindness out into the world.

Facing, working with, and dissolving or wearing out major and minor obstacles is also what creates the foundation for a good teacher and a good healer. The best horse may have more difficulty empathizing with the difficulties of others. For example, the best people to work with recovering addicts are usually recovering addicts. They know what it was like, the kind of mind tricks they played on themselves and their world when they were using, the suffering they endured and inflicted, and the difficulty of breaking away from the addiction and everything in their lives that accompanied it. The worst horse had to work long and hard and knows that learning journey well. Those who have successfully overcome or dissolved many of these obstacles can also help put apparent problems into perspective for others, reminding them that their problems aren't insurmountable.

A further implication of all this, by the way—one that may seem obvious but is often not understood—is that we are capable of radical change, and sometimes very quickly, even in the flash of a sudden realization. One potent insight can change the momentum of your life. As the teachers say, we all have Buddha mind. At the core, our basic nature is one of unconditional goodness—not in a naive, Hallmark card, pasted-on-Sunday-smile way—but the way we really are when we've landed on authentic presence.

It's as though we're actors and we get caught up into different characters. Buddhist teachers sometimes describe waking up as just basic sanity. Before that, we're all insane in some way, not really present, living by the ideas in our heads. Though we all have our talents and tendencies through thick and thin—at least in our current incarnation—beyond that, our behavior is highly mutable. Once we've seen the light these changes are often permanent. That old character is dead and gone, the logic driving him dried up and unnecessary.

This understanding has important implications for the way we educate children and the way we treat criminals. From this core understanding there is no such thing as a bad person, although of course "basic goodness"—or Buddha mind—can be deeply buried and apparently beyond reach in some people. The wise tell us we should never give up on anyone. Another

Buddhist teaching points out a kind of mathematical equation: the intensity of the energy moving in one direction, however negative, can be transmuted into unobstructed creative energy in equal measure.

That's great news, one of the wonders of the human mind: we can change, we're not forever stuck. Harmful, self-defeating patterns can be transmuted. I love that Buddhist teaching I mentioned before, the reminder that every moment offers the possibility of "fresh start." The clear awareness of nowness is always available in the gap, in the silence between our thoughts. Our problems aren't the impenetrable walls they appear to be. The demons don't deserve that much credit. Worrying about our failings and obstacles; thinking we're powerless; convinced we're victims of our own or others' negativity—just reinforces the solidity of the wall. Most of us have little or no experience of how things fall into place when we can get out of our own way.

Another favorite term is the "Mishap lineage." This is what we were told was our heritage as students in the Kagyu lineage of Tibetan Buddhism. I connect the Mishap lineage with the Worst Horse lineage, living as a child of illusion, bumping into things, making mistakes, falling, learning from the fall. We make messes—hopefully cleaning them up when we can—we pay attention, and we learn from the mistakes. As William Blake said, "If the fool would persist in his folly he would become wise."

Journeyers like you and me persevere. We develop patience and stamina. We continue to pay attention and to cultivate a nonjudgmental, observant mindfulness and awareness. We work on our mind-protection practice of seeing but not buying into the apparent solidity of fearful, discouraging, and harmful thinking. Then, as Suzuki reminds us, the worst horse can be the best horse.

13

Humble Accomplishment

Pride: the Christian teachings call it one of the seven deadly sins. It creates the conditions for a fall. Don Juan—Carlos Castaneda's teacher in his series of books from the 1970s to the 1990s—frequently reminded Carlos that his attitude of self-importance was a major obstacle preventing him from getting the message. Rinpoché talked about people being puffed up with arrogance. In fact, one of his early books was titled *Cutting Through Spiritual Materialism*, and in it he warned that the pride and self-importance that can accompany those on the spiritual path create the worst and trickiest kind of materialism in their subtlety and their ability to delude the seeker. Rinpoché cautioned his students against attaching ego-based importance onto their practice and study. He once reminded us in his typically sly way, "You think you're onto something. You're not."

In the Buddhist mind-protection approach, you simply observe attentively when these often slippery little feelings creep in. You think you've accomplished something valuable, skillful, compassionate. Great. But then here comes the self-important character. If you pay attention you can see him slip in the back door and take up residence in your mind. I make it my business to keep an eye on this guy whenever I can catch him. He steps in front of the Spirit and talks over the top of the prayer. Fortunately, he also runs from awareness and evaporates in relaxed, non-thought presence.

I've noticed that humbleness quietly sitting there when I'm able to drop my agenda, when I'm able to let go of my need in any particular moment to be heard, when I can release my judgments, my insecurity, my anger and my instinctive need to defend myself. At that point a subtle space—a softness—opens up.

Everyone knows this little word "humble." Some think of it in more or less negative terms, as a downtrodden condition or state of mind lacking in self-esteem. The Oxford Dictionary points at the cultural bias with some of its meanings, like, "having or showing a modest or low opinion of your own importance," and "of low rank." Probably not the kinds of character traits young people setting out to be somebody in the world would aspire to or admire.

Another almost shocking word is "meek." What do you envision when you read that word—a small, feeble, milquetoast person, perhaps? But then how is it possible that Jesus reportedly claimed "the meek shall inherit the earth?" That seems illogical. It looks like the strong and aggressive are ruling most of it and will continue to do so. Rinpoché also made some comments which put the whole view of humility or meekness in a different light. In his Shambhala teachings he discussed the process of developing authentic presence through the understanding of the *four dignities* of the Shambhala Warrior's path. As an aside here, I want to acknowledge that some people have trouble with the word "warrior" and its apparent military implications. As with much of his teaching, Rinpoché tended to take concepts already embedded in our culture, and turn them on their heads. Warriorship, in this cosmology, implies courage—not aggression or violence—but the rare courage to completely be oneself without ego, without the bloated sense of self-importance or the apparent lack of it that causes people to feel low and small. As the teachings say, the full realization of warriorship brings complete peace in the individual and society.

Meekness is the first of the four dignities and is used basically as a synonym for humility or humbleness. In this teaching, meekness is actually associated with relaxation, approachability, and unconditional confidence. The "warrior of meek" has no need to prove anything, no need to defend any territory, and is thus able to see clearly, to be touched by the world, and to proceed courageously—without being buffeted around, distracted or drained by the approval or disapproval of others.

When we see this quality in others, we're drawn to it, we're touched by it. To me, it's a sign of a person's spiritual development, a sign that the path has worked, has worn away the hard edges of self-importance. I've seen it here and there, particularly in people who have been on a powerful, effective path for a long time. I can see it in their eyes, in the way they carry themselves, in their tone of voice. At the shamanism conference in Peru I saw it in a number of the presenters. One who really stood out was Pablo Amaringo, he was an ayahuasca curandero for forty years. We could all see it. Even from a distance you could feel his humility and see through to his open heart. I believe this is what Rinpoché meant when he said: "What the warrior renounces is anything that makes him less accessible to others." People like that are inspiring and remind me that it's essential to persevere. Apart from their activities in the world, their simple presence among us is uplifting and encouraging.

Developing meekness frees us from the burden of our self-importance and the blinkered energy required to maintain and enhance ourselves. Maybe in that way it's possible to understand how the meek could in fact inherit the world. This is a process of coming back down to this Earth, out of our heads—allowing our hearts to soften. It's a path of rediscovering our place in the sacred web of all that is. Humbleness creates openings and connections. The vision is that, in the times to come, rulership will come from the heart, from a peaceful state of mind, and not from a dominating, aggressive mentality.

To be clear, genuine meekness is the opposite of weakness. It's been our confusion and disempowerment that have allowed the dominators to keep the rest of us off balance and unable to see through that game and our part in allowing it to continue. It's been said that you get the leaders you deserve. The word "deserve" has a whiff of guilt and punishment about it that grates on me though. Some of us may acknowledge that we deserve corrupt and visionless leaders but I don't. Maybe it's that we get the leaders the majority of people *allow* when they're disempowered and unable to see clearly. Humility, courage, and conviction—it turns out—are blood relatives. With clear perception undistorted by the fearful mind of ego, the most visionary and powerful prayers have a chance to gain prominence, to sweep away life-destroying blindness, and to create—with our determination and passion—the enlightened societies we know in the deepest center of our heart's wisdom we are fully capable of manifesting.

One way of looking at the situation is that the reality of awakened intelligence—Spirit, Creator, God or whatever other inadequate word we attach to this eternal presence—remains pure, remains in the still center. "It" observes with infinite patience the continual scurrying of us humans, lost in our unsettled illusion of separateness. The scurrying obscures the presence within us and all around us. It's impossible for this presence to interfere with the scurrying, to make itself visible to those who can't slow down enough to pay attention. The presence waits until the energy of confused mind exhausts itself, exhausts all other possibilities and strategies. It looks like that time may have come for many more of us. It looks like there are openings now.

The vision of the meek inheriting the Earth is the vision of the arrival of the best idea, the "aha" we've been waiting for, the meeting with the transcendental object at the end of the time-bound historical period—as the unsustainable energies of the past crumble and create new openings. This best idea goes something like this: There's no answer in the material world, no way to fill the hole. There's no escape, the samsaric mind has ensnared itself in an endless loop that never satisfies for long and now is bringing the whole enterprise to its knees. There's only one way: to stop, look, and listen, to constantly practice letting go, to develop confidence in the reality of the still center and do everything we can to uncover it in ourselves and others. Relaxing and opening into spacious mind allows us to feel that humbleness, that tenderness of heart, and that connects us to each other and to life altogether. From that state of mind, accomplishment can be skillful and beneficial.

Love's the only engine of survival.[1]
Leonard Cohen

14

Time and the Eternal Now

When you practice zazen, there is no idea of time or space.[1]
Shunryu Suzuki

The only experience of time that one can have is of a
subjective time that is created by one's own mental processes,
but in relationship to the Newtonian universe there is no time
whatsoever. One exists in eternity.[2]
Terence McKenna

My first clue that something was amiss in the culture's understanding of time came during my years at university. I'd been
hearing about LSD and its reputed ability to upend consensual
reality and open doors to wildly different realms. A friend told
me he had some and I was welcome to come over and take the
plunge at his place. On the appointed evening, I entered a small,
thriftstore-furnished apartment to find a cozy, domestic scene
with my friend's wife feeding the baby in the kitchen. About
thirty minutes after ingesting the small tab—while listening to
George Harrison's song *My Sweet Lord* on the record player—a
pure black emptiness opened above my head, and I experienced
in a flash the distinct sense that there was no time as I understood it. In some manner not easy to convey through language, it
was clear that everything happens at once, that there's no linear
movement of time, only now.

Of course that one experience wasn't nearly enough to break the chains of time in this particular mind. A couple of decades later I was stilling learning the lesson. One night a small group of us were in a Native American Church meeting in someone's living room. These ceremonies typically begin around 9 p.m. and continue well beyond the first light of morning. In the time-chained state the night can feel interminable. Round about 3 a.m., with a tight chest and crampy guts, I fell into that trap, wondering how long until daybreak.

The south wall of the room was dominated by a large picture window, looking out over a valley as the moon made its night-long journey across the sky. During that period I was training myself not to look at my watch. I looked up over my left shoulder at one point to see that big moon above a peak across the valley. After what I thought must have been close to two hours, I glanced that way again and was surprised and dismayed to see the moon exactly where I'd left it the last time. I foolishly repeated the pattern with equal surprise a couple of more times.

Time, for instance, did not exist, it had to be carried. The language has no word for time.[3]
Martín Prechtel,
(on the Maya he lived with in Guatemala)

It's been sweet relief to gradually give up that time-bound, linear mentality. After a few dozen of the Native American Church ceremonies over several years, I still get caught once in a while— especially when the energies become challenging to work with— but I stopped checking my watch (and it later fell off my wrist into deep water). One begins to realize that this present moment is all we ever have so we'd best enter it and appreciate it with full presence of mind. I'm repeatedly impressed by how many people I've met at those meetings for whom linear time isn't an issue at all. Some call it Indian time. There aren't a lot of watches around there.

The meetings are a great environment for learning that lesson. As in the old days of Rinpoché's talks, they rarely started on time and all that occurred over the course of the night in the tipi meetings continued in that relaxed mode. Nobody rushed. Events have their own progression. There are other priorities that make clock time all but irrelevant in this kind of work. Things need to be done properly, gracefully. When you're in that space for twelve to fifteen hours, suffering will teach you sooner or later to give it up, pay attention and stay out of your time-ruled head.

Here's another eloquently expressed anecdote to support the widespread human experience of the non-time state. In his memoir, *Memories, Dreams, Reflections*, Carl Jung described a period of severe illness late in his life when he was hospitalized for weeks—sometimes hovering on the edge of death—and experienced a number of visions: "It was not a product of the imagination. The visions and experiences were utterly real; there was nothing subjective about them...We shy away from the word "eternal," but I can describe the experience only as the ecstasy of a non-temporal state in which present, past, and future are one. Everything that happens in time had been brought together into a concrete whole. Nothing was distributed over time, nothing could be measured by temporal concepts."[4]

"Time" is an experience that is predominantly mediated by the left-brain hemisphere. In actuality, the experience of time exists only in a world dominated by the imbalance created by duality. As balance between the two [brain] hemispheres is created, instead of time we may expect to experience pure being moment by moment.[5]
Carl Johan Calleman

The elimination of time from your consciousness is the elimination of ego. It's the only true spiritual practice.[6]
Eckhart Tolle

Time, in our measured conception of it, lives in the discursive mind. It's tangled up with fear, ego, ambition, speediness. For many it's a straitjacket, a bully pushing and pulling. Linear time is the tool we use to maintain ourselves in the continuing state of unrest, the condition of always feeling like we're on the way to somewhere but never feeling like we've completely arrived. In the modern mind, time is often treated like a commodity—you know, the old "time is money."

Freedom from addiction to clock time really does bring sweet relief. Easing into organic time allows gentleness, creativity, indigenous soul. If you've traveled away from the clock-bound cultures into developing countries you've certainly come across the organic, no-big-deal mode of relating to time (although many countries used to be much more like that). How often has someone accustomed to all systems going on schedule gotten up in arms when the train or the bus or the boat are running on no-big-deal time?

Beyond the clock-ruled cultures you bump into that relaxed attitude frequently. The Tibetans I encountered during my years in close association with the Buddhist community were often like that. A favorite anecdote comes to mind about the sixteenth Karmapa, the head of the Kagyu lineage—one of the four major lineages of Tibetan Buddhism. This man was revered for his deep, authentic presence. He was considered a living representative of the lineage of the awakened.

The Karmapa loved birds and traveled with one or more of his small friends on a speaking tour in the United States. One evening, as the appointed hour for his talk approached, a young American attendant—those Kasung again—eager to do his job properly, reminded the Karmapa that it was now time to make his appearance. The Karmapa smiled, thanked him, and continued focusing his attention on his avian companions. As the scheduled time for the talk receded into the distance, the attendant became increasingly distraught and came back two or three more times to tell the Karmapa what time it was. Finally the Karmapa turned toward the young man with a scowl on his face, clipped him with a quick right hook to the jaw, and returned his attention unperturbed to the birds.

You see my son, here time turns into space.[7]
Richard Wagner
(from Parsifal)

I had numerous opportunities to observe my old teacher Trungpa Rinpoché in action. He operated mostly on Tibetan time and it was almost impossible for his students to keep him on a preset schedule. Whatever he was doing he did with his total attention. He may have been engaged in any number of activities—perhaps meeting with a student or working on a calligraphy. There was no point in telling him the talk was supposed to start twenty minutes ago. At our workshops and seminars we came to expect the unexpected. We had a joke that one of the Buddhist lies was "The talk starts at eight." We might be in the meditation hall for hours past the announced time for the talk before Rinpoché arrived. But once he was there he was completely there with us and gave selflessly without thought for time or comfort. If there were questions, he would patiently answer them into the wee hours of the morning and would sometimes stay up for twenty-four hours or more engaging with students back in his suite.

On the other hand, if he felt people were getting aggressively impatient, Rinpoché might even deliberately subvert the situation to force people to look at that mentality in themselves. At one public talk he appeared over an hour late and was met by a restless and irritated crowd offended by the wait. Rather than presenting his usual detailed and engaging address, he spoke for about five minutes, saying in essence, "Relax." One irate audience member raised her hand and asked, "Is that all?" Rinpoché merely smiled and said, "Yes."

You do what you like, and you do it well.[8]
Bob Dylan
(from the song *Buckets of Rain*)

The journey toward freeing ourselves from time is also intimately related to the journey toward uncovering the artist within us. Great artists show the rest of us that we've barely tapped our ability to enter deeply into the object or environment of our attention, to slip out of the bounds of time and ego and become one with it. These artists are the sensitives, the scouts who've gone ahead and returned with news of worlds beyond the previous experience of most of us. Over the years I've heard so many anecdotes about that ability to enter deeply that I've forgotten most of them. One of my favorites is about the now-legendary singer-songwriter Neil Young, an exemplary model of someone who has been true to himself on his musical path over the course of a very long career. He himself said, "I work for the Muse." Young told a biographer that while most of his friends and contemporaries were using psychedelic substances to shock the monkey out of its conditioning, he intuitively sensed that he didn't need that assistance, that he was already psychedelic. He described, for example, how he might be reading a book and he would zone in on a word on the page, then on one letter in the word, then on the individual ink dots that together formed the letter, and from there his mind would enter through that portal into other worlds.

There is a dimension parallel to time, outside of time, that is accessible only to the degree that one can decondition oneself from the history-bound cognitive systems that have carried one to this point.[9]
Terence McKenna

Relaxing out of the straitjacket of time is of course part and parcel of the vision for the new modality. Nowness and digital domination don't necessarily go together well. I mentioned earlier the Buddhist teaching on "One Taste," the practice of letting go of our insistence on one thing over another and just relating directly to things as they are from that unconditional, open state of mind. Teachings about duality apply here as well if we think of the attitude of duality as the state of mind that sees itself as separate from everything else, that experiences life as "I" and "other" where never the twain shall meet. Nowness, one taste, non-duality—all are teachings, practices, attitudes, and ways of life that help free us from the chains of time.

I'm presenting these anecdotes and insights to paint a portrait. In looking at the whole picture of who we are and where we need to go, our relationship to time is clearly one of the major elements that needs adjusting. It's as though we've been given a huge room to play in and we're huddling in corners building little walls around ourselves to contain our experience. It's all part of the same picture. It's all part of the disconnect and the journey back toward a way to live in the world that works, that's sustainable, that nourishes and uplifts all life.

If a thing loves, it is infinite.
William Blake

15

If You Meet the Buddha on the Road
On Students and Teachers

There's an old saying: "If you meet the Buddha on the road, kill him." It's an admonishment to remove any concept in your mind which tells you there is somebody or something other than your own mind standing between you and your awakening. All of us on spiritual paths—whether we're involved with religious institutions, shamanic ceremonies, or other healing environments such as psychotherapy—have to deal with teachers, leaders, authority figures at some points in our journey. How we work with such situations may determine how quickly we grow up spiritually, as it were.

Clearly, everyone learns and benefits immensely from teachers throughout life. For starters, we're all potentially teachers for each other. We can learn something from everyone if we're open, even if it's simply by observing, or even seeing what not to do. Over many years I've seen how people come into my life in heightened ways at certain times for the benefit of one or both of us. Our energy constellations converge and sometimes dissolve naturally when the focus shifts for one or both or the teaching is complete. Some relationships, seen in retrospect, appear to have existed exclusively for working through a particular gestalt.

There seems to be an unseen guidance that often directs these unexpected conjunctions. Books and other sources of information often behave like that too. Spiritual teachers and mentors also appear for periods of one's life, often introduced by an apparently small event. With some of these connections it feels like the complimentary pieces pre-existed the first known contact, like that old archetype "I was expecting you."

Martín Prechtel described such a meeting in his book *Secrets of the Talking Jaguar*. Before he left his homeland on a Pueblo Indian reservation in New Mexico at age nineteen to backpack around, he had a series of eleven dreams in eleven nights, several depicting the same village in vivid detail, even including a couple of small stores and the name of one of the owners. After wandering through Mexico for a year, a chance invitation for a ride took him to Guatemala, a country he knew nothing about. He immediately fell in love with the people—predominantly Maya—and the country itself.

Two months later, still meandering through Guatemala, his ride brought him to a large Mayan village in the mountains—the very one he'd seen in his dreams, including the details. After walking around town for three days unable to find accommodations, he felt two large hands clamp down on his shoulders from behind. The hands swung him around to face an eighty-year-old man who boomed out, "How come you come late Curly? For two years I've been calling you over here and you're just finally getting here."[1]

Martín later learned that this man was the most highly regarded shaman in the area and wanted someone to train and initiate for the purpose of taking these essential understandings into a wider world. The old shaman had correctly foreseen the coming violent destruction of his tradition and his community that ravaged Guatemala for roughly twenty years through the 1970s and 1980s.

My initial connection with Trungpa Rinpoché and my subsequent involvement with the community of students under his guidance also had that sense of synchronicity or even inevitability. Several years before I met him in person, a chance encounter introduced me to one of his books and before long I had read the first three books of his teachings, *Cutting Through Spiritual Materialism*, *Meditation in Action*, and *The Myth of Freedom*. I immediately became intensely interested in these books: they made brilliant sense, he felt like an old friend, and I soaked up the information. I did not consider myself at the time sensitive to psychic phenomena or spirit presences in any way. But once, a couple of years in, while reading one of the books, I had a very palpable sensation of warmth and compassion emanating from the page and the distinct impression that there was a presence there. I'd never experienced anything remotely like it.

Over a five-year period, I read each of these three books at least three times, but it wasn't until after that encounter that I noticed a brief mention in one of the books I'd completely missed in previous readings, no doubt because I wasn't ready to hear it. Rinpoché suggested it's important to have a sangha, a community of fellow travelers to associate with on the path. Distrustful of groups and group-think behavior, I hesitantly sought out and found a local community under the umbrella of Rinpoché's teachings and organization.

Traveling with Old Friends

There's a notion of extended spiritual families or brotherhoods that may transcend the narrow confines of one embodied life. I've come across other information that suggests this possibility, that we've known these teachers, these fellow travelers, before. For years I've felt that some of my friends and I are from the same brotherhood. It's the way we understand each other and at times provide useful insight and support. With these friends I can converse for hours and feel that we get what the other is describing. It's as though certain foundational understandings already exist and our minds move in patterns similar enough that we can let fly with the ideas without a lot of slogging.

Here's an intriguing possibility: At least with those of us actively on the path of awakening, it may be that we travel throughout the long stream of history in family groups. There's not necessarily any connection between these family groups and our immediate blood relations. The people in these groups may become separated and have no contact with each other throughout this particular incarnation. Or members of this extended family may encounter each other at some points during their lives: sometimes early and sometimes quite late in life. Working with this idea may require you to stretch your concept of the individual soul. Perhaps what we call an individual is actually a kind of semi-autonomous part of a larger entity. For example, it's been said that Tibetan masters have been known to come back in several different simultaneous incarnations.

These friends that I suspect are members of this larger "self" have in common a keen interest in spirituality, but beyond that have followed very different paths, not necessarily directly involved in religious study or practice of any kind. I could speculate that this larger entity breaks up like a group of friends to go off and explore different territories with the goal of bringing back various experiences and understandings to further the wisdom development of the whole.

My friend Geoff, a man of high integrity and intelligence, is a senior, well-practiced student of Trungpa Rinpoché. Although possessed of a poet's soul, he's a successful businessman and anything but flakey and naive about paranormal phenomena. A few years ago Geoff described a period in his life when he was engaged in a Buddhist practice that required him to form a highly detailed visualization of a deity. These practices, as I understand them, are employed to enhance and develop certain specific abilities and qualities related to spiritual development.

One had to hold this complex visualization for some period of time while repeating a chant. Geoff reported that he began noticing a presence, a kind of warmth that came over him in a manner completely unfamiliar to him and clearly not of his own making.

This spooked him a bit and made him curious about channeling, the experience or practice of receiving information from unseen sources, perhaps in a trance state. He read a book called *Opening to Channel* by Sonaya Roman, and began practicing the techniques suggested. It wasn't long before he began to receive information that was clearly different from his own imagination and patterns of thought formation. (Channelers often did this work for others as a psychic does. Geoff was just doing it alone.) He wrote down as much of the transmissions as he could keep up with. I still have a copy of some of this material on my bookshelf.

The crux of this story is that one day Geoff asked the speaker to identify "himself." An immediate and clear answer came back, "Oh, we're your old Shambhala friends. We've been traveling with you for a long time. At any particular moment some of us may be in human incarnations and others may be behind the scenes assisting, supporting, protecting, and teaching, as well as doing our own work in realms apart from this particular material environment."

I'd like to think that everyone who is interested and actively working to wake up is drawn to the right people, led to the appropriate guidance at the right time that matches the seeker's own way. I can't say how widespread that is but I'm convinced it has happened like that for me and a number of my friends.

Transmuting Energies

Rinpoché was a very controversial and provocative teacher. He referred to his lineage as the "Crazy Wisdom" lineage of Tibet, a school, as it were, of highly creative and daring souls who acted upon "first thought best thought," a spontaneous, intuitive skill-fulness that could easily defy conventional understanding. Some of the students were baffled and concerned by Rinpoché's unorthodox methods and behavior. I never was to any great degree. I thought I understood the larger picture. I could feel his rawness, his authentic presence. His unguarded heart was visible on his face. (Thomas Merton, the brilliant Trappist monk/mystic/writer described Rinpoché as the most unguarded, authentic person he had ever met.) His actions, spontaneous as they were, were the actions of a master artist. I saw a number of these first-thought responses myself and heard numerous stories from other students, who invariably said that Rinpoché's gesture in that moment cut through the bullshit and communicated the exact message they needed to hear.

The typical scenario might go something like this: You're having a personal interview with him. He asks you how you're doing. You start in, but because of your nervousness in his presence, because you've elevated him to a position of great authority, you ask a question that, had you had your wits about you, you know you could have answered for yourself. The teacher, attentive until this point, suddenly burps loudly, or tosses the lighter he's been holding so hard that it bounces off the ceiling and lands in your lap, or looks out the window and says, "Is that a lawn mower I hear?" The typical response from the student at that point is an immediate "Right, got it, thank you."

Rinpoché manifested the approach that I appreciated in people and aspired to in myself. His approach also represents a central theme of this book—combining a powerful under-standing and integrity with a fearless openness to inspiration from wherever it might come. He had a deep knowledge of his area of expertise. In his particular case he was trained from the age of three to be the Supreme Abbot of a group of seven monas-teries in Eastern Tibet. He had a an abiding devotion to and respect for that tradition, but was in no way limited by it or unafraid to innovate, not for any need to put his own stamp on the work, but truly from this fearless, creative mind, guided by muses.

I don't think I would have been drawn to or learned nearly as much from any other Buddhist teacher. More recently I felt the same way about Kanucas, the Native elder who leads many of the peyote medicine prayer meetings I've participated in. That world is so foreign to my own in some ways that I'm sure I never would have entered it or been welcomed without Kanucas's creative synthesis of deep knowledge and respect for his tradition, combined with a fearless openness to new information, to doing what the Spirit suggests is the most appropriate and skillful thing. I've heard Kanucas say a number of times that the Spirit talks to him and—when he's in the role of roadman at a meeting—gives him instructions about how to work with the group or with an individual.

The approach of these kinds of teachers is that rather than dogmatically or habitually adhering to one particular method or set of rules for proceeding, they're creatively alive in the moment to the needs of the situation and can draw readily upon the tools at their disposal. Kanucas, for example, is considered by some people I've spoken with to be unusually flexible within the Native American Church culture. My friend Anderson has "sat up," as they say, with quite a few different roadmen in different parts of western United States and Canada. He sometimes thinks Kanucas is not strict enough. I completely disagree. His approach is very similar to Rinpoché's. Whereas some Buddhist masters who came to North America have attempted to transplant their traditional experience and methodology unchanged into this landscape, Rinpoché's attitude was to meet people where they are, take the energy of the direction they're already going, and then create an environment where that energy can be transmuted and turned into positive, creative behavior and action.

One story of how he did that comes to mind: Policing and militarism are obviously a significant element of our society. These elements are not going away and neither is the energy of young men in particular. Most people would also agree that despite the abuses often perpetrated by these groups, there is a need for protection of the community and perhaps for warriorship as well. Rinpoché looked at these aspects of our society and considered how to transform them into enlightened activity.

He instituted a program as part of his teachings he called the Dorje Kasung. Again, the Kasung are, to put it simplistically, the protectors of the teachings and the teachers. In that Buddhist community they have a limited role in that they don't carry guns or in any way interfere with the activities of regular police. The principle is a vision for how we might eventually position this kind of function in an enlightened society. You take that warrior energy, both in individuals and in the structures of society, accept it as it is, don't judge or avoid it, don't push back against it. Then you nudge it toward an enlightened attitude.

Some of the core teachings for the Kasung, for example, are aimed at a kind of skillful meditation-in-action, dissolving self-importance and acting with an unobtrusive and fearless sensitivity to the situation you're in. One is taught particular skills about how to defuse situations, how to meet aggression with non-aggression and so on.

In a similar way, I had long wondered about the warrior side of the Native American traditional cultures, how that aspect of their societies fit with what was apparently a deep reverence for and understanding of nature and Spirit. How does that fit with fighting and killing? Charles Eastman (Ohiyesa) was born in 1858 and raised for his first fifteen years in the traditional life of the Sioux, including the complete training to be a warrior-hunter in the tradition of his forefathers. His description of the role of warriorship and combat among his people reminded me in some ways of the Kasung—that you take the ferocious energy of young males and direct it in disciplined ways that embody the wisdom of the tribe. Take a look at the following passage from *Light on the Indian World, The Essential Writings of Charles Eastman (Ohiyesa)*.

> Warfare we regarded as an institution—the "Great Mystery"—an organized tournament or trial of courage and skill, with elaborate rules and "counts" for the coveted honor of the eagle feather. It was held to develop the quality of manliness and its motive was chivalric or patriotic but never the desire for territorial aggrandizement or the overthrow of a brother nation. It was common, in early times, for a battle or skirmish to last all day, with great display of daring and horsemanship with scarcely more killed and wounded than may be carried from the field during a university game of football.[2]

Here's another example from Ronald Wright's well-researched and disturbing book, *Stolen Continents*, referring to the traditional ways of pre-Columbian Cherokee from the southeastern part of the United States. I'm confident that with a little research one could find examples like this from traditional indigenous cultures all over the world.

> Although they had no central authority, the Cherokees never warred among themselves. Disputes between towns were vented in tough games of lacrosse, "the little brother of war", which resembled the Mesoamerican ball game in its ritual and political functions.[3]

Again, I'm using these stories to illustrate the skillfulness of great teachers and healers—awake to the energies, tendencies, and creative possibilities inherent in situations—and the combination of knowledge/experience and fearlessness that underpins this kind of beneficial and often visionary action. In the case of the Sioux, it was the community's understanding that you can't ignore or repress that energy, but by giving it some room to express itself, it can be channeled into healthy activity.

Unfortunately, you can see the problems that arise in societies that ignore this energy. Young men often act out in destructive behavior without developing a meaningful relationship to the "tribe." Robert Bly explored that theme in his books and talks, the importance of having some kind of initiation process to work with those powerful energies in the young and to maintain the long-term health and survival of the community. Without channels, without mentors, in societies that have lost unifying myths, that energy can become violent and confused in some of the young as they seek outlets for it.

In the individual's journey toward awakening, teachers, guides, midwives are—if not absolutely essential—at least extremely helpful and likely to speed the path of discovery. Of course, apparent mistakes and wrong turns can teach one a lot as well. Remember the Worst Horse and the Mishap lineages— learning as you're falling off the horse. But I'm sure there are more than enough dead zones and wrong turns even with some skilled assistance along the way.

One aspect of this assistance has been called "mind trans-mission." There's a tradition in Buddhism—and no doubt other paths—which involves the direct transmission of awakened understanding from teacher to student. If the teacher is properly initiated and the student is ready, there can be a kind of "aha" experience where the student can fall into the egoless space created by the vastness of the teacher's mind, the Buddha mind. In its untainted form, the teacher acts as a clear mirror, an undis-torted channel of awakened mind. Like the indescribably powerful pure white light said to be the primordial uncondi-tioned abode that awaits those capable of total release after the death of the body, that power burns away ego and is then, of course, too strong for the undeveloped and so remains a challenge, an invitation, a call to the student.

You might well wonder about the difficulty and rarity of finding such people to work with. In our desertified society, where the lineages of deep wisdom have been in extremely short supply, that is definitely a problem. It may be necessary to go elsewhere, to look for hints and clues found only far beyond the borders of the culture's agreed-upon understanding. As an aside for the moment, this is another reason I believe that those who can handle it need to be open to looking at the plants as teachers. In particular, combining those encounters with the presence of living wisdom keepers and skillfully designed ritual settings has great potential in this challenging time. As Thaddeus Golas proclaimed, "Enlightenment doesn't care how you get there."[4]

If you meet the Buddha . . .

People need to be empowered, and you're not empowered by placing your spiritual development in the hands of a guru. You're spiritually empowered by taking responsibility for your spiritual development, by looking around and seeing what needs to be done.[5]
Terence McKenna

Obviously there are potential dangers in our relationships with spiritual teachers, as well as with religious groups and institutions altogether. There's an old Zen question about when your master is pointing his finger at the moon. Which do you look at, the pointing finger, or the moon? My experience with the Buddhist community showed me a few disheartening aspects of students' relationships to teachers, to authority figures. Too many of them, us, fell into the mistake of becoming fascinated with the finger. It was ironic in some sense that the teachings of Buddhism are considered non-theistic. Without going into an intellectual discussion, the practical application of that principle is that there is nothing other than our own choice to heal and awaken that will save us from our confusion. As Kanucas said one night in a meeting, pointing to his heart: "There's nothing out there that'll ever feel right to you until you feel right in here".

We were wildly theistic about Rinpoché in those days. People even mimicked his language and behaviors, even though Rinpoché himself cautioned us not to imitate his behavior. If I was any example—and I'm confident my experience wasn't so different from a lot of the other students—the pedestal upon which we placed our guru obscured our trust in our own intelligence and postponed our maturation. Other communities weren't so lucky. Rinpoché was a fully trained holder of a deep and ancient lineage, and not dangerously susceptible to aggrandizement in the face of all that transference. The newspaper archives carry the tragic stories of those who followed other leaders into the flames.

It was after Rinpoché died in 1987 that I began to see my own theistic transference. When I experienced his absence, a hole appeared and a questioning process began. Soon afterward our community had its own fires, when it was revealed that Rinpoché's appointed dharma heir, the Regent Ösel Tendzin, had been seducing young men in the sangha with some frequency and that he was—unbeknownst to his recipients but not to him— HIV positive while doing so.

This news sent shock waves through the community. Confusion and betrayal of trust severely rocked the stability of the organization, (for a few years anyway,) and for people like me it was nearly the death blow to our faith in groups. I asked myself how, in the face of the power and sanity of these teachings, did the one person Rinpoché picked out from all his students to carry on his work go so badly off the rails. To keep the record straight, it should be said that in the last few years of his life, Rinpoché did become deeply concerned about the

Regent. In *Dragon Thunder: My Life with Chögyam Trungpa*, Rinpoché's wife Diana Mukpo described him saying that the Regent had become "terrible" and should be "dismantled."

There's a peculiar thing that happens to groups, even when the teachings themselves caution against group-think. Remember Rinpoché's comment that "You think you're onto something, you're not." Our job, he taught, was to give up any ground like that—any crutches and false securities—and to learn to make a relationship with groundlessness, with shunyata.

Although the practice and study the students were engaged in were having excellent effects on the general well-being of many, it was apparent that there was also often a subtle—and here's the rub, usually unnoticed and denied by the group members—smugness. People did feel that they had found a home, a resting place, a relief from the anxiety of unknowing, the complete explanation of the predicament we're all in, just as the teachers were telling us to cultivate the "don't know mind," the "beginner's mind." Alan Watts once made the dubious claim that Catholics were the happiest people because they felt completely safe in their faith in the Holy Father God to look after them and tell them what to do. I confess that the years of my deepest immersion in that Buddhist environment were among the happiest and most lighthearted of my life.

Although most people recognize the dangers of group behavior—especially when not in a wisdom context with good people around who know what they're doing—I wouldn't dare to suggest that it's the wrong way to go, that people should stay away from groups. I steadfastly maintain that Rinpoché's teachings were brilliant and highly beneficial to many people. Many who knew him and his works would agree that he was a genius with an impeccable vision for enlightened society and the components required to bring that vision into manifestation.

And of course there's great potential in commitment and perseverance. The problem on the other side arises because the ego is so slippery, so clever. On the larger level one can observe how governments do it all the time. On the personal level, ego can outsmart your wiser sensibilities at every turn when it feels threatened. The stories you tell yourself can get you right out of any situation where that old bastard could lose his control of your spirit. The brilliant Buddhist teacher and writer Pema Chödrön tellingly titled one of her books *The Wisdom of No Escape.*

I return again, though, to the point that there are clearly obstacles and dead ends associated with groups and leaders. There's a Buddhist teaching, "Of the two witnesses, trust the principal one." That's the key concept. If you can trust your native intelligence—your intuition, your connection to Spirit even when it's not apparent—maybe you can successfully negotiate the seductions of thinking you're onto something and the often unacknowledged pressure to see things as everyone else in the group does. I suppose it's about keeping your wits about you, catching yourself when you realize you've been seduced by the attractions of the safe harbor.

Allons! Whoever you are! Come forth!
You must not stay sleeping and dallying there in the house, though you built it, or though it has been built for you.[6]
Walt Whitman

Some of us have to move on, follow our noses. Maybe it's partly because of the teacher in me that I was interested in what people from other traditions had to say on these matters. I was really into this Buddhist community for more than a decade. I paid close attention. I worked hard. I meditated daily, sometimes for several hours. I went to retreats, including the three-month long Seminary, I helped with administration and teaching. I took Rinpoché's teachings to heart. But I saw how I had put this man between me and the Spirit, between me and direct experience. I trusted that witness more than myself and I saw that I needed to grow up.

That was when I started to notice the other students doing the same, even some of the older, more experienced ones who also did a lot of teaching themselves. I'll pass on one story about this as an example. It was probably the final neuron falling into its receptor, after which I decided I needed to step way back and get in touch with my own guidance.

We were having a practice day at the center. This was a more advanced practice that students worked toward for several years. Only the more senior students were there. And we were all there because we'd been told to expect a brief visit during the practice session from one of Rinpoché's sons, Gesar. Before he arrived, a woman got up and told us that Gesar had been recognized by highly placed lamas as the reincarnation of a renowned Tibetan master and that we should behave toward him in a manner appropriate to that status.

A while later, a nineteen year old young man came shuffling in and took a seat. With all eyes and ears keenly focused on him, Gesar told us a long story of his travels in Tibet. I was open to hearing him, but he didn't sound wise to me. In fact he sounded like a somewhat whiny and altogether fairly ordinary teenager. There was nothing about his journey that was particularly insightful or uplifting. He complained a few times about the discomforts he had to endure and the treatment he received while there. Then there was a question period. A couple of the most experienced students asked Gesar questions that clearly showed they were giving him the authority to answer problems that they could and should have figured out for themselves. And he didn't have anything insightful to say to them anyway.

Turning Toward Internal Guidance

Rinpoché had taught that at some point the phenomenal world

becomes the guru, becomes your feedback mechanism. Again, it's similar to that metaphor of riding the horse. You may be in tune with the whole rhythm but at some point lose your balance and begin to fall. In the falling itself you wake up and correct yourself.

A teacher can only share what he knows, and no one teacher can teach us all we need to know. After one has learned the lessons that one teacher has to share, it is good to go on to the next teacher. Ultimately, our most important teachings come from two sources—our universal mind, with its eternal knowledge and cosmic consciousness, and our inner nature, which teaches us through our willingness to observe and interact with nature.[7]
Eduardo Caldéron Palomino,
Peruvian curandero

As a former practitioner of theism in the Buddhist sense of the term—looking outside oneself for salvation—I'm well qualified to comment on this journey out from under the protection of that umbrella. I've watched and felt myself grant final authority to "masters" and I gradually learned to see myself as an equal. As Golas says, "There ain't nobody here but us chickens." If you don't feel free to be yourself, if you're nervous around someone in a position of leadership, it's a good indication you need to keep looking at that.

People in those positions—unless they're charlatans who want to feed off your transference—don't want to be treated that way. They don't want people to be uncomfortable with them and put them on a pedestal. They want people around them who can relax and be themselves, who can play with them and speak their minds freely. The dark, usually unconscious, side of that theistic attitude, that poverty mentality, is that the student wants something from the master. The bizarre irony is that people often don't behave with sensitivity and respect to the very person they've placed above themselves. I've heard a few stories from people who were seen by others as having the Holy Grail in their pocket. The seekers invade their privacy. They do things like come creeping into their heroes' yards and homes uninvited to get some of this empowerment to rub off on them.

> Europeans, accustomed to hierarchy, assumed that all they had to do was seek out one "king" or "emperor" and make agreements with him...But the Cherokee Nation of the eighteenth century was a loose federation of sixty-four autonomous towns united only by language, culture, and kinship. Chiefs led by example; bad ones simply lost their following. "The Savages are an odd kind of people," one British officer noted disapprovingly. "There is no law or subjection amongst them... The very lowest of them thinks himself as great and as high as any of the rest, every one of them must be courted for their friendship...everyone is his own master.[8]
> *Ronald Wright*

The example of the Native American Church, a tradition not uncommon among Native Americans historically, may provide a workable model or template for how to view spiritual teachers, and authorities in general for that matter. Although some people are designated as ministers of the church, as I understand it that is for legal reasons in dealing with bureaucracy. One doesn't need to be a minister to run a meeting and you'd never be able to pick a roadman out in a crowd. I sometimes jokingly think of the NAC as disorganized religion, although there is definitely a natural organization in alignment with Spirit.

Born from oral cultures, the NAC has no books of church canon, no boards and committees that I've ever encountered. This church is fluid and light on its feet. Even the physical structures that house the gatherings are akin to Buddhist sand mandalas: here tonight gone tomorrow. The tipi goes up and comes down, the drum is tied and untied, the altar is built out of sand and erased in the morning. The church is maintained in the hearts and minds of the members.

Once, in a conversation with Kanucas, I referred to him as a teacher. He corrected me, saying that in his tradition people like him didn't view their role like that. He sees himself as a midwife, helping people through the transit from samsara to the awakened state.

The result of this attitude is that there are no avenues for personal ambition, for getting close to the "guru," for collecting followers. If you get too big for your hat, you might get brought down to size. They might just slap you down, perhaps even in a full tipi. What's honored is honesty, straight talk from the heart and dignified humility in the light of the Spirit. Anyone can potentially be a teacher for anyone else at any particular moment.

The shift back to internal guidance has begun.[9]
Ken Carey

To picture the trajectory of maturation at both the individual level and the societal—or at this point, planetary level—you could use the analogy of the development of a person from birth and infancy where there is complete dependency, through the stages of increasing independence, toward full adult maturity. In the early stages of growth one relies on greater authorities than oneself. With increasing maturity you come to see these teachers, guides, and mentors as valuable—even necessary to your development and the realization of your capabilities—but you've begun to filter the information through your own witness. Hopefully your attention moves away from the pointing finger and toward the moon, although hopefully you encounter a number of good and true fingers along the way. As the saying goes, when the student is ready the teacher appears.

Though the wise may always be students to some extent—maintaining beginner's mind—full maturity suggests that the relationship with the inner guru is fully realized and the phenomenal world becomes the guru. This is the message I'm hearing from all over. It comes up in the prophecies, in the voices of the teachers, and in our own understanding. It's time now for us "ordinary" folk to develop our own direct connection to Spirit and to manifest that realization in skillful, compassionate action.

This kind of maturation is also of central importance to the vision for the planet. It could of course be an extensive thesis of its own. Just let me say briefly here that the empowerment that many of us see underway at this time is absolutely necessary to the healing of the nations. There's a wonderful moment in the old film *The Wizard of Oz* where the travelers pull back the curtain and the great wizard is exposed as a frail old man amplifying his voice and presence with a microphone and a false, puffed-up image. As people around the world wake up to their own dignity and native intelligence, I believe (and pray) that the air will come out of the despots who still maintain control and inflict such unnecessary suffering in many countries.

Here's a last thought on the subject of teachers and personal awakening, from Dhyani Ywahoo: "In the past one found redemption through a savior, through a great teacher. These times call each one of us to manifest fully in alignment with the concept of savior, redeemer. Let us redeem through clarity of speech, purpose, and action, through harmonious living with respect for future generations."[10]

16

You Came Here to Get Strong

It's not a long stretch to imagine we'll be living in simplified material circumstances a few years from now. Many more of us may find ourselves getting around on foot or bicycle, growing gardens, relearning old methods for preserving food, and in general doing more physical work to maintain ourselves and our families. In any case, moving in that direction makes great sense at this time for environmental and spiritual reasons—slowing down and making relationships with everything in our lives instead of allowing ourselves to be dragged around by the kind of disconnected speed that drives much of the activity of modern societies.

An unexpected course of learning I've encountered in my experience in spiritually focused environments is the concept of getting strong. I don't intend to delve into a treatise on how soft the great majority of us have become in the highly technologized societies. I suspect most of us are aware of it. I also suspect most are glad we have the conveniences and comforts we have and wouldn't wish to return to the days when we had to do much more by the strength and agility of our own hands.

However, there's definitely something bracing and beneficial to the spirit that results from being placed in situations where the common comforts of modernity are less available or where one is required to exceed previous beliefs about one's stamina, perseverance, and ability to do without. Body and mind become stronger together when pushed beyond these supposed limits.

My own experiences are humble, but may serve here as instructive examples of how this functions. My first lessons came from my years in the Tibetan Buddhist community. When I heard about meditation practice I remember thinking that thirty to forty-five minutes would be a long time to sit still. Over the next couple of years that imagined limit kept extending. An hour didn't seem so long, then a day, then a week, and later a month of sitting for fourteen-hour days—though we did have walking meditation and a couple of other breaks.

I once participated in a three-month program called Seminary, which was divided more or less equally between periods of all-day meditation and sections devoted mostly to classes and talks on Buddhism. During the study section I had volunteered as Kasung. One night it was my task to watch the door at the entrance to the large hall where Rinpoché would be giving his talk. The problem was that everyone was required to be in the hall before Rinpoché's arrival, partly, at least, because it's considered disrespectful in his culture to walk into a talk after the arrival of the teacher.

The students—all four hundred or more—filed into the hall shortly after dinner for the talk that was scheduled to begin at 8 p.m. Remember the Buddhist lie about the talk starting at eight? I don't think Tibetans traditionally functioned under the rule of the clock and Rinpoché in particular was a dedicated practitioner of the attitude that everything has its own time, that you do whatever you're doing with full, relaxed attention until it's done. The result was that—though you never could be sure—a more likely starting time for the talk was sometime after 11 p.m. I attended more than one that didn't begin until after midnight and carried on well past two or three in the morning.

On the evening that stands out in my memory, we had also been up into the wee hours the previous night for the same reason, and had still begun the day's schedule first thing in the morning. I sat dressed in my Kasung uniform of white shirt, Kasung tie, navy blue blazer, and flannel slacks, face flushed from two or three glasses of wine over dinner. Due to the uncertain arrival time, there were no breaks for walking meditation. As the evening dragged on toward the midnight hour, the room became increasingly hot and stuffy—no tie loosening or jacket removal permitted—and I became more and more claustrophobic, exhausted, in need of a bathroom break, in danger of fainting, and generally distraught, until I really thought I couldn't bear another five minutes.

The commitment and pride to do my job properly and demonstrate respect for the protocols of the situation kept me sitting right where I started until the hall had emptied around 2 a.m. And of course, as you've no doubt concluded by now, I didn't faint, pee my pants, or suffer any psychic damage. What stayed with me was not the discomfort but the conviction that I was sturdier than I had imagined.

No doubt many of you reading this have much more exotic and extreme tales to tell of endurance tests of one kind or another. Rinpoché himself was a living demonstration of the ability to transcend conventional physical limits. When called to, he could stay up for days at a time. He once said that he had recently gone to the dentist to have a tooth pulled and refused anaesthetic because he wanted to experience the situation fully, not numbed. I also watched him sit unshaded on a podium for over two hours in blazing mid-July, midday Colorado mountain sun, wearing a winter-weight, worsted-wool, double-breasted, navy blue suit and tie, and never move or appear uncomfortable.

My exposure to the people in the Native American Church has been almost more remarkable and humbling. I've mentioned Kanucas' comment, "You didn't come here to get comfortable, you came here to get strong." Numerous accounts of the traditional life of the Native Americans indicate that they were indeed hardy. One old lady told a story of how in the days of her childhood, if a man fell into the icy creek water he would take his clothes off, roll and rub himself in the snow to "warm up," ring out the soaked garments, put them back on and continue his journey uncomplaining.

From crippling diseases and from body-crushing accidents during the wild and difficult days of their youth, a lot of the people I've met in that world are banged up. Kanucas for example, at age 62, is badly crippled from polio, has zero remaining cartilage in his hip sockets, is missing most of one arm, and has diabetes. One night he told us, with a kindly tone, that we, these days, are pathetic. He said that forty years ago when he first started participating in these all-night prayer meetings, he didn't understand how the elders could sit up all night, barely moving. After a few years he realized that it was through their unbroken focus on the prayer that they transcended or ignored those pains and discomforts.

Lawrence Littlehawk, another roadman in the NAC, was once dragged down a hill under his truck, broke most of his bones, and flatlined four times in the helicopter on the way to the big-city hospital. He also ruined his knees jumping out of more than a hundred—in his words— "perfectly good airplanes" during his military service. Now in his fifties, Lawrence lives with continual pain in much of his body.

One night in the tipi, Wakay, an energetic and powerfully built middle-aged Native man, leaned over and whispered to me, "The things I love the most, like being in these prayer ceremonies, are the things that hurt me the most. I've been injured in thirteen car accidents and fallen off two roofs." That community is full of stories like these that would humble most of us in astonishment and respect. I sometimes weep when I watch these dignified and courageous people stay upright and uncomplaining in the tipi for twelve hours and more.

Experiences like those definitely toughen you up and make you more flexible, less demanding of having the right temperature ("womb temperature" as Alan Watts once teased), the right amount of sleep, food and water on demand, etcetera. There's a freedom in that, not being as concerned about your own needs, more able to give all your attention and care to the situation at hand.

I'll pass on another striking example of the power of intention, concentration, and deep meditative states to transcend normal physical limitations. There's a Tibetan Buddhist practice called "Tummo," the ability to generate heat in the body. One source described it like this: "Tummo is taught as one part of the six yogas of Naropa. Stories and eyewitness accounts abound of yogic practitioners being able to generate sufficient heat to dry wet sheets draped around their naked bodies while sitting outside in the freezing cold, not just once, but multiple times."[1] A 1982 study by Benson et al. found that Indo-Tibetan Yogis in the Himalayas and in India "exhibited the capacity to increase the temperature of their fingers and toes by as much as 8.3 degrees Celsius."[2] — about 15 degrees Fahrenheit.

There's a wealth of stories of people who have had spiritual visions and deep experiences in situations of transcending the time-bound body. In many traditional Native American cultures the vision quest is an important practice for people at certain stages of their journey. According to written accounts and the tales of friends, a vision quest involves spending several days alone out in nature without food or water. As I understand it, the seeker prays steadfastly and often receives direct Spirit guidance in these situations. Here's part of Wallace Black Elk's description of the vision quest: "It takes prayers. It takes a lot of work. It takes a lot of courage. It takes a lot of patience. It takes a lot of endurance...Ninety-six hours is a mighty stretch! But what's really going to get you down like nothing is when you start thinking about time. When you go to Tunkashila, there is no time. There's no past or present or future time. Everything is the same. So when you understand that, then Earth time is nothing...But if you go there and start thinking about time, you're dead."[3]

The Sun Dance practice—also common to many native American tribes, past and present—is a similar, very powerful method of reaching beyond oneself and demonstrating one's trust in Spirit. The gods seem to like this kind of commitment and courage. Typically, the dancers are tied to a tree in the center of a kind of corral in a cleared "arbor." With assistance from supporters, they do a simple dance—accompanied by singing and drumming—in sessions throughout the day from sunrise to sunset. This usually lasts for four days, with the dancers taking no food or water. It may also be very hot, since Sun Dances are usually held in the middle of summer.

> We pierce in the Sun Dance or go without food or water in order to contact spirit. When that spirit comes, we have all the chance in the world. We could say anything we want there. So I have to prepare myself to be alert as to what I say, what I've been longing to say all my life.[4]
> *Wallace Black Elk*

Putting oneself through ordeals like these may seem severe, but I've been a supporter and drummer/singer at a few Sun Dances and I've seen the energy that can be created. At the first one I attended, the hard work, commitment, courage, and devotion of the dancers and the supporters brought a stunning power and tenderness into that shared contained space. I also saw some of the dancers in the months following and I never heard any of them say they regretted it. I've only seen how some have taken significant leaps forward in the strength of their spirits and their ability to manifest their prayers and visions. Kanucas once told me how he went for a week with no sleep, beginning with an all-night peyote medicine prayer meeting, followed by the Sun Dance for four days, and concluding with two more all-night meetings. He finished the story by saying that he wouldn't counsel anyone to do what he did. "It almost killed me" he said, "but I learned something invaluable, that I could transcend the limits of the body."

These examples of mind over matter indicate capabilities far beyond what most of us in the comfortable, more or less sedentary environments of modern societies would consider possible. They also point to the larger implications for ideas like Terence McKenna's theories of freedom from the monkey body, of "life lived entirely in the imagination." I've been chewing over a phrase McKenna used several times to encapsulate this vision. He imagined our future lying in the ability to "exteriorize the soul and internalize the body," a challenging concept that, put in the most simple terms, seems to suggest our potential for multi-dimensional exploration in an unbound eternal now.

For many of us, it's a powerful lesson to find out we don't need to be ruled so restrictively by what we consider to be the demands of the body. I'm not suggesting that people shouldn't look after themselves or should treat their bodies shoddily, just that in certain intense situations that could lead to a transcendent experience, we may need to have developed the strength to not indulge in fears and concerns about our physical comfort levels. We may find that the way forward demands a return to the kind of inner strength of body and spirit that many of our ancestors have had. We may need to rediscover our resilience.

This discussion has so far focused more on transcending apparent physical limitations and has only hinted at the emotional and psychological aspects of getting strong. We can cultivate those attitudes toward our mind states as well. One way of describing worry and fear is that these mind/body states get the better of us. We feel out of control in that regard. These states just sweep through us and often dominate our experience. Learning to have confidence in our strength also calls for developing the faith that our spirits are stronger than the stress experiences. It's not uncommon to think we have no choice or control over them. It may take discipline, hard work, and persistence, we may still have to ride powerful energies that feel difficult, but the message from the masters is that we do have that capability. Rinpoché had a slogan I'll address more in the next chapter, "Relax and change your attitude on the spot."

The spill-over effects of bare-attention meditation practices help train the mind to be present as these emotions and tensions arise. Meditation helps cultivate the ability to catch yourself in your discursive mind. Often you can let that mindstuff go on the spot, allow it to dissolve with the outgoing breath. There are also various practices and reminders that can help regain a calmer center in the moment, even in the heat of battle—ways to slow down, tune in to your breathing, release tensions that settled in while you weren't looking, while you weren't "in your body." This is not navel-gazing. Simply reminding yourself to pay attention to the body and breath only takes a second or two, doesn't have to disrupt your attention to the matters at hand, and can actually promote a less self-conscious presence.

Beyond just working at bringing ourselves back into the present, there is the practice and capacity to step into sacred space—prayerful space—feeling the whole space, feeling one's heart connection, as one focuses on Spirit and on praying for the benefit of others. There's an excellent Tibetan practice called tonglen—sending and taking on the medium of the breath— which can be employed briefly in almost any situation. I'll describe this practice in more detail later. In the simplest terms, it involves breathing in the suffering of others and oneself and breathing out blessing, kindness, prayerful thoughts.

That's our challenge and our strength in the years ahead, to rouse barely tapped levels of energy and determination, to step out of ourselves, reduce our demand on the world, on the resources of the planet—to "let go and let God". The potential for growth and new discovery in that field of learning will likely prove to be an exciting and invaluable blessing in the conduct of individual and community life.

17

Change Your Attitude and Relax

"Peeple of zee wurl, relax!" was the well-timed raspy reminder of Sailor the parrot in Tom Robbins' novel *Fierce Invalids Home from Hot Climates*. The concept is ridiculously simple on one level, yet central to the planetary shift and a message that still doesn't seem to have worked its way into the marrow for most of us. The good news lies in the remarkable potential for the "workability" of the human mind.

There's a Buddhist saying, "Change your attitude and relax on the spot." Though I heard that one a long time ago, it's a skill that takes time to develop, to become more consistent in recognizing when it's necessary, to become confident that we have that capability and can put it to good use. As Kanucas has told those assembled more than once, "However you say it is for you, that's how it will be." In the fine tradition of the Mishap and Worst Horse lineages, I and many of my brothers and sisters seem to have to trip over ourselves countless times while we're learning to get out of our own way.

And then of course there's the legendary "But . . ." response. We all know the "But" character. He's got a thousand good reasons, a thousand convincing stories. It's a circular argument though, a self-sabotaging apparent paradox. As soon as we "but", we're not there anymore, we're not on the spot, we've just sent the very message that will undermine our desire or intention. "But" happens when you're walking on water and you suddenly fall into doubt. Oops.

Part of the practice is called "mind protection"—watching your mind like a hawk to catch sinking feelings, discouraging words, negativity of all sorts. The little creeps that want to steal you away are always waiting for you to turn your back so they can sneak in and take over the controls. Some readers might be thinking here that this practice sounds like a self-absorbed, navel-gazing thing to be doing, but it's actually the opposite. You're far more likely to catch these saboteurs when you're alert, and that means present to both the inner and outer environments without compulsively spinning around in busy mind.

Like I said, I've known about this one for many years, but recently I've observed that I can sometimes just grab some sinking thinking pattern by the lapels and gently but firmly send it packing. It can flash through so quickly that I don't even realize it's happened until it's passed and I've perked up. At that point I sometimes then recall the exact moment when the quick thought-intention arose to change the habitual pattern.

Sometimes it feels like a sudden and subtle flash of determination, a shot of wrathful energy that sends a little electrical jolt through the system to clear out the deadwood of disheartening thought patterns. It's as if you put these words into a nanosecond: "No. Don't need to do that again, don't want to go there again. Cut."

There's another way I've observed the "change your attitude and relax on the spot" concept functioning. I think of it as seeing the space around situations, especially when there's conflict involved. My wife or I say something to each other which triggers the hot button and we start falling into anger and recrimination. Sometimes though, I have enough awareness in those moments to see the event occurring in a larger space. At that point I might not get taken over by the solidity of my position. The tension sometimes dissolves on the spot and is replaced by a sense of humor.

Humor is an important part of that dynamic. Being clear enough to see the field around those obsessive mindstorms allows the humor of the situation to become apparent. The gentleness that comes with relaxing in the moment walks hand in hand with this kind of humor. It's also a good sign that your spiritual work is having a beneficial effect. We're often drawn to people who don't seem to be taking themselves seriously. And that quality is closely related to the humility and accessibility we also tend to find attractive in people.

So there's encouraging news on the air waves. Every moment is a fresh start. At any moment we can relax, let go, pay attention, cut if necessary, and wake up on the spot. There are numerous little quick tricks around to encourage the likelihood of catching the moment and uplifting yourself: lifting your gaze, raising your dignity, looking around, checking in with body and breath, feeling your feet planted solidly on the ground, clearing your head and focusing with complete attention on the task at hand (or as someone said, "Forget it and focus").

Then there's the secret OM AH HUM practice that can be done in seconds anywhere anytime, where you say to yourself "OM" as you contact the energy of the heavens and the great masters in the sky above your head, "AH" as you bring that energy down into your body, into your heart, and "HUM" as you breathe and empty outward into the world and wake up yet again in the fresh start moment of nowness.

Whatever the trick or technique we bring to bear on the moment, the message from the elders and masters of the phenomenal world is that our beliefs about ourselves and our world—our habitual, conditioned responses to situations—are not solid. This message doesn't need to be shipped on as a belief. It can be field tested every time we don't like the state of mind we're in, whether it be an ongoing condition or a sudden arising of defeatist or conflictual thinking. Ego is synonymous with struggle. Though we often don't consciously recognize it, we're actively maintaining and renewing our stance.

Extending that thought, it might be good to pay attention to your attachment to the negative, painful, harmful patterns residing in your consciousness. They don't feel good but we want them anyway. We believe we have a right to our anger, our depression, our blaming. These thought-feelings seem to confirm us, they seem to justify us. Sometimes it really does feel like a surrender, like giving something up reluctantly. If we make the choice however, we can often release our thought bundles, we can relax right now out of the programs we're running at any particular moment, in any particular encounter. The programmed, habitual responses exist only in the virtual, ephemeral world of thought and are amenable to change...on the spot.

The Watercourse Way
A Field Study Assignment

Go to Running River School.
Follow a creek up into the hills,
to the source and beyond.
Observe the water easing out
of the body of the mountain.
Molecules join molecules,
form rivulets, brooks, streams,
reuniting with friends
as they travel toward the Ocean.

Watch them effortlessly find and fall into
the Watercourse Way,
without resistance or thought interference,
Surrendering again and again
to something larger.

Free running,
joyous running,
breathing out completely
and finally dissolving into the Mother Ocean.

Gaté, Gaté,
Paragaté,
Parasamgaté.
Gone, Gone,
Completely gone,
Gone without remnant.

"The voice of the river
    that has emptied
        into the Ocean
            Now laughs
                and sings
                    just like God."
                    Hafiz

Part 3

Roads Leading Toward Home
Tools and Techniques for Healing and Awakening

Introduction to Part Three

The first part of this book perhaps created a dramatic portrait of some of the central issues of our time—many would now say *the* central issue of our time—the need for large numbers of people to get the message quickly about who we really are and what we're capable of envisioning and manifesting. That portrait or survey is based on the understanding that all life is spiritual and all of us are in some relation to this reality, whether we are consciously aware of it or not, whether we are attuned to the call of awakening or are completely in the grip of our denying egos.

In Part 2, the information became more focused on specific teachings and concepts that may help with a shift in view, as well as provide good guidance on the journey of awakening. There were teachings about how to recognize a variety of pitfalls and distortions that can knock us off the path, as it were. There were suggestions for effective and sometimes on-the-spot remedies and antidotes to some of these obstacles.

In this section, I hope to engage you in an exploration of tools and techniques that can have a real and lasting impact—techniques that I hope may stimulate you to go further in your practice and to deepen your commitment to awakening for yourself and for all.

A caring consciousness that experiences itself freely as one with and at peace with everything—that puts the solution of problems and the creation of beauty ahead of selfish, ego-based motivations—appears no closer than an impossibly distant, frail, and even deluded fantasy to many of us. Maybe a lot of you who are reading this are working with a path that feels right and effective. No doubt others are thinking that all this talk is one thing, but how does an ordinary person get from A to B, from samsara to the awakened state.

To start with, it's safe to say that the awakened state doesn't manifest itself in our lives as a result of reading and studying, of gathering a body of knowledge, or of developing a belief system we're convinced explains life and our situation within it. Belief is especially tricky because it typically resides in thought—in ideational construction—and because it is often founded on an illusion, regardless of the accuracy of the information it's based upon. The illusion is that we have found the answer and that therefore we are safe in our knowing. But unless we've completely freed ourselves from ego's hold, there is something in us—the Buddha mind if you will—that knows what we're doing and threatens to undermine our certainty. So we're not completely open and relaxed and we sense that we have to defend this territory we've built up to soothe and protect ourselves.

Buddhist teachings equate ego with struggle, "the battle of ego" as it's been termed. We expend huge reservoirs of energy defending our belief, convincing ourselves constantly that we have "found it." The logical extension of that position is that we also feel the need to convince others we're right, in an unconscious drive to remove contradictions from our field of awareness and reassure ourselves that our view must be right if others also hold to it. It's no great insight to point out that in its unbridled versions, belief breeds violence. The tragic results of attempting to enforce a set of beliefs on others litter the trails of history with tracks of suffering and bloodshed. Great societies have been destroyed in the cause of someone else's belief.

Funny how things work out when we get out of our own way.[1]
Susan Littlehawk

In a different way altogether, the message coming from the wisdom carriers is that this awakening is completely accessible to us all because it is actually our true nature, the way we are when we dissolve the illusions that obscure the truth from our awareness, when the burden is surrendered and we land on what is. When we bring our mindfulness and awareness to bear with diligence, courage, and perseverance, when we pay attention and let go again and again, we might gradually relax into that unconditioned state.

In case anyone gets the impression I'm proclaiming my own great wisdom on such matters, I would just like to remind you again that my function is that of a lifelong student working with these issues. I'm in the trenches like many others and I'm acting as a journeyman and journalist—a channel for information I've sifted through and worked with all these years. This is information I have deep confidence in and am moved to share with others, with the intention and prayer that we all may wake up together.

> [Some] may come to attain the enlightened state simply by surrendering to divine grace. The intent and humility of each one of us will determine the outcome.[2]
> *Carl Johan Calleman*

Strictly speaking, the teachings and various anecdotes and stories suggest that one could wake up on the spot. There's an archetype of that kind of sudden illumination scattered throughout the literature. You probably know the famous Christian story of the flash of awakening experienced by Paul on the road to Damascus. One of my personal favorites is Charles Dickens' *A Christmas Story*, in which the hardhearted old Mr. Scrooge is shown—in a series of vivid dreams that seem to last the night—the causes of his bitterness and his withdrawal from love, the cruel impact of his present behavior, and the tragic future consequences of his current direction. I always weep when I see the old film with Alistair Sim and the joy and delight he experiences upon "waking" on Christmas morning. We long for that kind of catharsis, to be free of our burden, once and for all.

Realistically, however, for most of us, the journey will be gradual as we undo the layers of illusion and self-protection; as we let go a little and let be; sometimes get scared again and fall back into habitual patterns; let go a little more and let be and learn to relax into what is, until we have complete and continuing confidence in the awakened state. With and without the guidance and direct instruction of wise teachers and of Spirit allies, humans have found numerous methods of uncovering the true nature of mind. I'm quite sure there are various paths and techniques with whose efficacy I'm unfamiliar. I have, however, had experience with a few of the most widely practiced techniques, as well as some that are more obscure and even controversial but probably equally as potent and perhaps more powerful than those better known. In this section, I'll also briefly discuss some methods of dissolving ego, transcending the monkey body, and contacting Spirit wisdom that I've had little direct experience with but have studied enough to intuit that they have potential as good awakening tools.

As I understand it, the connecting link between various spiritual practices that truly work is that of uncovering natural mind, quieting the obscuring noise of the ego, stepping into the gap between thoughts, and connecting to the unconditioned primordial reality that—from the point of view and the known experience of conventional mind as it is understood by most people—is truly in the realm of the unknown. Our practices, I believe, need to shine the light directly on the truth, provoke us to look clearly at the obstacles in our minds, and help us surrender to that unnameable presence, without dogma, falling upon "Buddhadharma without credentials." What follows is an exploration of a few of the most effective techniques of awakening that have been received, practiced, and taught in various places by many awakening and wise souls.

18

Nothing Happens Next
On Mindfulness/Awareness Meditation

As one sits and stills the mind, subtle means of knowing are revealed in the mind, in the light, in the stars above the head. There is a way of knowing that passes through all realms: to be fully present in the moment, that what is above may manifest below. That is our choice.[1]
Dhyani Ywahoo

Reminder: Waking up doesn't occur as a result of collecting, believing in, or articulating a body of knowledge—no matter how brilliant and compelling those teachings might be. Enlightenment doesn't unfold in us as the result of intellectual knowledge at all. We don't get sane because we believe in our religion, in our God—no matter how passionately we believe, no matter how convinced we are of the truth of our chosen path, no matter how airtight our case for the unassailable logic of our religion's explication of life. According to Buddhist and other teachings which people have worked with diligently for millennia, we awaken by learning how to uncover the existing wisdom already within us. And with that understanding, very simple mindfulness/awareness meditation practice is, as Suzuki Roshi reminded us, our true nature.

There are many kinds of meditation practices. You probably

194

knew that. In this discussion I'm making a few general distinctions, first, between meditation and prayer—although some meditation techniques look a lot like prayer. Perhaps the link between the two is chant, where seed syllables, words, phrases, and longer passages are recited or sung, either in silence or aloud, alone or in groups. The repetition of these utterances is, for example, what the Transcendental Meditation (TM) people call meditation.

Without drawing too tight a line around matters, I also want to make a distinction between meditation practices that have a focus—sometimes called one-pointed meditation techniques— and what might be called "emptiness" or "bare-attention" meditation practices. One-pointed practices may involve chanting, as well as visualizations and even physical movements, such as the Tibetan Buddhist ngondro practice of prostrations. And if you were prepared to stretch your conceptual boundaries a little, you might also note that intense, unbroken concentration directed toward any number of tasks— such as artistic creation and performance—could also fit the description of one-pointed meditation.

I'm by no means a scholar of meditation practices, so although I've experimented with a few and practiced a few in-depth, I can't comment on the efficacy of those techniques on the roads not taken. During my years of intense involvement with the Kagyu lineage of Tibetan Buddhism, my main practice was, and still is, the mindfulness/awareness practice called *shamatha*, or *shamatha/vipashyana*. Practices very similar in technique and intent to the versions I learned have been taught and practiced over the last two or three millennia throughout Asia—in countries such India, Bhutan, Burma, Thailand, Laos, Cambodia, Vietnam, China, and Japan, to name some of the main ones. Japanese Zen meditation practice—perhaps the practice most well-known by name in mainstream Western society—is very simple and direct, and much like shamatha practice as it was taught to me.

I also spent several years doing other Buddhist practices in that community, such as mantra and chant recitation and the invocation and visualization of deities, which, I was told, were representations and even manifestations of certain energies. The students were to work with these energies to develop or cut through particular aspects of our minds and to make a relationship with the qualities being invoked. Although I was diligent with some of those practices, I finally concluded that that route wasn't for me. My developing intuition was that the complex elaborations of the Vajrayana practices didn't suit my more simple nature. Perhaps I was just too thickheaded or impatient to tune into the subtle and invisible energies.

So if you want to be Phoenixed, come and be parked.[2]
James Joyce

The one practice that completely made sense to me from the beginning is the basic meditation technique mentioned above. This, and other similar variations of mindfulness/awareness techniques, are about as close as you can get to *no* technique, as close as you can get to simply being present and trusting in your own clear mind as a way to live your life. Numerous books explain in detail the Buddhist understanding of how our minds work, how we create confusion for ourselves, and how these practices work with the samsaric, mind. A brief explanation:

You'll recall we normally see ourselves as entities separate from everything else. This is at bottom a highly insecure state of mind no matter how successful we've been in establishing our place in the material world. Ego is a kind of synonym for struggle. We actually know, though we may keep the awareness buried, that underneath all the obscuring clutter and denial, this separateness is an illusion—a serious game we're playing—and that our success is always conditional, at risk, in need of maintenance and protection. As Rinpoché described it: "Ego is imagination of a centralized nest that gives secure protection. You are frightened of the world outside of your projections, so you just go back into your sitting room and make yourself comfortable."[3]

In the egoic state we're continually compelled to generate thoughts and energy to maintain the illusion. The noise we create to obscure clear mind may seem to keep the threats to our comfort at bay and out of sight. But generating constant mental activity is at best a bandaid approach that doesn't touch the real obstacles, the "sticky web of attachments that seem to provide something we lack" and that work us over every day. It's said that samsara—the confused ego-ruled state of mind—is endless. Traditional Buddhist teachings even claim that without seeing these thought patterns clearly and exposing them to the crisp air and light of awareness that allows them to dispel and dissolves the chain, souls can remain stuck in samsara for thousands of lifetimes.

Mindfulness/awareness meditation could be described as a gradual and, for the most part, gentle way to preside over the dissolution of the ego. Ultimately, we envision being free of the tyranny of this busy mind, relaxed, and fully present with awakened heart continuously. I'll remind you again here that Eckhart Tolle suggested the ideal relationship to the thinking mind is not to be ruled by it—not hurtled along by obsessively overlapping thoughts in an endless project to cover over the threat of ego's nonexistence—but that instead we could pick up the thinking mind when we need to use it as a tool, and set it down when we don't.

I wouldn't claim that everyone needs to engage in a formal meditation practice to reach that state of functioning. For example, Kanucas once told me, without judgment, that in his experience white, European people in general had much busier minds than the Native Americans he had known throughout his life. However, it's probably of great benefit to most people to do this kind of practice, if only, for starters, to make the commitment to putting aside some time to observe discursive mind and allow it to settle down and clarify a little. The beauty of the practice is its simplicity, its naturalness, and its proximity to living in the now in the midst of daily activity.

I was told a story by one of the early students about the way Rinpoché first presented this meditation practice to his American students. Rather than introduce them right away to rigorous traditional practices, he told them to just sit down on a cushion and try to be present—without busy minds. He sat with them and it became apparent soon enough that their minds were jumping all over the place. So then he added one element of technique; pay attention to your breath, with a light touch, perhaps with about twenty-five percent of your attention on the breath and the rest simply being aware in the environment. It's hardly a technique at all, since breathing occurs continually as part of the autonomic nervous system and requires no conscious effort or attention from us. Our breathing is real and basic and paying attention to it brings us back into the present moment in a palpably grounded way.

As the story goes, Rinpoché observed that with this simple technique his students still continued to have a hard time with their wild minds, and so he added one more refinement to the technique. You almost never notice when you begin to drift into thought and out of full presence. But there is an exact moment when you realize you've been in thoughtland. At that point—he taught—lightly, silently say to yourself, "thinking," and gently bring your attention back to the breath, without a big deal and without praise or blame for the content of the thoughts. That helps make a really clear distinction, often not recognized before, between being in your head and being present. There's nothing abstract about it.

Although you would get more detail if you went to a formal meditation instruction session, and that's highly recommended anyway, the other key aspects of the method I was taught are to sit up straight and to keep the eyes open. Again, these are natural activities. Sitting up straight—perhaps with hands resting on thighs or folded in front of you so you don't have to think about what to do with them—is the best way to stay awake and diminish pain from poor posture that puts a strain on muscles. A straight posture also symbolizes and models a wakeful, alert, and dignified state of mind. We were taught a simple, effective reminder for this posture; "firm back and soft front," representing and encouraging strength and openheartedness. We were also taught to keep our eyes open, our gaze slightly lowered and softly directed toward the floor several feet in front of us, not staring or concentrating on one spot. Nothing against closing the eyes, but the principle again with the open-eye method is that it's very close to normal daily activity. This whole method of practice is nothing exotic or unusual, just the least amount of detail needed to sharpen up our already existing innate awareness.

We were also taught a simple technique to use for walking meditation, for example when we were doing all-day group practice sessions: not as intensively following the breath and labeling thoughts, just holding one hand cupped over the other in front and noticing the movement of one foot in front of the other, landing heel, toe, heel, toe while attempting to be aware of the surroundings without any special focus. And that is one "step" away from walking down the street with a similar degree of presence. You could even make the claim that that's where the real practice is, where the majority of the real work gets done. Eventually, with persistence—probably after many years of regular meditation practice in this way—the formality of the technique might gradually ease and dissolve, perhaps without our even noticing, into a more or less continuous meditative presence while moving through the day.

A caution might be helpful for some at this point. It can be tempting, especially when things seem to be going well in your life, to think that you don't need the formal technique anymore, that your mind is mostly clear and thoughts aren't frequent. I've noticed, both in myself and from descriptions by others, that this can be tricky, that there's a kind of murky grey area in there somewhere. The discursive mind can be subtle—running in the background—especially if you're not paying close attention to its processes. It's probably good advice for most students of meditation that even when it feels like things are flowing, to periodically check in with the specific, narrow discipline of following the breath and labeling thoughts, or whatever similar variation you've been working with.

This kind of natural and simple practice brings us back to ourselves and helps us to clarify and work with the thought patterns that have been ruling our lives. We come to see these thoughts as insubstantial, non-solid, temporary upheavals and delusions. Rinpoché once called the disturbed mental activity "temporary vomit." We come to notice the driven, overlapping functioning of our discursive minds and how it keeps us unsettled and dissatisfied.

People in my culture—urban and suburban North America— talk a lot about stress. Although the grounding and mind training of a formal sitting routine is a great help, don't underestimate the value of paying attention throughout the day, checking in with breath and body, softening the chest, feeling your feet solidly on the ground. Eckhart Tolle made a suggestion I've employed at times. He suggested you can do this anywhere; "notice your toes." Simple as it sounds, that tends to trigger a body awareness all the way up and including one's breathing and mental attention. It's that reminder again to relax and change your attitude on the spot.

Hopefully, by practicing a simple, bare-attention type of meditation with commitment and perseverance, the disturbances that plague us come to be seen clearly and understood as not being solid and insurmountable, but passing clouds obscuring our naturally awake minds. My old teacher compared this journey to walking in your shoes for so long that you eventually wear them out. You eventually wear out this ego. You learn to preside with patience, perseverance, and dignity over its gradual dissolution. Emptying out in this way allows something new — what some call Spirit or God, others call reality or awakened heart — to enter, like Jesus' teaching that you can only pour new wine into a vessel which has been emptied.

There's a crack, a crack in everything,
That's how the light gets in.[4]
Leonard Cohen
(from the song *Anthem*)

For anyone considering working with this kind of meditation technique on their own, I'd like to suggest a couple of things to keep an eye out for. First, it's essential to persist through all different states of mind. The ego considers this dissolution to be a threat to its very existence and since it's that mind most of us have primarily or totally identified ourselves with, any opening may trigger bouts of extreme cleverness from the fear-based self. The survival instinct kicks in. The ego drive can convince you of its airtight logic. It's extremely slippery. An easy trap to fall into is to think you're doing so well or so poorly that your practice is either not necessary or not working at all. A regular practice and a commitment to oneself that trumps the daily doubts and rationalizations can be extremely beneficial.

Second: Meditation doesn't necessarily offer obvious rewards. In fact, it's common to judge that you're doing worse than you were before you ever began to meditate. Seeing through your illusions — through ego's constructions and strategies — and facing down your formerly ignored, repressed emotions and habitual thought patterns isn't always a walk in the park on a sunny day. Many of us have created a one-sided picture of ourselves in which we're the good guys, the innocent, or the victims. These illusions are part of the personality package we've put together for coping with the world and we often employ them unconsciously to prop up and puff up our highly conditional self-esteem. Without the crutch of this false ground—the lie of personality, as Otto Rank labeled it—practitioners sometimes understandably feel depressed. Ego is often equated with self-importance. If it's not being fed it sulks and strategizes. The path of meditation teaches us to learn to observe the arising and dissolving of our mental patterns and to preside with dignity and without judgment over the twisting and stuttering journey of emptying these elaborate constructions of self-importance and self-protection. The naturally existing state underneath all that is a compassionate, unconditional appreciation of ourselves as we are and of life *as it is.* I think a lot of us already know that even if we don't know that we know.

And since this emptying feels like death to the ego, we just have to persevere, developing the confidence that all states of mind are workable. We're taught to develop this acceptance of everything that arises in our minds—gradually relaxing into an unconditional kindness to ourselves which naturally begins to flow outward toward others.

You could say that this kind of simple mindfulness/awareness practice is a universal meditation. You might even go further and call it the ground practice of the one true religion of nowness. People around the world who are awake to the living presence of Spirit in their lives would no doubt agree that there has to be a gap in the discursive mind to allow that unconditioned presence to manifest. In fact, I hear similar comments again and again from people from indigenous cultures as well as those where something like the Buddhist understanding of mind is still pervasive, or where a quieter, Earth-connected spirituality and lifestyle still lives. My friend Stephen, for example, who has been living in Thailand, a nation with deep Buddhist roots, tells me that his Thai friends tease him about thinking too much. They say they often see that in Westerners.

The masters keep reminding us that we all have this innate, primordial mind of wakefulness. These methods attempt to encourage and sharpen Buddha mind with the least possible overlay of technique, to bring us back to that natural condition. At some stage, farther down the road for us travelers still partially in the grip of the fearful mind, you could imagine even these simple crutches falling away as we learn to relax into a stable state of nowness. I like to think of this beautiful simple practice as a very generous stepping-stone to full presence.

This practice started from beginningless time and it will continue into an endless future. Strictly speaking, for a human being there is no other practice than this practice. There is no other way of life than this way of life. Zen practice is the direct expression of our true nature. Of course, whatever we do is the expression of our true nature, but without this practice it is difficult to realize.[5]
Shunryu Suzuki

19

A Channel Between Voice and Presence
The Power of Prayer

Handed down from my people was a story that the only duty left to us from the ancient ones was the duty of prayer, so I became a prayer person.[1]
Agnes Pilgrim

While the practice of bare-attention meditation may be the natural, universally available root practice, the spiritual practice that's truly universal in its regular application among humans is of course, prayer. The Oxford dictionary defines prayer as "a request for help or expression of thanks made to God or a god, an earnest hope or wish," and in all its glorious and sometimes crazed variations and intentions it's centrally important to every religion and to individuals everywhere whether or not they're involved in formal, organized religion. I think many of us in the modern secular societies, though, have been ill-educated spiritually, and so have missed the value and potential of certain kinds of authentic, powerful prayer. Cynics and skeptics in the modern materialistic cultures even write off the whole idea of praying as a simplistic, childish, and fruitless appeal to imaginary projections.

The way prayer was taught in the mainstream Christian religions probably didn't help for many of us. I grew up around it in the Anglican Church in the 1950s and 1960s, but the potential of prayer never really took hold, as I suspect was also the case for the great majority of my contemporaries. We were never presented with compelling, first-hand evidence that there was anyone listening to our prayers and that any result would come of them. For several years, when I was between about six and twelve, my mother monitored me closely and insisted I say my prayers before getting into bed each night. Looking back, I appreciate the intention, but at the time it was too abstract for me. I couldn't connect the implied concepts with my real life experience. "Now I lay me down to sleep, I pray the Lord my soul to keep. If I should die before I wake I pray the Lord my soul to take." There's some serious philosophy in those words for a young child to wrap his mind around, not to mention the unsettling implications of the possibility one might not make it through the night.

Then I was to ask God to bless my mother, father, sisters, other relatives, and friends. These are powerful sentiments and unquestionably good for the soul and possibly the recipients if said with sincerity, but my culture in general didn't experience Spirit anywhere else, didn't believe in the living intelligence of anything on Earth other than humans, (and to a very limited degree, animals), and laughed at the idea of ghosts and any other beings invisible to the modern eye. By the age of eight or nine children have already been jaded by one major shock when they discover they've been duped all those years about another mysterious superbeing who was supposed to circumnavigate the planet in one night, bringing gifts to all the children of the world. So, for most of us in the new, primarily secular and consumer-oriented middle classes of North America after World War II, there was a vague possibility that God existed, but we had little confidence in the proposition or in what He would do about blessing people if He did exist.

Nor did anyone instruct me in how to reconcile the other

feelings and thoughts I might be having with this intention to have friends and family blessed by the highest authority. My sister and I were periodically at each other's throats during those years. I didn't always feel like having God bless her. If my true feelings were included I might have asked him to knock her down a peg or two before I got to the blessing part. I'm being glib, but the point is there was a superficiality or naive one-sidedness to the process that didn't deal with the real blood and guts issues—not that I was conscious of any of that at the time. I just didn't get it and wasn't interested.

Martín Prechtel described how the Maya of Santiago Atitlán in Guatemala during his time there in the 1970s and 1980s sometimes felt sorry for the earnest American missionaries trying to sell a dry, boring, fear-mongering religion to a people with wild and strong hearts and an ancient, powerful, and ecstatic connection to Spirit. That description about sums up the kind of religion we were exposed to—bloodless. A commonly held view among members of the Native American Church is that the whites go to church to talk *about* God and the Indians go to church to talk *to* God and *with* God. It's obviously not the case that people in the "white" religions don't at least sincerely attempt to talk to someone they imagine to be God. But the evidence isn't clear that a real, functioning relationship has been widely established in the dominator societies and understood by a people who in general aren't manifesting the living heart-connection to Spirit that initiated people in indigenous spiritual environments say they have experienced directly. It seems the dominant cultures have wandered far from the knowledge of intelligent communication from and with the Earth, the animals, and the unseen spirits. I offer myself and the community of my upbringing as Exhibit A in the making of this argument.

I now know enough about that other world, especially through my experience with the Native American Church, to say that the aphorism about talking with Spirit isn't just a belief or a clever turn of phrase. Though my own experience is limited as I gradually undo the conditioning of a rational reductionist culture, I've seen enough and heard enough to be confident that the mysterious Spirit is immanent, and readily accessible, especially to many of the experienced elders of that environment. Kanucas has said a number of times, to remind those of us who've not yet experienced that presence clearly, "When I say that Spirit talks to me, I mean it just like that."

My contemporaries and I didn't experience any revelations "like that" in the white, middle-class suburb and Protestant church of my youth. The sermons didn't raise the blood flow and the whole environment seemed to me, even at that tender age, to lack something essential, some authentic spark. As I recall, there was also a distinct scarcity of humor there and so it was a delightful revelation for me years later to discover in the Buddhist community a lot of laughter, lightheartedness, and even mischievous irreverence. Until then I had no idea religion could be funny and didn't have to be somber and serious. Now I would say that a spiritual environment without a liberal sprinkling of humor is no spiritual environment at all.

Also confusing in those days was the behavior of most of the people in the church community. In general there wasn't a lot of charisma emanating from the adults who were supposed to be embodying and communicating the information and worldview the young were supposed to accept and inherit. In fact, the lack of manifestation of authentic awakening was more in line with the Buddhist view that until we free ourselves from our confused state we're mostly engaged in mutual group-imprisonment. Even at that young age I sensed a disconnect. Of course, as I said, this was the WASP, middle-class suburbia of central Canada in the 1950s. I could rest the case there or pile on with the acerbic observation that that version of life in North America at the time has been described as the nadir of Western civilization.

Prayer in Buddhist Practice

In any case, by the time I'd reached young adulthood, I'd come to think of prayer, when I thought of it at all, as a quaint idea that had little or no application to my life. My reintroduction to it came when I joined a Tibetan Buddhist community a few years later. Though the word "prayer" wasn't in common use in that environment, there were many chants. The chants were verses, paragraphs, shorter and longer passages—most of which had been translated into English—which were employed to accompany a variety of events, sessions, and other practices. We read them aloud together, recited them from memory, and included them in our private practices. These chants were reminders of the power of the truth (Dharma,) invocations of wisdom energies, pleas for the banishment of negative forces, and stories of the achievements and dedication of great masters. The chants were also expressions of devotion and gratitude to these masters and to the wisdom of the teachings, as well as appeals for the awakening and blessing of all sentient beings.

As always, there can be an energy aroused when a group focuses its attention in that way. Some of the chants were short phrases repeated for several minutes or longer. Some were as simple as seed syllables like "OM AH HUM" or just "OM." Repetition of sounds like these can cut through the mental chatter, create a trancelike state, and energize prayerful intention. Some claim that the vibrations of the syllables themselves can create an altered state that deepens and heals. Traditional Buddhist teachings say the voicing and visualizing of these seed syllables in meditative practice is a method of rousing the presence of deities—or archetypes—and in some sense melding with those energies.

During those years, though I was sincere and often passionate in my recitation of the chanted passages, I still hadn't grasped the potential of prayer. I didn't have any direct sense or confirmation that what I was chanting would have any impact on anything other than my own intention. I saw this chant recitation as expressions we made of our commitment and devotion to the beauty of the teachings of enlightenment and to the masters who had exemplified that wisdom and kept it alive from generation to generation. For most of us, the feeling we were able to muster for these chants was strengthened in particular by our love and admiration for our teacher.

There was, however, one form of what I would call prayer that really stood out among the Buddhist teachings of those years. We called it by its Tibetan name, "tonglen" — the practice of taking and sending on the breath. It's a way to actualize one's intention and compassion in physical, mental, and symbolic form. I'm presenting it here for information and inspiration, and not as complete instruction on the details of the practice. Talks can be found in books and online by a number of Buddhist teachers. One of the clearest is Pema Chödrön, a senior student of Chögyam Trungpa and the author of several excellent books on Buddhist and Shambhala wisdom. Here is part of her description at shambhala.org:

We begin the practice by taking on the suffering of a person we know to be hurting and who we wish to help. For instance, if you know of a child who is being hurt, you breathe in the wish to take away all the pain and fear of that child. Then, as you breathe out, you send the child happiness, joy or whatever would relieve their pain. This is the core of the practice: breathing in others' pain so they can be well and have more space to relax and open, and breathing out, sending them relaxation or whatever you feel would bring them relief and happiness. However, we often cannot do this practice because we come face to face with our own fear, our own resistance, anger, or whatever our personal pain, our personal stuckness happens to be at that moment. At that point you can change the focus and begin to do tonglen for what you are feeling and for millions of others just like you who at that very moment of time are feeling exactly the same stuckness and misery.

There's a beautifully active, creative, and visceral quality to that practice, and although it's often done more formally as part of group or solo meditation sessions, it can be called up anywhere, anytime, by taking a moment to focus one's attention and compassion on a particular situation of need, or as an antidote to negative thought patterns that arise in oneself. For example, when you notice yourself indulging negative thoughts toward someone, it may help to breathe that energy in and imagine yourself sending it back out as kindness, forgiveness, and so on. Sometimes that simple gesture acts to diminish or even reverse the momentum of the negative feeling. In some respects, tonglen is also similar to the spirit of prayer in ancient indigenous practice—a potentially powerful assistance to the kind of heart and mind concentration required to invoke beneficial healing energies and spirits.

An Unexpected Revelation

It wasn't until I began participating in the all-night prayer meetings of the Native American Church that I began to understand something about the real power of prayer. This was a different approach. From the very first meeting I attended, it was evident that here were people who knew how to speak their hearts. The songs that accompany praying throughout the night are also carriers of prayer and I'll come back to that. At this point, I'm speaking of people expressing themselves in their own words—or as some elders have said—in the words of the Spirit coming through them.

Each meeting has a particular purpose, generally determined

by the "sponsor" who has requested the meeting. During the night there is a lot of focused prayer toward that purpose. There's also ample time to pray for the benefit of people in the lives of the rest of us. Sometimes the prayers are visualized and expressed silently during the course of the night. At other times, there are specific prayers expressed aloud by one individual. The chant-like prayer songs that many take turns singing or leading are also meant to be the wings of the heart's intentions.

One clear instruction that hit home with me was Kanucas' teaching that in the order of things there's a natural hierarchy of attention and intention. God or Spirit is first, the people are second, one's own family is third, and oneself is last. It makes sense that you first make your openhearted connection to the mysterious presence of the Creator to establish the foundation for all other prayer intentions. I also liked the reminder that I put myself last in that sequence. When I get caught up in suffering, it helps me remember to refocus elsewhere. In the presence of the powerful peyote medicine Spirit, there have been nights when I've experienced an instant shift from uncomfortable physical and mental suffering to relaxed compassion and joy as soon as I remembered to drop the "self" thoughts and concentrate my attention and prayers on Spirit and others in need of assistance.

This spontaneous-expression type of prayer has been a revelation. I've been deeply impressed and moved by the authenticity of people in these meetings. There are a few times during the night when someone is called upon to speak in that way and sometimes they talk for as long as an hour without hesitation, without "ums" and "uhs." I've made mention in this book of the Mayan belief in the use of "delicious words" to court the spirit—the ones who feed us. According to Martín Prechtel, the Maya of his experience lived their lives from the conviction that we keep life going by our commitment in that way, by our gratitude, devotion, and praise. Kanucas says, "Our life is a prayer."

Rinpoché spoke of "good head and shoulders," maintaining an upright, outward looking, dignified bearing with a soft front and a firm back. Whenever I remember, I straighten up a little, raise my head a little, pay attention, come up—or down—out of the discursive mind, and allow my heart area to soften. Sometimes I visualize something like a thread or beam connected between my heart and the feeling of that presence out there. It may not be literally true that there is any such thing as a presence "up there" or "out there," but that practice often helps me reconnect with my heart in a humbling way. That kind of prayer is wonderfully light on its feet. You can pray anytime. You can come back to your heart. You can turn your thoughts and feelings to those you care about.

Some people may think, "Sure, it's probably good for your spirit to think that way, but that's as far as it goes." There's another whole level to this kind of prayer though. Again, from my own experience—combined with stories, testimonials, and teachings from authentic, intelligent, grounded people with no axes to grind, no need to persuade or proselytize—I'm convinced that committed, heart-fueled thought intention directed to the Creator, or whatever word you prefer, has powerful effects in the real world.

This capacity is one of the ideas that our conventional scientific establishment hasn't been able to come to terms with yet, although there are cracks in that edifice where light is leaking in. The influence of the scientific worldview in the modern dominant cultures has been an obstacle for many people trying to make this connection and develop those practices. There's reason to respect skeptical intelligence and a hard-nosed approach to examining the truth of an idea or hypothesis, but it's been said before that science doesn't have much to say on the deepest questions of life. Can science prove or disprove the existence of God, of love, of the effects of sincere intention on the material world? For some things you just have to put away your measuring stick and pay attention. People from indigenous cultures that have kept alive threads of their ancient practices know the truth of the power of prayer, in their hearts, in their bones, and in the evidence they see around them, like the Buddha putting his hand on the Earth and saying, "This solid Earth is my witness."

Healing Power

I've heard a good number of powerful stories of healing resulting from prayer in just my few short years among the people of the NAC and I have no doubt that there are countless more from around the world. I've seen some things that could be called miraculous and I've been told stunning stories of healing that have been corroborated by reliable witnesses: reports of people brought back from the brink of death, healings from cancer and other serious and life-threatening diseases. Some of these stories and testimonials describe healings that defy the rules of conventional medical science. People with cancers go back to their doctors for tests. The tests come back negative and the doctors are bewildered. Though I might lose a few of you on this next one, I'm going to share it anyway because it might be the most extreme example I've heard of the contravention of the known laws of physics. I asked several of the elders about the story and they confirmed its veracity.

One night a young Indian man, known to some of us as Wild Willy, told me he'd had a bullet lodged near the base of his skull for a couple of years. Surgeons were unwilling to attempt removal because of the bullet's delicate placement and the fear it would cause other serious damage if moved. The bullet wasn't deep enough to be life-threatening in the near term, just embedded enough to cause bad headaches and other unwanted symptoms. A special healing ceremony was held for Willy, accompanied only by a few of the most experienced elders. All ate the peyote medicine, smoked prayer tobacco, prayed and sang hard, and performed other healing rituals. Willy was wearing a small medicine-bundle pouch hanging from a cord around his neck.

The ceremony lasted all night and in the morning he noticed the pouch felt a bit different. He then reached in and was astonished to find the bullet. If it helps the skeptics at all, I want to make it clear that this was in no way a commercial or public transaction. The elders who confirmed the story had nothing to gain from any fabrication or exaggeration. In fact, the general rule of thumb in that environment is that it's unacceptable to charge money for this kind of healing work.

We are made of holy speech.[2]
Martín Prechtel

One of the elders told us that when you have complete confidence in the power of your prayer—the power of your intention—it *will* manifest. But people often wonder why their prayers don't seem to be answered. There could be a lot of reasons for that. Some people's faith in God seems predicated on the belief that God can snap His fingers any time He wants and stop wars and similar great tragedies and disasters. Maybe He can, but it makes more sense that the wisest teacher must allow us to make our own mistakes and learn the lessons that will bring us to wisdom and compassion. If we're going to grow up, we're going to do it by cultivating our own innate intelligence.

Lack of energy, of sustained concentration, or of unshakeable faith can also be part of the reason that prayers fail to make their journey. There are attitudes and contexts that appear to create a stronger foundation or launching pad for the energetic transmission of intention. There is also the aspect of gratitude to Spirit, to life, of sending our delicious words and our beauty to the gods, to those who feed us, who sing us into life and maintain us.

As Leonard Cohen wrote in his song *So Long Marianne*, "I forgot to pray for the angels, and then the angels forgot to pray for us."

And then there's the reality that a great many factors are in play in any given situation. As the saying goes, the Spirit moves in mysterious ways. Rinpoché once said, "Make your offering and disown." In other words, we don't have any control over what happens once our prayer has been sent—no matter how true and concentrated our thoughts have been. Kanucas reminded us as well that we can't interfere with anyone's free choice or personal responsibility for their life path. Those forces operate beyond our understanding and control. We can only do our best to send the energy of our love and our wish for the recipients of our prayers to have it the best way they would like it to be for themselves. We can ask that the Spirit bring support, encouragement, and all good blessings onto their path, but the individual also has to appeal to Spirit with the same level of commitment. Kanucas also said, "However you want it to be for yourselves relatives, that's how it will be." That clearly implies total responsibility for our own minds. On another occasion he told us, "When you say you're well, you're well."

The mysterious ways in which the Spirit moves may also bring changes that aren't obvious or don't appear on an expected timeline. It may take years for the prayer to take effect and Spirit may have other ideas for what the recipient of the prayer needs at any particular point. A brief anecdote about my cousin Ross may help illustrate this. Ross called me out of the blue after we hadn't seen each other for nearly thirty years. During the course of a brief stopover in my city, he told me he had Hepatitis C. I arranged to sponsor a healing meeting in the Native American Church for him. What Ross didn't tell me (or those at the meeting for him) was that he had also been deeply in the grip of alcoholism for many years.

A ceremony similar to the one I described for Wild Willy was held a couple of months later. That was three years prior to this writing and until recently I had assumed that Spirit's intention with Ross was to get him away from the booze, since he never again took a drink after that night. Meanwhile, the hepatitis, while showing signs of improvement, did not seem to be going into complete remission. Then, after having no contact with him for another year and a half, Ross again recently appeared in my life, announcing that new tests showed absolutely no evidence of the hepatitis and that he'd never felt better in his life.

Developing Confidence

I'm well aware that these are radical and far-reaching concepts to the conventional view of the modern mind, my own included. There's been a lot of discussion in the past few years in spiritual work about the idea that we each create our own reality. That's a demanding and tricky concept, no doubt one of the key elements of life that can't truly be understood until experienced. The concept has also been used and abused by people with partial understanding—self-styled gurus of the so-called New Age movement suggesting that we can and should apply this principle to accumulation of wealth and personal power in the material realm—or in other words—for strengthening the grip of ego in the guise of spiritual advancement. People also make the mistake of thinking that if they accepted this view they would have to heap blame upon themselves for their inadequacies, failures, and even illnesses and infirmities.

What we do have to do, I think, is look at our attachment to the status quo. We may not be happy in our situation, but the impetus of our fear of change, of stepping out of our cocoons, is often greater than the energy and determination to change. We need to make the connection in the moment between our thoughts and the results they create. Doubt creates its own results, fear creates its own results, "but" is one of the strongest words in the lexicon. These thoughts are often lightning fast, beyond or below our normal horizon of awareness. Mindfulness/awareness practice on a daily basis helps clear the air enough to catch these habitual patterns. We have a choice at any moment whether or not to get hooked back into these habitual, fear-based patterns, or step into openness, into the unknown groundless now.

It's been said that the journey of awakening is one of gradually—in most cases—shifting allegiance from the dictates of this ego to the larger, egoless, intuitive guidance of Spirit, or awakened heart. Therapists often have stories of clients who come to them claiming they want to change but who are not willing to actually make the changes, not ready to let go of the attachments. We have great difficulty taking a panoramic perspective. We like our stories, we like to complain, we need to justify ourselves and our current beliefs, we find our misery strangely comforting. Again, the practice of tonglen can be very helpful when we see ourselves thinking in these ways. If we could proceed on our shaky faith that what we see is what we get in life, as spiritual teachers have been telling us for millennia, perhaps time and further experience would reveal greater depths of truth in this way. I like this encouraging reminder from the writer Philip K. Dick, "Matter is plastic in the face of Mind."

In the context of the NAC prayer meetings, working with the assistance of Grandfather Peyote, it's been suggested that we start small. Kanucas has told us to speak directly to the medicine spirit, to tell it what we want, tell it to be gentle with us. The medicine can sometimes make you feel nauseated and, following that instruction, I've had several experiences where I felt that nausea coming on strong and I prayed hard to Grandpa that I wanted to keep the medicine in me and be able to make use of it. How many times have you flipped from feeling on the edge of throwing up to suddenly, instantly having a completely settled stomach? That's exactly what happened those few times. In that small, simple example there was a direct and immediate response that I could take as encouragement as I developed confidence in the power of prayer. It was a reminder as well that the apparent solidity of the physical world is open to question. Change isn't necessarily limited by what we understand to be the laws of physics. As the elder said, if you believe wholeheartedly in your prayer, it will work.

There is a channel between voice and presence,
a way where information flows.
In disciplined silence the channel opens.
With wandering talk, it closes.[4]
Jelaluddin Rumi, 1207-1273

Prayer is similar to meditation in that regard. There has to be space in the overlapping busyness of the discursive mind. When the mind quiets there can be a crack for something else to get through. Though prayer suggests language—formulating thoughts of intention—it could be said that the engine of prayer is this space that allows softening, allows the heart to activate. Sometimes simply placing one's attention on others, and perhaps thinking about what they may need, can generate the energy needed to send a beautiful and powerful prayer. Like most people who attempted it, I couldn't manage to slog all the way through the large and dense book *A Course in Miracles* a few years back. But I did come away with a central theme from it, that what we want for ourselves we must wish for and work for for others. If we want peace, forgiveness, and healing for ourselves, we aim to give those to others.

Tools of the Trade

Chanting and singing are world wide shamanic practices. The shamanic singers navigate through a space with which we have lost touch as a society.
Terence McKenna

There are numerous other techniques and aids to create a prayerful space, many of which I'm sure I've never heard about and a few that I have come into contact with. The all-night tipi ceremonies of the NAC seem to have brought several of these tools together in a powerful synthesis. One of them is singing. The songs of this church, practiced in many places, contain mainly vocables: short syllables that may have had specific meanings long ago but today are thought of as chant-like carriers of the heart's intentions. (Lines like, " Hey ah wen ah hee yo nah hey ney yo ay." are typical.)

During the course of the night, in the context of the main prayer for that meeting and the other concerns of the participants collectively and individually, instruments are passed clockwise around the tipi, beginning and ending with the roadman. In the meetings of my experience, the instruments consist of the roadman's staff, a small sage bundle which is held with the staff while singing, a gourd shaker held in the other hand and shaken rapidly in time (one hopes), with the beat kept on the water drum. The water drum is a small metal pot, six or seven inches in diameter and about as deep, partially filled with water, covered with an animal skin, ritually tied and untied for each meeting, and struck with a small hardwood stick by the drummer for the night. The drum is said to be the heartbeat of the prayer. Skilled, experienced drummers say that it is a being that the drummer can communicate with and employ to empower healing and blessing energy (or perhaps the spirit of the drum employs the drummer).

As the instruments go around, each person who knows some songs is invited to sing a four-song cycle. Songs come from all over and so some are known to many in the meeting while others may be new to the ears of the assembled. The rest of us are welcome to and often do join in with the person leading that cycle. The singers may touch on the intended recipient of a prayer—perhaps visualizing the person—or may simply sing with as much heart and passion as they can arouse. From the first meeting I attended, I was moved and impressed by the conviction with which most people sang, a conviction that often transcended limitations in musical skill and singing ability. When the energy in the tipi is strong, settled, and clear, when the presence of Spirit is felt by those present, the singing can be impossibly sweet and rich.

> When I express prayer through song, the universe seems to listen in and—in some fashion unknown to me—I and all things around me seem to come together...when I sing the song of a plant in the rhythms that have come to me, the spirit of the plant comes alive.[6]
>
> *Stephen Harrod Buhner*

It should be pointed out that the influence of the spirit of the plant sacrament—in this case Grandfather Peyote and around the world a variety of other plants employed in indigenous ceremonies and healing sessions—is considered an essential element of the power roused by prayer songs. The plant is said to lend its assistance and direction, blending with the energy and concentration of the singer(s) to empower the prayer and carry it to its intended destination.

And then there's something about the dawn of the new day. Whatever physical and mental struggles and issues have arisen during the long night, the morning is a time of gratitude, tenderness, and celebration of life. In a full tipi, the heart-carried singing of the morning sometimes invokes a heartbreaking and gentle beauty that infuses the atmosphere. Those who've experienced something similar know there is nothing in this world quite like the sound and feeling of people connected in their hearts and blending their voices together in song.

Songs like these are employed to invoke the Creator and the helping spirits, to call those presences to come hear the prayers and carry them to the aid of the intended recipient. There's a powerful traditional plant medicine found throughout the Amazon jungles regions of South America known most commonly as ayahuasca. Shamans typically go through a lengthy and rigorous training regimen learning to work with this medicine in healing ways. It's said that the spirit of the medicine teaches songs, called "icaros," directly to those worthy of doing this work. When a shaman is gifted with icaros she or he can use them to call for assistance in healing.

According to stories from traditions like this, the spirit can appear in a great variety of forms. I remember one story told by Wallace Black Elk about when he was asked to help a young white boy more or less permanently bedridden in hospital in a condition of chronic pain and severely restricted movement. The boy had been born normal but within a few months was unable to move, speak, or eat. At the time of the story, he had been in the hospital for four years. His parents had tried every conventional treatment and several experts but nothing had had any impact and no one knew what the problem was. In desperation, they called upon Wallace, who agreed to perform a healing if he and his helpers could set up the hospital room the way they needed to without interference.

With the room completely darkened, and with prayers, songs, tobacco, and other offerings, he called for assistance from the spirit world. According to Wallace, there was an audible boom and the spirit appeared. Wallace said, "Tunkashila, nobody knows what's wrong with this boy. We ask you to help us help him." The spirit walked over to the boy, studied him, and returned to report that the boy's muscles were tied up in a knot, in a tangled spider's web that choked off the flow of energy. He told Wallace that he would have to call in a spider spirit—an iktomi. They sang a spider-calling song, the spider spirit appeared and went to work untangling the web strangling the boy's throat area. Before the afternoon was out, in the presence of the bewildered doctor and nurse, the boy had begun to eat and drink, make rudimentary vocalizations, and move around.

> O Wakan-Tanka, this smoke from the sweet grass will rise up to You, and will spread throughout the universe; its fragrance will be known by the wingeds, the four-leggeds, and the two-leggeds, for we understand that we are all relatives.[7]
> *High Hollow Horn*

Even a cursory examination of traditional healing and spiritual rituals and practices around the world will reveal their widespread use of various plants for burning and for smoking. Native American elders say that the Creator taught the people the use of natural herbs like tobacco, cedar, sage, and sweetgrass. These traditions run deep and house teachings often fully understood only by those well-steeped in the knowledge and experience of their use. There's a beautifully symbolic, metaphoric quality to the burning of plants in this way: the transformation of solid, earthbound matter into the realm of the intangible and the invisible.

Tobacco is said to bridge the physical and the spiritual realms, the visible and the unseen, from roots that reach into the earth to the smoke that dissolves into the atmosphere and disappears as it rises to the heavens, to the Creator. This plant is considered by many connected to Native North American traditions to be the most highly honored and respected plant and its use is nearly universal in the spiritual practices of these peoples. In the prayer meetings of the Native American Church, tobacco is typically used throughout the night to carry the prayers of all those assembled as the meeting begins, to accompany the praying of the sponsor and others with particular serious concerns at that point in time, and to support the in-depth spoken prayers of principals at several key points during the night. Praying with tobacco is regarded as one of the most serious, reverential elements of a meeting.

In the NAC prayer meetings, when the morning water is brought in at dawn and the water woman begins her prayers, all participants who are physically able are expected to be up on their knees listening closely to this praying, and to put their minds and hearts fully into the water woman's prayers to help strengthen them. As she kneels before the water, she begins to roll some tobacco in a section of corn husk and speak freely of the heart matters that arise spontaneously. When the tobacco is lit, she directs her voice to the Creator and repeatedly blesses the water in the bucket as she expresses her prayers at length for everyone to hear. She doesn't inhale the smoke but in the exhalation gives and sends the smoke completely, offering it up to God and to Grandfather Peyote as well as blowing the smoke across the water, which will later be passed around the tipi to bless all present as they drink a ladle-full. When she has finished expressing herself she passes what remains of the lit tobacco to several other of the meetings "officers" to add their own prayers.

It should be mentioned briefly here that some people make an important distinction between commercial tobacco—especially with its numerous chemical additives—and the traditional tobaccos of indigenous peoples. There are over sixty varieties of this plant that often grows wild across North America. Commercial tobacco is a specialized variety and many consider the attitude behind it and the methods of preparation an abuse of a sacred plant. According to information from the Red Road Collective: "Sacred herbs are powerful, but when misused or disrespected, their power consumes us. Tobacco can be a healer or a destroyer. When used in a sacred way, it can promote good health and assist with spiritual guidance and growth. The Creator's spirit is in tobacco. When used in this sacred manner the spirit as smoke enters the man, refreshes him, and then travels to the sky laden with thanksgiving."[8]

In native North American traditions there are numerous other uses of tobacco for blessing, gratitude, purification, and healing. Those familiar with the rituals of other groups could add many similar accounts of detailed, reverential use of tobacco. To my knowledge, it's employed in these ways up and down the Americas and has been for as long as anyone can imagine. Throughout the Amazon, for example, tobacco has been central to shamanic healing and prayer ceremonies and sessions, and employed for these same purposes: to purify, to bless, to heal, to facilitate the opening of the channel to Spirit. Some shamans in the Amazon consider tobacco the little brother of ayahuasca and they actually consult its voice for guidance. Healers in that region, for example, often blow tobacco smoke over someone they are working on.

> For Black Elk, the Sacred Pipe, or Chanunpa, is the center and heart of his ritual. It is his link to the spirit world. With the Chanunpa he begins and ends the ceremonies. With it he talks to Tunkashila, he calls on the spirits, he asks for help and health for himself and for his people.[9]
> *Betty Stockhauser*

Many other herbs, like cedar, juniper, sage, sweetgrass, copal and other types of incense have been used for similar purposes around the world, from the jungles of South America to the high plateaus of Tibet. The Tibetan Buddhists I practiced with used generously burning copal and juniper smoke to bless, cleanse, protect and purify a practice space and the practitioners within. Incense is burned on the shrine throughout sessions and ceremonies. In the tipi meetings of the NAC, someone is designated as the cedar person for the night, throwing cedar on the fire to purify ritual objects and gifts, for those entering from outside, for those in need of a blessing while experiencing difficulties, and periodically to raise the spirits of all those assembled. Sage is used in various ways for similar purposes: to petition the Creator, for purification, for smudging or using the smoke to cleanse the body and the practice materials, and to drive away negative energies or thoughts. In the tipi meetings sage bundles travel with the instruments and are passed around for people to bless themselves with. The traditional use of the sacred pipe—the "Chanunpa"—in native North American spiritual and healing work is deep and powerful, a body of knowledge in itself and too far beyond my personal experience and understanding to speak about here.

This section on prayer wasn't intended to be in any way an exhaustive or balanced survey of approaches. My hope is that through these brief glimpses, some may be stimulated to create new practices or recover old ones for themselves or their communities that assist in reestablishing our place in the cosmos, in nature, in the circle and cycle of life. Rinpoché frequently spoke about "sacred world," the idea that one can live with the attitude that every moment and everything in this world is sacred and therefore worthy of our attention, our respect, our appreciation, our love. As well as its healing capabilities, prayer can be understood as a central activity in remaking the connection. We work to awaken ourselves and to express the naturally arising intentions of our hearts in gratitude and compassion.

In terms of the central theme of this book—the vision for planetary healing nurtured by joining the attention and intentions of people from around the world— prayer would seem to be the foundation and the vehicle for the manifestation of this vision. According to the elders of the wisdom traditions, when enough individual and collective intention can be focused and fed by the power of compassion, anything is possible.

The Earth is your Grandmother and Mother, and She is sacred. Every step that is taken upon Her should be as a prayer.[10]
Black Elk

20

Through the Looking Glass
Substances that Heal and Reveal

We cannot afford the luxury of wasting their potential [the entheogens and empathogens] . . . for they constitute precisely the kind of remedy that we need as we approach a new collective Red Sea crossing.[1]
Claudio Naranjo, M.D.

In his keynote address at the Fourth Annual Amazonian Shamanism Conference in Iquitos, Peru in July 2008, Dr. Dennis McKenna told us that he and others have received the message: "You monkeys only *think* you're running the show." He continued to say that it's the plants that are running things, that it's the plants that sustain life on this planet, and that the plants are also our teachers.

After a lifetime of studying and exploring healing/teaching plants, Dr. McKenna has arrived at the conviction that he and others of like mind now "work for the plants." The plants are calling us, he said. They are using us to spread their teachings around the world. They are telling us that we have only an extremely short amount of time left to wake up to our deep relatedness to the whole and manifest this understanding in the material world.

The use of plants, as well as a few laboratory-synthesized

chemical compounds, is without doubt the most controversial topic and set of techniques related to spiritual awakening. In most quarters it's a very poorly understood issue. Deep and long-standing prejudices make open discussion of these substances extremely difficult in the wider public arena. A lot of people with little knowledge or appropriate experience—even many of those committed to spiritual practice—have their minds firmly made up and won't even consider the possibility that what they call "drugs" can produce genuine spiritual experience.

For this reason, this is the topic I've given the most careful and thorough thought to before venturing into the writing. I've done much research over many years—through the literature and through personal exploration—and I've become convinced that what many call "sacred plants" have proven a great benefit to humans for millennia and hold exciting promise for the years ahead. In fact, it may be correct to state that the use of plants in spiritual practice is by far the most undervalued and underutilized set of methodologies available to us. Some would go so far as to suggest that the planet is in such peril right now that the teachings of the sacred plants may be essential for enough of us to get the message loud and clear and act upon the information.

> Oh soma-drinker, drink of the soma-wine; the intoxication of thy rapture gives indeed the Light.
> The Rig Veda

What remains of the anthropological, historical, and archaeological records clearly shows that visionary, healing, spirit-invoking plants have been widely used since time immemorial. The evidence is extensive: from the archeological findings of shamans buried ten thousand years ago with their pipes and plant residues beside them; to the iconography of ancient cave paintings; the use of soma in the Rig Veda of ancient India; mushroom stones of Kerala from over two thousand years ago;

the visionary sacrament at the heart of the annual ceremony at Eleusis in pre-Christian era Greece; Byzantine-era religious frescoes in Northern Africa, and a great deal more. The spiritual use of plants has continued right up to the living traces of practices still employed by indigenous groups tucked into the jungles, forests, plains, and mountains, as well as the determined personal and scholarly explorations of the "new people." We know that there are and have been peoples all across the planet who knew the uses of nearly every single root, stem, bark, leaf, berry, fruit, and fungus in their environments and how to prepare each one for shelter, clothing, food, medicine, divination, and spiritual insight.

Fear of the Truth

A sizeable congregation of intelligent, responsible, caring individuals is now convinced that we need a radical rethink on this topic. It's not too difficult to see a strong correlation between the repression and suppression of wisdom-plant use and the other versions of suppression discussed in this book. For too long now the religious and secular enforcers and power brokers of the dominator cultures have been denigrating and eradicating the knowledge and practices associated with plant spirituality wherever and whenever they've been able to extend their influence and authority. And this is the same mindset that has attacked, suppressed, and ignored indigenous wisdom, women's wisdom, and Earth wisdom.

In many cases the emissaries and enforcers of the worldview of dominator cultures were so convinced of the superiority of their own civilizations and religions that they simply did not see the wisdom and beauty of what was right in front of them. One of the most egregious crimes was—and still is—the active criminalization and punishment brought down upon groups of people whose spiritual practices included the use of plants. Laws were enacted to banish the practices of the indigenous people encountered by the conquistadors and religious proselytizers and enforced with the most severe punishments imaginable.

The conclusion of a great many practitioners and researchers has been that plants can give people a direct experience of the divine—of an authentic spiritual universe completely hidden from the normal ego-based mindstate—and that this potential has been seen as a direct threat to the power structures, often ostensibly religious but certainly abetted in willing participation by secular authorities.

Dr. Ralph Metzner, a leading researcher and elder statesman in the field of plant spirituality, had this to say about some of the causes for the eradication of the use of ego-dissolving visionary plants. In this particular discussion he had been talking about the disappearance of the use of Soma, a plant-based sacrament mentioned frequently in one of the world's oldest religious documents, the Rig Veda of ancient India:

> My theory about what happened then is the same as what happens now, that the use of soma, which was a genuine religious intoxicant in the sense that it produced a religious experience and direct knowledge of God, was stamped out systematically by the priesthoods, who were primarily intent upon maintaining their own power structure. If people could have a direct experience of God by taking mushrooms or any other plant they would not be interested in priestly power structures—they couldn't care less. Why should they talk to a priest if they could talk directly to God.[2]

It's this potential for dissolving boundaries and opening the doors to direct perception and understanding of spiritual wisdom that explorers of the sacred plants claim is one of the main obstacles to their acceptance by the power elites and other vendors of the status quo illusion. Whether they are conscious of it or whether they are primarily motivated by unacknowledged instinctual fears, those whose agenda it is to control the flow of power and the wealth of nations do not want the rest of us to wake up and see things as they are. They say that these "drugs" are a threat to the social order—and from their point of view they probably are. The power elites—the "cloud minders" of Empire, as David C. Korten calls them in *The Great Turning*—act to keep the populace off-balance, confused, and afraid so we won't see what they're actually doing. Empowered people are not shaken off their seats by bullshit, and somewhere in the dim recesses of their minds the elites sense this.

I don't mean, of course, to suggest that all leaders are con men. However, I think most people who are able to think for themselves can see that the political establishment of many of the most influential countries often functions mainly to preserve the wealth and power of a relatively small number of people at the expense of most and at devastating cost to the planetary environment on every level. I can't resist quoting again the ever entertaining Terence McKenna on this issue: "In a genuinely civilized society, one would think that putting the bottom line ahead of the entire civilization and planet would be a hanging offense."[3]

The war on drugs is the quintessential example of the kind of dissembling and hypocrisy at play. In 2007, there were 870,000 marijuana arrests in the United States—the highest number ever recorded. More than 85 percent of these were for possession. Recent statistics indicate more than 50,000 people in U.S. prisons for marijuana offenses at any given time, with approximately one third of these in for possession only. Many more are serving time for other minor offenses, such as possessing a couple of plants or selling a small amount to a few friends. This for a plant with an ancient and widespread history of medicinal, spiritual, and safe recreational use. It's as though the more the veil is removed, the harder the fearful dig in their heels and the more absurd the whole situation looks. The war on marijuana, to take that highly visible example, is a culture war, a clash between the intolerant and the tolerant, between the controllers and those who would stand on their right to cognitive freedom.

This kind of rearguard action notwithstanding, there's good reason to believe that plants will play a much greater role in the awakening process in the years ahead. If that's true, the real questions then become: Where do we go from here? How can we effectively and safely incorporate the use of mind-manifesting, entheogenic, healing plants into the awakening process at this crucial time in the crisis and transformation nexus on planet Earth?

Thankfully, the darkest hours of the dark age seem to be lightening in the past decade or so, at least in much of the West, where the possibilities for sanctioned research are opening up again and a number of groups of people are extending their explorations of the religious and otherwise spiritual and medicinal use of these substances. Organizations like the Santo Daime Church of Brazil, for example, with its use of the entheogenic brew ayahuasca, are rapidly gaining credence, legal approval, and membership in North America, Europe and other parts of the world.

Como Se Llama?

As this introduction is leading into a large section of this book, I want to clarify a few points before proceeding further with this topic. The first is the issue of nomenclature. There are a lot of words being tossed around these days to name the general class of substance under discussion here. Language can of course be extremely important in establishing the ground of a discussion and, in this case at least, in honoring the substances of our attention. Referring to a plant as sacred, as a medicine, as an ally, or naming it by the spirit it calls forth will tend to create very different associations in the mind than calling it a drug. A perfect example of that is the phrase "the war on drugs." No distinction is made in that statement between dangerously addictive substances like cocaine and heroin on the one hand and the healing and awakening medicines on the other. In the United States, most of those two wildly different kinds of substances are consigned to the same hellhole, known as Schedule One of the Controlled Substances Act. The result of that kind of manipulation of language is that most people who don't look past such slogans tend to buy into the view that all drugs are "bad," unless they're sanctioned by the authorities.

> I think it is vital to distinguish between the consciousness-contracting, antisocial nature of addictive drugs and the consciousness-expanding, psychotherapeutic nature of psychedelics and hallucinogens.[3]
> *Ralph Metzner, Ph.D.*

The crucial difference lies in the all-too-obvious truth that all psychoactive substances aren't alike. Some do promote unexamined, habitual behavior and some do not. Some, like cannabis, straddle both camps, with spiritual as well as abuse potential. Excessive use of cocaine, heroin, and alcohol, to name a few of the worst offenders, clearly fit Metzner's description of drug and have the potential to lead to tragic dead ends and muddied and muddled experience without promoting insight into one's psychological obstacles. In the novel *Fierce Invalids Home from Hot Climates*, Tom Robbins' protagonist Switters put another insightful slant on this distinction as he turned down an offer to snort some cocaine: " 'Thanks, pal, but I tend to avoid any substance that makes me feel smarter, stronger, or better looking than I know I actually am.' There were, in his opinion, drugs that diminished ego and drugs that engorged ego, which is to say, revelatory drugs and delusory drugs; and on a psychic level, at least, he favored awe over swagger."[4]

Then there are those plants, and a few compounds synthe-sized in the laboratory, that have the potential to awaken the mind and promote insight, reexamination, healing, and lasting positive change. These plants are not only *not* addictive but often function—through the sometimes hard insights they provoke—to break patterns of addiction. The peyote cactus, for example, has been granted legal protection by the U.S. Congress for bona fide religious use by Native Americans. Why has that right been firmly upheld at the highest level of government in a country with powerful and persistent forces aligned against this very kind of substance? In no small part because the record shows impressive—even dramatic—results in helping people break free of addiction to alcohol and other substances, with no harmful consequences to individuals or threats to society.

Back now to the question of what to call these agents. "Psychoactive" is a term you hear sometimes but it's too general to be of practical use. It simply means, "affecting the mind or mental processes" and is used in medical circles to describe any drug that has any affect on the mind, or perhaps more accurately, the brain. Aspirin, for example, is considered psychoactive in this respect.

"Psychotropic" is another word with a related meaning and is—again for the same reason—much too general. The noun "hallucinogen" and its adjectival form "hallucinogenic" are often employed in this context, sometimes with an understanding of the meaning and implications suggested but often not. The word has potential but can also be misleading for two reasons. The first is the implication that the visions seen under the influence of certain substances are artificial or unreal, "just" hallucina-tions, less or other than reality. The medical profession tends to associate the term hallucination with pathology. But a wealth of evidence from experienced journeyers indicates the potent reality quotient of visions. These experiences are often described as more real than ordinary reality. Second, some of the plants used for spiritual purposes are not particularly known for inducing visions, especially in the dosages employed in their ritual contexts. Elders in these traditions might say that it is often more an issue of opening the heart and mind to Spirit presence and seeing things clearly as they are that is the essence of the experience rather than visual content. Ayahuasca curanderos and curanderas often stress that their work is about healing, and that visions per se are not the main feature.

Then there's the famous—or infamous—term "psychedelic," meaning literally "mind manifesting." Some researchers and advocates in the field prefer this term for its relatively straight-forward meaning. But the word "psychedelic" still carries the burden of leftover cultural baggage that can make it tricky to use. For that reason there's been a move in the field in the past decade or two to supplant it with the term "entheogenic," which means "becoming divine within," or "generating the spirit within." Though not every one in the field is comfortable with describing the plant teacher/medicines as entheogens, it may be the most serviceable compromise for the time being.

There's another class of substances, a group of semi-synthetic substances, the most significant of which is MDMA. These may be marginal to the discussion at hand but may also have a useful role to play in healing work in the right circumstances. MDMA, although capable of invoking experiences of unity and peace, is generally not considered a psychedelic or entheogen and, except in rare cases, does not induce visuals. The most common label for this class is "empathogen," which means "to create an empathetic state."

I asked the third specialist, Usi Kamarambi, [at a conference in Peru], why, in his opinion, gringos have difficulty under-standing that plants contain spirits. He had a joyful, ageless face. "Because they just do not know," he replied...Lack of knowledge to understand nature...lack of know-how about how to see visions, what to drink, how to do it.[5]

Indigenous people generally have very different kinds of words from the mainstream cultures to describe the plants they use in spiritual practice and healing work. The most common element of this kind of language involves references to the spirit of the plant. In this context the agent is sometimes given a particular name or description. In the Native American Church the peyote plant is often called Grandfather. Maria Sabina—the Mazatec Indian curandera encountered by Gordon Wasson in his ground-breaking research in the 1950s in Oaxaca, Mexico—called the psilocybin-containing mushrooms used in her ceremonies "the children" (Los Niños), or "the saint children." The Mexican plant Salvia divinorum is also known by the name "the shepherdess." In the Brazilian Amazon, cannabis is sometimes called Santa Maria. The ancient Aztecs of Mexico referred to their sacred mushrooms as "God's Flesh." Examples of this nature are widespread in the traditions of indigenous experience, as are terms that describe the plants as teachers, as healers, or simply as medicines.

In the Care of the Elders

There is no denying that these are potent substances not made for casual use by the unprepared...Substances that are, for the most part, benign and socially constructive when used in their original cultural contexts can become harmful when transplanted to our modern and far more disorderly, neurotic, and surreal landscape.[6]
J.P. Harpignies

The other concern I want to address at this point in the discussion is the crucial distinction between using plants and other mind-manifesting substances in recreational versus controlled, knowledgeable therapeutic and spiritual contexts. One of the reasons for some of the current prejudices against plant spirituality is the ample evidence—however sensation-alized by the media—of sloppy, unprepared, and even dangerous use of these powerful agents. Ironically and unfortunately, much of the reason for this kind of abuse is the very fact of prohibition. The wisdom-engendering plants have been cast into the nether-world of illegal and illegitimate. Open, honest, knowledgeable discussion and education have been made impossible. The abdication of the cultural authorities has left the dissemination of these substances in the hands of people outside the law, people outside the counsel of experienced elders, people who often know or care little or nothing about the effective, safe, spiritual/medicinal use of the plants and chemical compounds they are dealing with.

Even worse, with laboratory created compounds like Ecstasy (MDMA), mescaline, LSD, and others, the illegal status has often resulted in uncontrolled, incompetent, and unethical production methods. Albert Hofmann, the discoverer of LSD, was a chemist with Sandoz Laboratories in Switzerland. During the 1960s—and especially after 1966 when it was banned in the U.S.—police were sending him samples of confiscated LSD for analysis. Hofmann was surprised to find that the majority of the samples were not actually LSD but a corruption of the formula. The recent history of the use of Ecstasy has also been notorious for unpredictable reliability of product. DanceSafe, an organization that attempts to minimize harm associated with illicit use of Ecstasy, at raves in particular, frequently reports the sale of other potent and very dangerous substances like PMA (Paramethoxyamphetamine) and DMX (Dextromethorphan) posing as Ecstasy.

We're not generally wise enough and openhearted enough to take that type of medicine on our own, for casual use, without a teacher, a healer who can show us how it really is medicine.[7]
Kathleen Harrison

So-called recreational use of entheogens was by all accounts extremely rare in traditional contexts. They were and are generally considered sacred in these cultures, to be used with great care, knowledge, respect and reverence. I've encountered story after story of untutored psychonautic adventurers casually ingesting hefty doses of potent agents like psilocybe mushrooms and LSD with no attention to set and setting, no supportive environment or guidance, and no notion of what kind of territory they're entering. A not-at-all uncommon result is that people reach the threshold of ego dissolution and experience the terror that feels like death with no idea that that moment is the gateway to realities beyond the ego, beyond the known. The instinctive tendency at that point is to pull back in fear, to scramble for safe ground, to desperately seek confirmation that one does indeed exist as a separate ego entity. Once fully in the grip of a powerful entheogenic substance, people find that there *is* no middle ground and that resisting creates serious problems; anguish and suffering, fearful visions, the classic "bummer" experience. For anyone who's seen or experienced that, it's not something to be taken lightly (though I have to admit I've learned a few valuable lessons from those bouts of anguish and suffering.)

Iboga is very powerful and that's why it is absolutely impossible to use it without the rigorous control of those entitled to administer it[8]
Vincent Ravalec

Among those who have worked responsibly with these substances, it's well known that without experienced guidance, people can and have become stuck in difficult places they've bumped up against and been unable to handle, unable to move through. The role of the protected ritual environment and the trained guide or shaman is to employ time-tested techniques to assist people through that very transition into an unresisting state where healing can take place or where the supplicant may encounter realms of gnostic information beneficial to the spiritual unfolding process.

What I'm about to say may sound highly provocative or even blasphemous to some. Given these extremely urgent conditions, this is not a time for refined, cerebral debates about what tools and techniques are valid. The house is on fire. The plants work when used wisely by people equipped to handle them. It's as straightforward as that. There just may not be enough time for a great many journeyers on the paths to stick with *only* the non-entheogenic practices of the various religions, not enough time for twenty years of psychotherapy, or a lifetime of only a daily meditation practice.

There seems to be no doubt that there are paths such as Buddhism, that, when practiced intensively and wholeheartedly for a lifetime, are completely capable of unraveling the samsaric mind. However, the deep inner traditions of these religions—the mystic, esoteric traditions—were historically practiced by a small minority, and simple observation indicates that, at best, that's still the case. Those of us who have the inclination and circumstances to devote major portions of our time to religious practice, intensive retreats and so on remain small in number. One of the messages in the air now is the idea that we are in a remarkable window of time where a leap of awakening is both possible and necessary for a surprisingly large number of people. We're all Buddhas and at this time we have a number of powerful tools and techniques available to us.

The healers know that at this level of awareness there are no absolute cultural boundaries: Catholic and chthonic, cave and book, ancestors and mushrooms, indigenous and international—all are working in a vibrating tapestry of *la medicina.* Not everyone knows how to ask for medicine or how to receive it, they tell me, but there is no one in the world who does not need medicine in their lives.[9]
Kathleen Harrison

This awakening is, underneath the noise and confusion, our deepest longing—to be well, to be free of disabling chains, to be in love and at peace. We're calling ourselves into the light of reality. There's wide agreement in a range of related fields that this is it, right now, as I'm writing these words. The window of time left for driving in the wrong direction is shrinking faster by the month. There are tools at hand that can help us wake out of our collective bad dream and reconnect ourselves to the living, intelligent Gaian mind. This is no time to allow these remarkable tools and allies—these gifts from the planet, from the Creator or Creators—to be passed over because of the misinformed and manipulative mindsets of societal authorities.

Again, those knowledgeable in the use of the entheogenic allies readily caution that they are not for everyone by any means and not to be employed without the utmost care and respect. That's the way plants have been used for millennia around the world. But we might need bright, committed, bravehearted people to set aside assumptions and conditioned prejudices, take a risk, and step forward to learn firsthand about the potential of these plant sacraments. It's for each other, for the planet, for the Creator. The elders say to get your relationship with Spirit right so you can help others. As I mentioned elsewhere, Kanucas told me once that people like him function as midwives, helping the willing through the challenging and sometimes frightening crossing from the flatlands of illusion to the shores of awakening.

The information is out there and accessible. Committed groups of people are springing up all over the place.

Intelligent, stable, responsible adults operating under appropriate conditions of set and setting have to be trusted to draw their own conclusions about the validity and applicability of the information released, about the alterations of perception that overtake them. That seems to be a key point. If there are experienced, intelligent, caring people out there suggesting there is something to be learned—that the insights available may be highly useful and important, and that there is a deep reservoir of untapped healing potential—those who claim to be serious about the awakening process may need to put it to the test themselves. There is no other way of knowing and the unguided experiences of one's youth may have provided no indication of what the potential is when these agents are employed wisely.

The Medicine Wants to Meet You

The chief peyote is pretty tough. It watches what is going on. It keeps everything straight. It is a plant but it can see and understand better than a man.[10]

Lipan Indian,

Anonymous

To those who would claim that entheogens are an easy and therefore somehow invalid path toward wisdom, I would simply say: no, that is not the case. Yes, a person on his or her first voyage into the unknown may have incredible insights that are life-altering in a lasting way. However, the most common experience of even the most spiritually athletic is that the ego is dissolved over time as one gains insights into the manner of one's self-imprisonment, learns to recognize and trust awakened mind, and allows the layers of self-protection to peel away. In my experience and research, sacred-plant medicine teachers are no less demanding than the clearest mirror held up by an enlightened teacher inhabiting a human form. In fact, there may at the core of it be no essential difference.

I remind you of Kanucas' comment about the Peyote Spirit, "This medicine wants to meet you, but it can only meet you on its terms." Peyote has also been described by the experienced elders as a medicine that will enter you in gently if you open to it without resistance but will kick you around pretty hard if you fight it. "Enlightenment" or "God" or whatever name we employ to describe this awakened state can only be unbending. It is what it is and can only remain pure and true—eternal and indestructible as Buddhist teachings say. It's we who decide and learn how to remove the veil and move closer to understanding reality.

The Tibetan Vajrayana Buddhist path has been described as the fast route to enlightenment. Teachers have said that it can bring a practitioner to awakening in one lifetime. However, the truth is that most people surrender old patterns very slowly and it's not uncommon for longtime Buddhist practitioners to feel that the changes in their lives have been subtle, even after decades of ongoing meditation practice and study. The vision afoot now is to learn from everything that comes onto your path and to join the four directions together by following intuition, by following the whispered guidance of Spirit. A case can be made that for many spiritual practitioners of stable mind, the disciplined, intelligent use of entheogens, especially with the support of other mindfulness/awareness practices and teachings, may at this time be the most direct path to awakening. Again, not because they are easy, but because they are "God's flesh," and the space they create during the time of one's encounter with them is real, unequivocal, and very powerful.

There is no way around that reality. One either opens to it in that moment or struggles against it. Various meditation practices—if undertaken diligently—will most likely dissolve ego gradually. Entheogens can dissolve ego on the spot, though not likely finally and forever. Tibetan Buddhist practice is sometimes described as a preparation for the moment of death, in the hopes that the practitioner will have surrendered obstacles and illusion enough to enter realms of greater reality after slipping out of the mortal coil. In the right conditions, the entheogenic sacraments invoke and draw the supplicant to and beyond the gates of those realms right here and now. In those situations, you simply cannot fool yourself about your spiritual condition. If you keep coming back, the plants will show you — like the clear mirroring teacher — exactly who you are and what your relationship to awakened mind is.

> Iboga is a doctor-initiator that has a job to do...It knows exactly what it has to do and its task flows from that[11]
> *Vincent Ravalec*

There's one more issue of clarification needed before moving on into the specifics of some of the major entheogens. The focus of this book is, of course, toward spiritual awakening. But when it comes to the use of plants, it isn't possible to separate spiritual from medicinal — or healing — activity. In the worlds of many indigenous groups and ancient cultures, the two are often the same. Problematic medical conditions are said not to be isolated events apart from the whole being. There is, in this under-standing, no division between mental, or spiritual, and physical.

In the Native American Church of my experience for example, the peyote plant is often referred to as a medicine and that medicine is considered a living presence, so it is also called Grandfather Peyote, or Spirit. The plants are both doctors and teachers and shift effortlessly between those two apparently differing roles as the situation requires.

This is not to suggest or claim that all medical problems, injuries, and diseases have a psychic source and must or even can be approached that way — and much less to suggest that people heap judgment upon themselves for causing their own disabilities and infirmities. There are clearly medicines and techniques, both traditional and modern, that can successfully address certain specific conditions and injuries by means of what appear to be purely physical interventions. But I'm neither inclined, for the purposes of this book, nor qualified by training to wander very far into that complex subject.

What follows is by no means meant to be a complete tour through the pharmacopoeia of plant and other chemical teacher/healers. Based on my experience and my research, I've selected out several with—for the most part— a history of human use and the greatest potential applicability for helping us wake up.

What if He came back as a plant?
Would you let Him in,
Would you let Him into your heart?[12]
Guy Mount

21

Vine of the Soul
Ayahuasca

Overpowered by a tsunami, healed without knowing it by the magical song of a shaman, and saved from the misery of my resistant ego by a kindly jungle cat who took over the controls just long enough to free my mind and usher me into the joyous presence of the spirit protectors and teachers—that was my first encounter with the acrid-tasting jungle tea. I'll tell you the rest of the story later, but first, I'd like to introduce you to the astonishing plant admixture that triggered these events.

This brew has been utilized for at least hundreds and most likely thousands of years in a vast area of South America that includes parts of western Brazil, eastern Ecuador, Peru, and Colombia, as well as sections of the Orinoco basin where Brazil and Venezuela meet. It's typically associated with the Amazon jungle and the multitude of tribal groups that have long inhabited the region. Among its many names, ayahuasca is the most commonly used today, as well as yagé (pronounced "yah-hey" and also spelled yajé or yahé).

Numerous sources of information already available describe in detail the composition of the brew and the methods of preparation. Here I'll just skim the salient points for the purposes of this book. Ayahuasca is a mixture of two essential elements with the possible addition of others. The key ingredients consist of a jungle vine known as Banisteriopsis caapi and a DMT-containing plant, most commonly Psychotria viridis, also called Chacruna. The DMT—or dimethyltryptamine—is said to be the active, vision and information-provoking agent in this mixture. DMT is orally inactive in humans, because it's neutralized by the monoamine oxidase, or MAO, found in the stomach. The Banisteriopsis caapi vine contains MAO inhibitors that allow the DMT to be absorbed into the bloodstream and activated in the brain. The two plants are prepared together, often in lengthy, complex procedures that themselves are often considered an essential aspect of the experience.

As an interesting side story: researchers have wondered how the native people of the region happened upon these two complementary plants—or two complementary chemical reactions—among the many millions of possible combinations available in the jungle environment. The indigenous people of the region often answer that it was shown to them in visions, perhaps induced by other plants.

The word ayahuasca has been translated as "vine of the soul" or "vine of the dead." The "dead," in this context, is said to refer to the spirits of the dead that copious reports have suggested are encountered in the ayahuasca intoxication. From the evidence of a great many accounts, we can assume that the phrase "spirits of the dead" means that drinkers have seen, heard, and communicated with non-incarnated beings of great variety. What is indisputable is that this medicine is extremely powerful and has immense potential for healing and awakening.

The reason ayahuasca is included in this description of spirit plants is both because of this inherent potential and because of factors suggesting it could have a future of widespread benefit. As another side note, part of this hopeful outlook depends upon the availability of the plant material, and part of that availability will depend upon the will and determination of people to limit the destruction of forests like the Amazon jungle. As ethnobotanist/anthropologist and valuable spokesman for biodiversity Wade Davis has pointed out in several of his books, we are losing species of flora rapidly and risking the loss of an incredible storehouse of plant medicines and the knowledge of their use.

Simply speaking, there are two main streams of usage of ayahuasca. Its historical use by shamanic healers of the Amazon has been documented repeatedly since the arrival of Europeans in South America some 500 years ago, and all indications are that that use extended back into the long distant past. A common scenario describing the way ayahuasca has been used shamanically might go something like this: It's an oral tradition where the knowledge is passed from a fully initiated and extensively experienced elder shaman to one or more apprentices. The traditional training is usually long and arduous, involving intense discipline and firm commitment. The apprentice will often be required to undergo long periods of restricted diet, sexual abstinence, and isolation, as he or she—usually a male in the historical context—comes to know ayahuasca and other medicinal plants from personal experience.

An ayahuasca shaman, or ayahuasquero, will often work with one person or a small group. In one-on-one work, the focus has usually been on treating illness of one sort or another. In some traditions only the shaman drinks the brew, in other situations both the client and the shaman drink. Now, as information filters out to a larger community, non-indigenous people from the region and beyond—particularly North America and Europe—are finding the ayahuasca shamans and participating in sessions with the goal of spiritual healing. Most researchers would agree that the continuity of this tradition has been seriously threatened in recent decades, as the old ayahuasqueros find it increasingly difficult to find young apprentices among their own people who are willing to undergo the rigors of the traditional training. I mention this partly as a reminder of the long reach of the modern technological, consumer-focused cultures that have left no group on the planet untouched.

At the same time, however, there seems to be an uncanny archetypal scenario unfolding, as it is in regard to indigenous wisdom all over the planet. Just as the last threads of ancient knowledge and practices are in danger of disappearing, a renaissance of interest and vision is arising both within and outside these traditional cultures. With ayahuasca, some significant developments are unfolding which may save this knowledge from disappearing and lead to it playing an important part in the rebirth of sanity. These developments involve the discovery of ayahuasca by new groups of people, not limited to the Amazonian region. In the Brazilian Amazon non-indigenous and mixed-race rubber tappers became acquainted with ayahuasca, and a church—the Santo Daime—was formed in the 1930s, using the brew as its central sacrament. In the 1950s and 1960s, two other religious groups were founded in Brazil to work in this way, the União do Vegetal, or UDV church, and the Barquinia, each with its own set of ritual practices.

Remarkably, in the contemporary environment of ignorance and fear around the use of mind-manifesting substances, the Brazilian government, in 1987, made ayahuasca legal for use in religious practice. According to Charles S. Grob, Brazil thus became "the first nation worldwide in almost 1600 years to allow the use of plant hallucinogens for spiritual purposes by its non-indigenous inhabitants." This environment, along with the explosion of interest that came out of the 1960s in the use of spirit plants and the practices of ancient cultures, contributed to the dissemination of information about ayahuasca to, in particular, North America and Europe. There is work being done, some of it bearing good fruit, toward the legal recognition of Santo Daime in particular and the use of ayahuasca in general as a religious sacrament. There is good reason to hope that this direction will continue and expand in the years ahead as the dominator cultures are gradually dragged out of their caves.

The Holy Daime is not for everyone. The rituals of the Daime are not meant to be an "experience", but rather to provide a chance to interact intimately with a Divine being of unimaginable intelligence, compassion, clarity, and spiritual power. They require us to bring our whole selves to the work. They provide an opportunity for seeing truth, gaining knowledge, and to transform oneself, one's health, and one's life. What we get out of them depends on our level of readiness and our willingness to surrender our ideas of separation and enter into a new relationship with ourselves and with the Divine.[1]

Alex Polari de Alverga

I'll return here to a repeated theme in this book: my conviction and concern that these practices be treated with the utmost respect and discipline. In our wealthy, toy-infested societies there's a tendency to grab onto new ideas as though they're consumer items and jump in without even a minimal understanding of the complexities and even dangers involved. As recent history has demonstrated clearly, irresponsible practice with these radically powerful substances can cause individual harm and perhaps more importantly in regard to the serious work being done on the larger scale, can provoke backlashes among authorities all too ready to capitalize on the flimsiest of pretexts to demonize and squash nascent movements of this nature.

There's ample evidence of poorly tutored and self-promoting would-be gurus and healers setting themselves up to offer programs superficially rooted in deep practices from indigenous cultures. If religions like the Santo Daime are to move forward successfully, we will need thoughtful, respectful people with proper training and experience to lead the way. The rest of us interested in these pathways will need to keep our wits about us and proceed with our eyes wide open, on the lookout for those without proper grounding and throwing our support to those situations that can demonstrate the knowledge, experience, and right-attitude required to have a beneficial role in this work.

> For the Jivaro of the Ecuadorian Amazon, the supernatural realm, which can only be accessed through the door of the ayahuasca induced experience, is seen as the true reality, whereas normal waking life is simply an illusion.[2]
> *Charles S. Grob*

Because of the foundation that the ayahuasca churches have established, and thus the potential to expand into new environments, it's especially important to stress the power of this particular substance. It's been said that of all the major plant hallucinogens, ayahuasca may be the most unpredictable. Although some experienced with similar plants may question that statement, nonetheless accounts abound of utterly convincing experiences with ayahuasca that pull the supplicant into realms ranging from the glorious light of ineffable divinity to the depths of hell and terror. That statement alone should be enough to send a few readers scurrying and provoke others unfamiliar with the territory to wonder why anyone would be foolish enough to subject himself to such psychic danger.

The answer to such doubts is similar, in its unique version, to the promise of plant teachers like peyote, psilocybin, iboga, and others. In the right set and setting, these plants temporarily dissolve the ego into vast realms behind the veil of samsaric obscuration in ego's domain. They can put you into contact with noetic realities and potentially life-changing information that unambiguously does *not* stem from the library of your previous experience. As Benny Shanon described in his excellent scholarly treatise on the phenomenology of the ayahuasca experience, *The Antipodes of the Mind*, one of the most commonly heard descriptions from experienced drinkers of the brew is that what is experienced is "more real than real."

According to a large number of individual reports from both indigenous and non-indigenous drinkers—and in a wide variety of settings from the carefully controlled environments of the ayahuasca churches, to the darkened huts of the shamans, to the apartments of urban supplicants—ayahuasca seems capable of addressing any question, problem, or issue. People have been shown the origins of life on this planet, the secrets of DNA, the workings of all kinds of organisms, the processes of birth and death, and the diagnoses and treatment of life-threatening illnesses. Journeyers have uncovered the events of their psychic lives that need addressing and healing, seen landscapes and architecture of surpassing beauty in visions fully detailed beyond the wildest imagination of the uninitiated, and been given specific, clear information leading to further developments in their creative work as artists or academics.

For a concise assessment of ayahuasca's potential as a tool for awakening, I don't think I can do much better than this passage from Shanon:

Under the intoxication, it seems that a tremendous force permeates and animates everything around. Over and over again, in different locales and contexts, I have heard people comment that this energy is the force that sustains all Creation. The powerful energy is also regarded as the source of all wisdom and knowledge, and the ultimate fountain of health and well-being. Typically, people feel a direct tie to this energy and come to appreciate that their very own livelihood comes into being and is nourished by it.[3]

In traditional settings would-be drinkers are often asked to undergo restrictive diets and practices for several days prior to and sometimes following a session, often avoiding meat, salt and sometimes other foods and spices as well as abstaining from sexual activity. Prayer, meditation, and in general focusing one's mind and energy are also frequently prescribed. Rituals during the session—whether in a church environment like the Santo Daime or under the guidance of a shaman—can be extremely helpful for bringing drinkers through difficulties, preventing them from getting stuck and drifting astray, or from simply missing the potential of the gift being offered.

Though my own experience with ayahuasca is limited, I'd like to tell you more about that first one, as a good example of the value of the shaman's presence in a controlled setting. I found out through friends in the network that an American ayahuasquero who'd been training in Peru would be leading a session in rural Washington State. This man was said to have undergone a traditional training for the previous seven years under the guidance of elder masters. When we gathered in a large yurt on the Friday evening in question he explained to the assembled— about twenty of us—that he had mixed the brew the day before and had no way of knowing its potency until it was tested. He proceeded to dole out very small portions that evening which, according to everyone I spoke with, created barely a ripple of perturbation on the seas of normal consciousness.

We reassembled the next evening for the main event. Among other bits of relevant information he passed on to us, the ayahuasquero, who I've called Robert, held up what appeared to be a small whiskbroom or duster and told us that throughout the Amazon, groups who had never met each other had independently discovered the particular palm leaf used to make this instrument. He said that it was employed throughout the region to clear energy and that when the focus of a particular group was right, people could see light beams extending several feet from the points of the leaves. One use of the instrument—known in some areas as a shacapa—was to shake it around the perimeter of someone's body, especially the head and shoulders area. Robert said that he and others had seen black balls attached to these light beams when the shacapa was withdrawn from the person. He then told us that if we felt we were having trouble, to come up to him and request a clearing.

About forty-five minutes after ingesting the tea, I felt an onrush of heavy, confused energy overwhelming me. I remember thinking that this was not what I had imagined I would be seeing and feeling. It was powerful and frightening and I decided to take Robert's suggestion of requesting help. I was so shaky that I didn't trust myself to walk the twenty or so feet to the mattress Robert had placed in front of his spot, so I crawled across the dimly lit room and whispered my request. He told me to lie on the mattress, and here I have to tell you about the ayahuasca songs, called icaros (EE-kah-ros). Robert and others have said that a genuine ayahuasquero is taught icaros directly by the plant spirit for use in ayahuasca sessions. He seemed to have three or four that he cycled through over the course of the night. He had a lovely light tenor voice and the songs were beautiful.

Robert leaned over me as I lay face up on the mattress and shook the shacapa rapidly around my head and shoulders while singing an icaro. After a couple of minutes, he stopped singing, directed me to sit up, and whispered in my ear, "When you feel like that, it's fear, it's the ego holding on. You have to trust the medicine and try to relax into it." I muttered "mm- hmm," looked around to my own mattress across the room, concluded that I felt no different than I had when I came up there, and decided I still needed to crawl back. Everyone else remained lying down around the perimeter with eyes closed. As I crawled, I still felt dizzy, weak, and somewhat overwhelmed. But about six feet before reaching my spot, something completely unexpected happened. In a transition so quick and silent I hardly knew what had occurred, I suddenly felt like a large cat, a jaguar perhaps. I actually felt that I had become this cat or that it had taken residence in my body.

Those of you who've read about ayahuasca may know that jaguars and snakes are common themes reported by ayahuasca drinkers. I didn't know that at the time though, and prior to that moment had experienced nothing remotely similar. It wasn't in any way ambiguous. Without any effort or involvement on my part, I was immediately shifted from feeling unsteady and stunned, to a condition of total relaxation and gracefulness as I continued the last few feet to my mattress. My friend Martin, who was lying next to my spot, felt a sudden urge to look up at that exact moment and told me later that for a second he was convinced he was seeing a jungle cat approaching him, the movement was so natural and catlike.

When "we" reached the mattress, the cat dropped me and disappeared as suddenly and smoothly as it had arrived. However, I was now in a state of joy and delight—the cat spirit had brought me across the threshold. For the remainder of the evening I remained in that state of mind. Though there were no visualizations, I felt the distinct and irrefutable presence of a being or beings of wisdom and kindness hovering over the space. I felt I could ask any question about my path and receive an immediate telepathic answer. I kept throwing my doubts at this presence and having them gently corrected. They let me know that they were there to support what was going on, to help prepare us for future work toward the healing processes necessary on Earth.

In that regard, I noticed at several times during the session—maybe forty-five minutes apart—that I would feel a wave of intensity. At the same time, people around the room would shuffle and move, creating a rustling of sleeping bags. Each time that occurred, Robert would get up and walk around the room, shaking the shacapa and singing an icaro. After his round, the room would settle right down. In the morning I asked him if he had noticed that, and he replied that he didn't work with any agenda but that he would just have the feeling it was time to get up and do that. My sense of it was that the spirits just mentioned were sending waves of empowering energy to the assembled group every now and then and that these waves caused some discomfort which needed grounding.

One of the themes Benny Shanon explored in *The Antipodes of the Mind* was the often repeated point that the path of ayahuasca is a school, and that one rarely breaches more than the shores of a vast continent on the first encounter. His own experience and that of many of his "informants"—as they're called by anthropologists—has been that there is an ongoing course of instruction that builds upon previous learning. What I experienced that Saturday night was a beginner's entrance into those realms of learning. Even so, it contained several classic elements of the experience. First, the—in this case—essential involvement of the shaman to help me through the barrier; the use of apparently magical techniques like the shacapa and the icaros; the appearance of a guide or helper in the form of an animal; and the presence of wise and kind spirits, whether visualized or not. In fact, on the issue of visualizations, for those of you who have worked with ayahuasca or read some of the many trip reports, Shanon was repeatedly told that the visual experiences "are not at all the most important facet of the ayahuasca experience."

> Benny Shanon's list of qualities for a good leader in ayahuasca sessions: solidity, patience, a non-judgmental attitude, psychological sensitivity, the ability to say the right thing at the right time, and a good sense of humour...The presence of a leader is paramount in Ayahuasca sessions....a good leader will radiate security and induce an ambience of trust.[4]
> *Benny Shanon*

For anyone considering working with ayahuasca, a few more points should be made about the two streams mentioned above. The shamanic style I've described in my own experience is not untypical of the kind of situation one might find oneself in these days. Until recently, opportunities to participate in ceremonies of this kind have mostly been limited to those with the time and money to go to South America. However, it's encouraging to see that ayahuasqueros are now coming in increasing numbers to North America.

For those who are able to make the journey to South America, there are numerous small outfits that organize programs for foreigners. A typical one may involve coming to an ayahuasquero's encampment for maybe one to three weeks, often engaging in the dietary preparations, and then participating in several group sessions with the ayahuasca brew, under the leadership of a (hopefully) highly trained and experienced ayahuasquero. Some of these programs also involve counseling between sessions and some include side trips to the surrounding areas and beyond. Again, *caveat emptor*—let the buyer beware—applies here. As you may well imagine, where there's good money to be made, people of dubious motives will no doubt be found. Including transportation and program costs, a two or three week visit in Peru from the U.S. can easily get up to $6,000 or more. I've also been told by one sincere ayahuasquero working in Canada and the United States that about eighty percent of those claiming to be ayahuasqueros and leading shamanic sessions in North America do not have the necessary training to make that claim with full integrity.

I live in the Forest
I have my teachings
I don't call myself Daime
I am a Divine Being

I am a Divine Being
I came here to teach you
The more you ask of me
The more I have to give you
Santo Daime hymn

The other main avenue of approach to the teachings of ayahuasca is through these churches like the Santo Daime. As of this writing the Santo Daime has gained legal status in Holland and has made good progress in this direction in several other countries, including the United States, using the precedent of Supreme Court protection for the use of peyote in the Native American Church. There is good reason to hope for a lot more accessibility to this path in the years ahead.

There appear to be some significant differences in approach between the traditional jungle shamanic practices and those of churches like the Santo Daime. With the ayahuasqueros, one may have access to hands-on healing interventions during a session similar to the one I described with Robert. There is usually no organization or doctrine involved and there may be a greater flexibility in the structuring and unfolding of a night's session. Lighting is usually kept very low or snuffed altogether to enhance the clarity of eyes-closed visions.

Santo Daime services, for regular members, typically occur twice per month and are highly structured. Lights are usually left on, people sit in chairs, and men and women are separated. From the information I've gathered in my research, it appears there's much less time for silent inner reflection in the Santo Daime meetings than in many shamanic sessions. There is a leader who periodically speaks to the assembly, but the rest of the group is usually expected not to talk with each other. Much of the service is taken up with the singing and playing of music, accompanied by dancing.

The music and dancing are clearly a central focus of the meetings. It's been said by participants that the energy of the group and the music and movement have a powerful supportive and enhancing function in the ayahuasca-induced state. The songs are hymns and prayers, and it's easy to see how that could help people keep their focus on spirit—on celebration and praise— and cut through tendencies to fall into self-involved difficulties cycling through one's head. Benny Shanon described how sublime the music often was in these ceremonies. He was convinced that in general people in the spell of ayahuasca sang and played much better than in the normal state. He says that he was allowed to record this music a few times and found listening to the recordings later confirmed his subjective experience during the meetings.

Though the form of Santo Daime meetings and the presence of others in a communal experience seem to be very valuable, there doesn't generally appear to be any direct intervention or individual healing work that takes place during a service. The leader may come around and ask in a ritualized way how you're doing. The expected answer is, "fine," but Shanon claims even that has often helped participants who are struggling feel the benefit of a protected, loving environment within which to do necessary inner work.

The real question is whether or not participation in services like the Santo Daime results in lasting change and improvement in people's lives. For that there is a great deal of encouraging evidence. As with the Native American Church, a lot of people come around when things aren't going well—frequently when they're in the grip of addiction with alcohol and other substances. Both extensive anecdotal evidence and a couple of well-designed studies have shown marked change for the better in the lives of people who remain in the church for any period of time.

Though they may be recent, churches like the Santo Daime are also in a lineage that extends deep into the past. A number of scholars have made compelling cases for the historical presence of plant sacraments in the early days of a number of religions. There's a strong likelihood that a great many religious experiences have been invoked with substances in ritual environments. I mention again such evidence as: the frequent reference to soma in the Rig Veda of ancient India; the annual ceremony at Eleusis, near Athens, where the political, religious, intellectual, and artistic leaders—including names we still know today—participated in rituals involving a powerful plant sacrament; the visual evidence of sacred mushrooms on the world tree found on mosaic frescoes in the ruins of early Byzantine church walls in northern Africa; and of course the evidence of indigenous use of plant sacraments around the world and far back into the past.

Ayahuasca provokes a full range of experience: powerful insight into one's own obstacles to awakening and the possibility of direct, unmediated experience of divinity in all its seemingly glorious and limitless variety. Again, churches like the Santo Daime are called syncretic churches, meaning, according to the Oxford dictionary, "the combining of different religions, cultures, or ways of thinking." If we're clear on what we're doing and we stay behind the Spirit as we proceed, we can learn from—and sometimes judiciously combine— the best and most powerful practices of groups from all around the planet and scattered throughout history. We can sing freely and wholeheartedly, we can dance in deep ecstasy, we can meditate and open up in stillness and silence to spirit-infused reality.

My brothers and my sisters,
Please start unraveling yourselves
I am small and I keep my word.
I'm showing my truth.[6]
Santo Daime hymn

Heart of the Great Spirit
The Peyote Cactus

We know whereof we speak.
We have tasted of God
and our eyes have opened.[1]
Albert Hensley,
Winnebago

My first encounter with the peyote medicine spirit, ten years before I met it again in the Native American Church (NAC) ceremonies, demonstrated and presaged in a gentle and humbling manner what it could do. I was visiting an old friend, Alan, for a couple of days. Alan mentioned that he had one peyote button which he'd kept in a jar for about ten years, and he offered to share it with me and another friend of his. One peyote button for three people is not much, to say the least. When Weston La Barre traveled the west learning about the NAC in the 1930s, he found that participants commonly ingested from four to thirty or more buttons in a ceremony.

Alan took this dusty old peyote, cleaned out the hairs in the center that he'd heard were poisonous, and steeped it in boiled water for some time. The three of us shared the soaked button and drank the resulting tea in silence while sitting in big, overstuffed chairs in Alan's now darkened living room. We remained like that for an hour or two before Alan broke the silence and asked us what we'd experienced. We found to our surprise that each of us had undergone something strikingly similar. There were no indications of being "stoned." We all felt sharp and sober. That one little peyote plant had led all three of us on a clear, gentle, and nonjudgmental tour through our own faults. None of us felt belittled or depressed by this exposé. Instead we each felt a similar quiet humility and gratitude from the experience.

> The peyote spirit told me one night,
> "I am a safe way for you to come home."[2]
> *Nancy Littlefish*

To be frank, I'm a little nervous about sharing details regarding the Native American Church at all and have considered not including it. The reason for this concern has to do with the incredible difficulties that the church has had to overcome and the extreme amount of suffering visited upon the indigenous peoples of North America by the European invaders of the past five centuries. This church is—as religious philosopher and teacher Huston Smith has described it—a story of great triumph over adversity, and now exists as a refuge of sanity in a disturbed land and a lifesaving sanctuary of healing and wisdom for hundreds of thousands of Native people. It's a sacred treasure to be protected and nurtured with the utmost respect and sensitivity.

My fervent prayer and intention in writing about these matters, as I've alluded to throughout this text, is to pass along information and inspiration toward a renaissance of awakening and reattunement to reality on this planet. From that point of view, the information is intended to be received in the larger context of the main thesis of the book: that we're in a time of wrenching change and upheaval; that there are reasons we've reached this point; that there may not be much wiggle room anymore—planetary or personal—and that it's both possible and probably essential that we (whoever we are), open ourselves to and manifest awakened-heart vision. It looks like the whole planet is rapidly becoming one community, and that we're all becoming part of the same story.

Grandfather's Guiding Hand

Sparse as it is, the information I'm sharing here about peyote wisdom and peyote religion is not breaking new ground or giving away heavily guarded secrets. There are classic texts, well-known to anthropologists and other interested parties, that contain detailed information on the habitat, the pharmacology, and the historical and current use of peyote. Some of these are listed in the bibliography for this book. I offer here a very brief background summary of that story in the hope of providing some useful context for understanding the power and authenticity of working with the sacred peyote cactus and other similar entheogenic plants.

Lophophora williamsii, as the academics have dubbed it, is a small, spineless cactus whose natural habitat is the Chihuahuan Desert area extending from north/central Mexico up to southern Texas. The peyote cactus has most likely been helping humans with great kindness and wisdom longer than anyone will ever know. Some Native origin stories place it at the beginnings of human existence, as a gift from the Creator to help the people remember who they are and where they came from. Native American deification of the plant is thought by scholars to be about 10,000 years old. Peyote cactus buttons uncovered in Shumla Cave in southern Texas have been radiocarbon dated to 5000 BCE.

It's believed that the peyote pilgrimage of the Huichol (or Wixaritari as they call themselves) Indians of central Mexico may have been in place as early as 200 CE. Scholars consider it the oldest sacramental use of peyote in North America. The annual pilgrimage, a practice continued until today, takes members of the tribe, under strict rules of discipline, away from their homeland on a walking pilgrimage to Wirikuta—the "field of flowers," 400 kilometers to the northeast— to gather the spirit cactus and return with it for ceremonial and medicinal use. Several other Mexican tribes, including the Tarahumara, the Cora, and the Tepehuan (or Tepecano), also have a historical relationship with peyote.

There is some evidence of pre-Columbian use of peyote in the United States and one Spanish author, Velasco, wrote in 1716 that he had observed Indians of present day Texas drinking "pellote" as part of their ritual dances. The Lakota people today live mostly in the states of North and South Dakota. According to a Lakota elder of my acquaintance, the Lakota say that they have had this medicine since time immemorial. However, as far as researchers have been able to ascertain, the major diffusion of peyote's use northward appears to have occurred in the mid-nineteenth century, when it spread into the Great Plains of the U.S. through the Mescalero Apache and other tribes.

It may be more than coincidental—and in fact in keeping with the uncanny powers of the peyote medicine spirit—that the most rapid diffusion of its use unfolded at the same time that Native American cultures all over the western states were being destroyed and dismantled. As one tribe after another fell to the American soldiers and settlers and had their lands stolen and their traditional customs and practices denigrated and even outlawed, this sacrament quickly spread throughout the region. As Weston La Barre put it in his landmark ethnographic study *The Peyote Cult,* the first edition of which was published in 1938, "Thus, ironically, the intended modes of deculturizing the Indians have contributed preeminently to the reinvigoration of a basically aboriginal religion."[4]

This deculturizing program—the expressed intention of American government policy of the late nineteenth and early twentieth centuries—severely weakened the hold of the older tribal religions without actually undermining widely held Plains religious beliefs. At the same time, placing formerly scattered and diverse groups on reservations together and forcing their children into state schools brought members of various tribes into contact with each other in new ways.

By the 1890s, it had become apparent to the Indians that they would have to organize to protect their right to make use of this sacrament. Movement toward that goal coalesced in Oklahoma under the leadership of Quannah Parker and others and resulted in the formal adoption of the Native American Church by 1918. As of the 1990s there were chapters of this church in every state west of the Mississippi river with members from over seventy different Native American nations. Estimates of current membership range from 250,000 to over 400,000, and growing.

A brief mention of the legal situation may also be of benefit here. Since that time in the 1880s and 1890s there have been repeated attempts at all levels in the U.S., from local to federal, to prevent the religious use of peyote. One could suspect the wise hand of Grandfather Peyote again in this battle for recognition and protection. Each time a dire and lasting threat approached implementation, support arose from unexpected quarters to stop or overturn a particular measure. More than one attempt to pass laws through Congress failed in the early twentieth century. During the period from roughly 1910 to 1930, a number of states passed laws criminalizing the use of peyote until John Collier, the newly appointed federal Commissioner for Indian Affairs, applied a more enlightened attitude, sending out a Bureau circular in 1934 which stated that "no interference with Indian religious life or ceremonial expression will hereafter be tolerated."[5] The last Congressional attempt to quash peyote use died in committee in 1963, thanks in part to the support of anthropologists. When new, draconian laws were brought forward in the late 1960s, culminating with the dreaded Schedule One classification—substances deemed to have a high potential for abuse and no currently accepted medical use—for psychedelics of all kinds, peyote use for Native people in sanctioned religious practice was specifically exempted and protected.

The most recent, and hopefully final, furor arose in the late 1980s with a case called *Employment Division of Oregon vs. Smith* that went all the way to the U.S. Supreme Court in 1990, where, in a decision many consider to be a low point in the history of that court, the protection of freedom of religion was all but reversed. The devastating decision sent shock waves through much of the American religious community and forced practitioners of the NAC underground. Thankfully, a large number of groups and individuals, both Native and non-Native—including other churches who felt their rights threatened—worked passionately to get that decision corrected by an act of Congress, a campaign that was ultimately successful with the passage of the "American Indian Religious Freedom Act Amendments of 1994."

When I say "hopefully final furor," I have to add that in 2009 there is still no certainty of the long-term protection of this sacred rite/right. People closely connected to the harvesting and distribution of the peyote cactus have told me that there has been a recent upsurge of obstructionist behavior on the part of the Drug Enforcement Agency. Administrators have apparently been adding extra layers of bureaucracy which, if fully implemented, will have the effect of making access to the medicine much more difficult. It's also been reported that the D.E.A. has engineered ploughing of the peyote fields in Texas so that only a limited supply will be available through strictly controlled licensing of diminishing acreage. In the eyes of true justice, this direction, if not reversed, would have to be seen as criminally cruel in its potential consequences.

An Inspiring Model

Approaches inspired by the principles and the practices of the NAC ceremonies may prove to be an excellent model for the development of new and revived forms and rituals for the use of entheogenic sacraments where the knowledge from the traditions has been lost. It's very important to make it clear before going further however that nobody from outside should be messing with the existing forms of NAC ceremonies. In my experience, only those who have received a direct transmission of empowerment are sanctioned to act as the roadmen who conduct the ceremonies. The elders tell us that everything in the ritual has been put there for an essential purpose, under the direct guidance of Spirit.

These ceremonies are a synthesis of several powerful forms for healing and awakening: working with prayer and intention; using music to give wings and strength to that prayer, including singing and something akin to shamanic drumming; an encouragement toward a meditative mindfulness and awareness; developing compassion and commitment toward the benefit of others; and of course the potent assistance of the holy sacrament itself, the peyote medicine Spirit.

The church is also light on its feet. It has essentially no professional, paid clergy and no written canon. The only school for learning its ways and wisdom is the school of experience. The church lives in the understanding of those who've opened themselves to the teachings of Grandfather Peyote and especially in the knowledge of the authentic roadmen who have been given a "fireplace" and carry with them a deep understanding of the forms and meanings of the church and its ceremonial rituals. The altar and fireplace of the church are living concepts, even living presences. The house of worship—the tipi—is normally only raised for meetings and usually taken down immediately after. The roadmen generally prefer to see themselves as midwives rather than teachers, as people who help others make the daunting and often lifesaving transition from painful dis-ease to awakening heart. In my experience, there is precious little preaching in a meeting. Each individual is to find his or her own direct experience of awakening, peaceful heart, and prayerful communion with Spirit.

> It's said that "the peyote spirit is like a little hummingbird —
> when you are quiet and nothing is disturbing it, it will come
> to a flower and get the sweet flavor. But if it is disturbed, it
> goes quick." Hence the admonitions to sit quietly in meetings
> and "study" to see if you can "maybe learn something."[6]
> *Weston La Barre*

At the same time, in the context of this barely organized religion, there is a powerful tradition of knowledge which has been handed down from generation to generation. With minor variations, the main forms of the ritual have remained consistent for over 120 years. Those experienced in these ways have a deep respect and sensitivity toward every aspect of the practice, beginning with the peyote itself and extending to the various rituals and sacred objects. Based on what I've seen and learned in the ceremonies, I would say that the purpose of this careful reverence toward the forms and materials is to create and maintain the most sturdy, safe, and conducive container for the meeting of human minds with Spirit wisdom as well as to keep alive for future generations an ancient prayer and commitment. The rules for a meeting, I've heard repeatedly, are few and simple and are based on the learned experience of not interfering with the movement and nurturance of Spirit in the tipi.

What do I mean by "Spirit" in this context? After more than seven years, I still consider myself a relative novice in the NAC, reporting the stories passed on to me and strengthened by my own experiences of moments of great beauty, stillness, and love that often pervade the atmosphere in the tipi. As I've been told numerous times, talk of Spirit presence in meetings is not a matter of belief but is testimony of real encounters with presences that appear in a variety of guises—from ear-whispered guidance, to forms of light, to birds and animals, to entities in human form. This again is the source of the admonition to pay close attention, attempt to remain quiet on both the outer and inner levels, and keep one's mind focused on the main prayer and the energy going on in the tipi.

> This [holding up a peyote button] is the heart of the Great Spirit, sent here for all of us.[7]
> *Aurelio Diaz*
> *Tekpankalli*

This issue of Spirit highlights some of the major differences between the religious practices of the mainstream cultures and the direct encounters of indigenous religions like the NAC. At one meeting there were five or six first-time participants, in a group of about thirty-five. In the morning, when the energy softens a little and a hard-earned new dawn arises out of the work—out of the praying, healing, and upheaval of the deep hours of the night—Kanucas greeted us, "Good morning relatives," he said. "New people here might wonder what you've encountered. I can tell you but it doesn't make much difference. You have to find it on your own. What you've encountered here is reality." As mentioned before, I've also heard him say a few times that under the influence of the peyote medicine, the Spirit talks to him and gives him instruction on how to guide the meeting and how to work with individuals in need of assistance.

I'd refer you to the above-mentioned book by Weston La Barre if you're interested in a detailed account of the typical format and sequence of a meeting. I would just like to offer another brief summary here in the hope of providing some useful context. A meeting is normally called by someone who is then referred to as the sponsor for that meeting. The sponsor may be responsible for finding the location and the "officers" needed to run the meeting. He or she may also be required to organize the medicine, the firewood, and the tipi. The officers consist of: the roadman, who runs the meeting, typically a very experienced member of the church who has received a fireplace from another roadman; a drummer, who is responsible for tying up the water drum for the meeting and accompanying the singers around the tipi; the cedarman, who throughout the night periodically throws ground cedar onto the fire for purification of materials, people coming and going etcetera; the fire chief or fireman, who tends the fire thoroughly according to traditional guidelines; the doorman, whose job is mainly to oversee comings and goings and to watch over the group; and the waterwoman, usually the wife or close relative of the roadman, who is called upon to speak during the meeting and to say an extended prayer with a tobacco over a bucket of water at dawn. I share these details as evidence of the level of care involved in creating and maintaining the container for the ceremonies.

The range of purposes that can be set by the sponsor is quite varied and can range from a request for physical or spiritual healing, to a birthday, a baptism, an expression of gratitude, or in some cases even a celebration of life. These meetings are sometimes called prayer meetings, and I've explained a few things in the chapter on prayer about the approach one encounters in this environment so I won't repeat that information here. I'll just say again that these prayers are spontaneous, a kind of channeling of the voice in the heart. Many times I've been moved to tears by the sincerity and fluid eloquence of prayers shared during meetings.

The prayer established by the sponsor is called the main prayer, and the participants are requested to focus their attention on that prayer for much of the night. Elders would say that the power and consistency of that attention from those assembled goes a long way to invoking Spirit and bringing forth the realization of that prayer. I continue to be amazed at the stories of what would conventionally be called miraculous healing I've heard from various people at meetings and read in accounts like Guy Mount's *The Peyote Book*. Weston La Barre, writing in the 1930s, was told by his native informants that they considered peyote a panacea in doctoring, with successful healing of conditions like cancer of the liver, hemorrhage, tuberculosis, respiratory diseases, goiter, and one I came across of a boy who had been unable to speak until treated with peyote medicine.

One Mind

In our prayer songs that bring our hearts together, we offer our single, united heart to the Great Spirit.[8]
Reuben Snake

The bulk of the night is carried by the peyote songs that participants take turns leading as the instruments go around the circle, typically two or three times depending on the size of the group that night. The singing is periodically interspersed with other types of prayer and testimonials. As the morning light approaches, the assembled are invited to pray for their own families and friends and finally to ask the Creator for anything they need for themselves. After the prayers offered by the water-woman at dawn, the prayed-over water and ritual foods—corn, meat, and berries—are passed around the circle. As the meeting draws to a close, people are often invited to express themselves. In my experience, although many of us are a bit weary and sore from the long night's journey, that time of the morning is often exquisitely sweet, sometimes heartbreaking, and people's personal testimonials at times eloquent and poignant.

It may be worth noting that, although as discussed above, the peyote cactus is an emissary of Spirit and can therefore be very challenging to any resistance we have to surrendering and opening, in another sense it's quite different from some of the other major entheogenic sacraments. I'm thinking here of ayahuasca and psilocybin in particular. Both, as with peyote and as described in other chapters, have deep traditions of healing, shamanic, and ceremonial religious use. Though I'm certainly not the ultimate expert on the question, from all I've learned I think it's safe to say that peyote is more subtle and perhaps gentler, especially in the doses commonly employed in NAC meetings. For example, the mushrooms and ayahuasca are both well-known for their intense visual qualities, and when ingested in what might be called committed doses will often hurl the user into completely altered and sometimes very strange visual landscapes, sometimes even with eyes open.

Overall, there seems to be more emphasis on eyes-closed journeying in traditional rituals that employ those plants, with more solo time to go inward. Peyote meetings usually keep the focus outward and eyes tend to be kept open most of the time. Participants are often encouraged to pay close attention to what's going on around them and are sometimes called to step forward and assist. In my experience, these meetings are definitely not set up for long periods of solo inner journeying, but rather devoted more to the healing of body and mind that can be powerfully assisted by the care and attention of the group. It is truly a shared work in many respects.

I have heard people describe visual experiences with the peyote medicine, sometimes quite relevant and instructive, and as I mentioned earlier, for the brave and the experienced who are so attuned and who may have eaten a lot of medicine that night, presences or entities often appear. Kanucas has mentioned that sometimes in a meeting he'll have "one foot in this world and one foot in the other world." He also told me one morning about a brief (in our time) journey that took him out into space to see the celestial configurations before being led down, in through the door of the tipi, across the fire, and inside the chief peyote, which sits on the crescent moon altar, so that he could see that "as above so below" and "as the greater, so the lesser."

Others, however, rarely speak of visual travel, and when I cast my eyes around the tipi, I generally see people who look sharp and attentive and are able to speak coherently and powerfully and carry out ritual tasks without in any way appearing inebriated or diminished in cognitive or motor functioning. Reports in the literature regarding NAC meetings sometimes confirm that impression, such as this from Patricia Mousetail Russell, a Southern Cheyenne: "I have never seen colors or experienced delusions of any sort while taking Peyote. What it feels like is that I am sitting right by God the Creator."[9] Or this, from Virginia C. Trenholm: "Those who have unpleasant reactions or see fantastic or frightening objects during a meeting are said to have allowed their thoughts to wander. By controlling one's thinking, one finds inspiration in the quiet meditation of a meeting."[10]

One shouldn't draw too sharp a distinction between the experiences with different entheogens however. Ayahuasca in particular, as described in that chapter, is being employed by large numbers of people in religious gatherings like those of the Santo Daime of Brazil. The dosage level in those meetings is said to be moderate, not as large as sometimes taken in traditional native Amazonian jungle environments. A group experience somewhat similar to that of the NAC meetings has been reported, with less emphasis on the visual experience and more on the opening of the heart to Spirit in shared ritual space. The core experience of most value must be this awakening to reality.

The peyote filled me, gave me a sense of depth and dimension, a sense of opening, of oneness with the universe. Everything, the beadwork, the room itself, the faces of the others, grew visually intense; every detail came into focus. I became an eagle, soaring with the chant, over a lake of clear blue water. My veins filled with love, and the drumbeats entered, became one with my pulse. The Great Spirit was everywhere. Time had stopped and we were ancient beings, without need of language.[11]

Sun Bear

It is said by elders of the Native American Church that the voice—the teachings, the healing power—of the peyote medicine Spirit is active on the planet at this time, working behind the scenes and beneath the radar, whispering guidance to the attuned, empowering and participating in the spread of the vision of the joining of the four directions, and guiding the unfolding of the prayer for planetary healing and awakening.

23

Teonanácatl
The Sacred Mushroom of Immortality

I don't consider myself a hero of the high seas of the mushroom cosmos. But while working on this chapter I decided I'd best refresh my memory of those realms with a personal excursion. I'm always a little nervous before encounters with the mushrooms—I know something about their power. My friend Dan and I decided to venture forth together and made sincere efforts to create a safe, comfortable environment. We set up a makeshift shrine on the livingroom coffee table with candles, gourd shaker and drum, and a few personal objects. We petitioned the mushroom spirits, prayed with tobacco, lit sage to cleanse the space, stated our intentions, and ingested about 2.5 grams each of dried Psilocybe cyanescens which Dan had picked the previous fall.

We knew that two to three grams is generally considered a midlevel dose. Dan said he'd heard that the strength of an encounter with the mushrooms was fairly accurately indicated by the rapidity of their onset. Within twenty minutes we could both feel energies moving in our bodies and subtle shifts of tone in visual and auditory perception, and we guessed, correctly, that this one would be powerful. By forty-five minutes, the full force of that power was almost fully in place and not too much later we both found places to lie down.

It's hard to describe the way the energy moves with the mushrooms unless you've experienced it yourself. With eyes closed, the visuals become remarkable and alive. In this case my eyes-closed visual field was dominated by beautifully patterned moving serpentine figures colored in rich blues and golden yellows. Sometimes they snapped into place and stopped completely, then resumed flowing, toying with concepts of time. The power of the mushrooms often comes in waves and when I was able to stay loose with the rising energy there were sublime moments of peace and stillness.

Sometimes I found it very difficult—in spite of my best efforts—to remain still. I believe the most skillful and courageous mushroom warriors are able to keep letting go into increasingly powerful energies coming through. Mushroom veterans like Paul Stamets and Martin Ball have both counseled getting up and moving to ground the energy, so periodically I did do that. Ball said he likes long walks. But Dan and I both had a sense that we wanted to meet "the thing in itself" on this particular pilgrimage—remembering Terence McKenna's charming admonishment to "Sit down, shut up, and pay attention."—with as little distraction from the outside world as possible, so we tried to stay with the presence of the mushroom in that way to the best of our courage and ability.

But getting up to move periodically did indeed help. I'm also a musician and have learned a couple of dozen songs from the Native American Church. I found myself directed to my frame drum and I began to sing a song that felt like one of those but was actually a different variation than any song I'd ever heard or learned. My voice was unusually strong and clear, the music was coming through effortlessly, unbidden, with emotion and intensity. I noticed the effect immediately. It felt like a healing song and a wave of relaxation and grounding moved down through my body. Dan, who had gone down to his bedroom in his suite two floors below, felt the song and its power. And then I would go back for another round with eyes closed.

Mushroom travelers talk about communication with and especially *from* the mushroom spirits. I began to receive silent messages: teachings, information, reminders. The messages seemed to be directed both at me, for my own spiritual growth, and at the community of humans in general. Like this: "You're playing with powerful energies, be careful." Or this one, which especially seemed to be aimed at our collective behavior toward the gifts of the planet: "You can't just take, you have to give back." Having recently read passages like some of those later in this chapter that spoke of the voices of the living Gaian mind appealing to us to heal the ravaged Earth, I interpreted those messages in that way.

And then a lot about love. When I could handle the energy, this love came through powerfully, and carried messages. At one point I broke out in spontaneous song, "Take this love, silly monkeys." And other reminders like, "It's free, it's limitless, it's the only thing left on this planet that *is* free. But remember, you can't hold it, you can only dance with it and pass it on. Let this love come in. We forgive you, we forgive you for everything. Now, do something with it. Forgive yourself. Let the healing happen."

At one point I sat down at the window of our kitchen on the second floor and looked out at the beautiful and majestic trees I've often appreciated in our neighborhood. They were alive with beings. Multiple eyes looked out from the huge oaks across the lane. I focused in on a lovely, full-figured maple about fifteen metres high and saw something sitting in the middle of it. The closest I can come to describing this vision is that it had serpentine qualities, was multicolored and patterned, and remained fixed in that spot for at least a couple of minutes until I focused elsewhere. This stable vision was much different, for example, than the continuously shifting figures we often see in clouds.

When the power had diminished significantly, about five hours from ingestion, Dan and I reconvened around our little shrine to close it with prayers, songs, and thanks, and then began to talk about the experience. The usual boundaries and reticence about revealing very personal feelings and issues left the room for a while as we shared our heart stories with each other. Neither of us had crossed the threshold of total ego-dissolution and freed ourselves completely from the chains of the samsaric mind for more than short periods at a time, and we had to remind ourselves that it's an ongoing path of development. The repeated message for me during the journey was: "When in doubt there's one answer. Do it for love, with love, bring in love, call on us, we're here for everybody."

Out of the Shadows

As with numerous other ancient indigenous teachings and worldviews, spiritual traditions that included psilocybe mushrooms as their sacrament were nearly wiped clean from the pages of history. In fact, although scholars were aware of the use of these fungi among Native peoples of the Americas prior to the coming of the Europeans, it was believed by most that the practices were eventually eradicated by the conquerors. Some scholars even believed that the sixteenth century Spanish friars who documented the Aztec use of teonanácatl — "God's Flesh" — had gotten it wrong and were actually referring to the peyote cactus. So, again, just when it seemed that ancient knowledge of the power of this sacrament was lost forever, new explorers discovered that the practices had not disappeared among the indigenous people but had gone deep underground, or actually, deep into the jungles and mountainous regions, hidden away from the punishing eye of the conquistador.

Some credit Richard Evan Schultes for sparking the modern psychedelic revival through his discovery of the use of sacred mushrooms in Mexico in 1938. In the mid-1950s, R. Gordon Wasson traveled to Mexico with photographer Allan Richardson in search of these "magic" mushrooms and happened upon a Mazatec curandera (healer) named Maria Sabina in the mountains of Oaxaca. Maria Sabina was a lineage holder of the ritual use of the mushrooms for spiritual development and healing. She invited Wasson and Richardson to participate in a ritual—a velada—which, after 500 years of Spanish Catholic intrusion into all corners of Mexico, now incorporated elements and icons of Christianity into pre-Columbian practices. As Wasson described the encounter, "We had come from afar to attend a mushroom rite but had expected nothing so staggering as the virtuosity of the performing curanderas and the aston-ishing effects of the mushroom."[1]

Wasson's powerful revelatory experience with Maria Sabina stimulated him to write a detailed account of the adventure which was published in *Life* magazine in the United States in 1957, including a cover photo of the velada. The feature triggered an explosion of interest that spread across the culture and brought eager seekers into the mountains of Mexico—and later across the fields and pastures of America—in search of these mushrooms.

As with other entheogenic sacraments, the history of psychoactive mushroom use among humans goes deep into the past. Given that most ancient peoples living close to the land were certainly familiar with everything growing in their environment, it's safe to suggest that the potential of psilocybin-containing mushrooms was discovered very early. We have evidence from around the planet going back at least several thousand years. Rock paintings in the Sahara Desert dated to between 9000 and 7000 BCE contain repeated images of mushroom effigies. An effigy of a mushroom—most likely a fly agaric, and part of a shamanistic scene—has been found on a rock engraving at Mount Bego in France and dated to around

1800 BCE. Large mushroom stones still stand in the state of Kerala in India that date back to the civilizations of the Megalithic period (3500 to 1500 BCE). Similar evidence has been uncovered in other areas of Asia and Europe. In northern Africa, frescoes from the ruins of Byzantine era Christian churches from the early centuries of the Christian Era display clear images of "mushroom trees." In the Americas, mushroom iconography that locates the sacrament firmly in the center of their spiritual life is clearly evident in the stone carvings of the ancient Maya. A Franciscan friar, Bernardino de Sahagún, who accompanied Hernando Cortés to Mexico in the sixteenth century, spent fifty years documenting extensive use of the visionary mushrooms among the Aztecs, rituals that certainly went back many hundreds or even thousands of years.

> When we look at the narratives about the sea change of our society throughout the Western world in the last forty years— issues such as the new attitudes towards minorities and other cultures, the roles and rights of women, the environment— one key factor in that change of outlook is consistently expunged from the record: the fact that millions of us laid prostrate before the gates of awe beneath the power of one of these plants.[2]
> *Wade Davis*

To those who scoff at the suggestion that a "drug"—that is, a plant or a chemical compound—could have and has had anything to do with spiritual awakening, I would say this: Why not? The elders, the guides, and the shamans who have deep experience with these substances are telling us, unequivocally, that the presence of Spirit is immanent and available. I myself, a mere journeyman, have had direct experiences and encounters with states of deep love and peace, seen miracles of healing performed, and watched as lives have been radically altered for the better on paths strewn with wisdom plants. According to Walter Pahnke (famous among students of entheogenic sacraments for the Good Friday Experiment in 1962): "a study of the literature of spontaneous mystical experiences reported throughout world history from almost all cultures and religions" demonstrates that people claiming to have had mystical experiences through other means typically described the details of such phenomena in ways identical to those who have had experiences of mystic power and divine connection through the use of entheogens.

Where these mushrooms have appeared, and that has been nearly all over the world at various times, they would have been discovered, they would have been eaten, and their messages and teachings would have been experienced. This knowledge would have spread to others and become part of the cosmology of the people, except of course in times and places where powerful groups and individuals have attempted to control and mediate the spiritual experience of the people.

When I have ingested psychoactive plants and mushrooms, there is one message emanating from this world of plant spirit consciousness that comes to me loudly and clearly virtually every time. That message is that we are part of an "ecology of consciousness", that the Earth is in peril, that time is short, and that we're part of a huge, universal biosystem. And I am far from alone. Many people who have taken these substances report receiving the same message.[3]
Paul Stamets

Paul Stamets, author of the book *Psilocybin Mushrooms of the World* and possibly the world's leading expert on identification of these mushrooms, has been a diligent and devoted student of the mushroom teachers for several decades. During the years of his research, Stamets came to the realization of a powerful symbiosis between humans and the visionary mushrooms. Accompanied by these messages from the plant teacher, he observed that, rather than growing in the forest where one encounters most other varieties of mushrooms, the psilocybe genus is usually found in conjunction with human habitation, in "disturbed environments" as they say. They appear in gardens, in proximity to common plants like Rhododendrons, in wood chips, in cleared pastures and fields, and around cattle and sheep—to list a few of the more frequently observed habitats. The suburban sprawl of recent decades has been accompanied by the proliferation of these psilocybe mushrooms. Stamets described how the grounds surrounding his local county courthouse and sheriff's department are among his favorite spots to find the little ones, along with college campuses, utility substations, hospitals, office complexes and ornamental gardens. He further claims that by the mid-eighties, whole cities on the West coast were teeming in psilocybes, from Vancouver in Canada down to San Francisco in California.

Numerous other researchers and explorers of plant wisdom have noted this interconnection and the urgency of the messages coming through. A repeated theme in this book is the historical disconnect of the dominator cultures from the Gaian mind, and the resultant spiritual and environmental distress we find ourselves facing now. The message of the indigenous wisdom carriers and the plant teachers themselves is that the planet is alive in all its various forms and that it is in peril and in need of a rapid awakening and commitment among us. Plants and fungi, like these small mushrooms, are emissaries of the living vegetal mind, and, according to people with deep experience, are speaking to those who will listen—who will be mature, coura- geous, and open-minded enough to avail themselves of this infor- mation. The spokespeople for this vision say that belief is not enough, that what's required is direct experience of the relationship between us humans and the living Gaian mind.

Another quote from Terence McKenna may serve to drive this point closer to home: "The greatest gift of the vegetable mind to the human order is the psychedelic experience because it allows the dissolution of boundaries, and it is going to be necessary to dissolve those boundaries in order to coordinate the metamorphosis of the human world."[4]

There are some eighty known species of psilocybin-containing mushrooms, the majority of them in the Western hemisphere. According to Paul Stamets, they can be found in all temperate and tropical habitats with high annual rainfall amounts. The psychoactive components identified in psilocybe mushrooms are psilocybin, psilocin, baeocystin, and norbaeocystin—the latter two being much less common. Psilocybin and psilocin were identified as the primary psychoactive components by Albert Hofmann in 1958, the same Hofmann who discovered LSD some years earlier. Psilocybin is a remarkably stable molecule which converts to the unstable molecule psilocin after ingestion. It's among the class of entheogens known as tryptamines. As with other entheogens, it's very similar to existing brain chemistry, seemingly well suited for a meeting of minds. Other tryptamine molecules found naturally in the human body include tryptophan, 5-hydroxytryptophan, serotonin, melatonin, and N,N-dimethyltryptamine (DMT).

There's something very elegant about a small mushroom that follows us around as we expand our footprint; fits remarkably smoothly into appropriate receptors in our brains; has a toxicity level so low that it's a non-issue; does not need our assistance to grow in abundance; requires no laboratory to prepare it for human consumption; can be stored in dried form without rapid degradation; and which, upon meeting our minds, imparts immensely valuable information. For these reasons it appears that these humble fungi could have a crucial role to play in the reconfiguration of human understanding required for us to move forward successfully.

To Face Your Soul

If this vision has potential, there are a few important considerations and cautions to examine. First, the mushrooms are indeed plentiful and available to all without the mediation of the marketplace. However, a learning process is strongly recommended before people blithely traipse through fields and gardens picking and swallowing little brown fungi. In the Pacific Northwest of the U.S. and Canada, for example, over four thousand species of mushrooms have been identified. Among these, approximately twelve are of the psilocybe genus. According to Paul Stamets, toxic mushrooms greatly outnumber psilocybes anywhere in the world. For example, mushrooms of the deadly poisonous genus Galerina can look very similar to several species of psilocybe and often grow in close proximity. Stamets urges seekers to obtain guidance and be certain of identification before consuming any particular mushroom.

Then there's the repeated theme in this book regarding the all-important "set and setting" issue. Again, "set" refers to the whole of the mindset of the would-be seeker, that is, one's overall, ongoing mental and spiritual condition as well as current state of mind. "Setting" refers to the physical environment, the ritual preparation, the presence of experienced guides etc. All the researchers I've encountered in my reading caution against casual use and stress that these mushrooms are by no means appropriate for everyone. This issue is so important—especially if we hold a vision that sacred plant sacraments may prove to be central to the call to awakening—that I think it's worth letting some of those with deep experience speak for themselves. First, Paul Stamets: "I don't think everybody should ingest psychoactive plants. Many people are not mature or centered enough. I think the plant spirits have a lot to teach willing students and serious people who are ready to listen, but these plants have been dangerously commercialized and popularized, and that can pose real problems. Mushrooms and these other plant medicines make you face your soul...Are you ready to look at who you really are, including your deepest fears and failings? I know lots of people who are not ready."[5]

Kathleen Harrison has made a life of studying plants and humans' relationships to them. She teaches at several American universities, has done field work in Latin America for over thirty years, and is cofounder and director of Botanical Dimensions—a nonprofit organization whose mission is to preserve knowledge of medicinal and shamanic plants. Referring to the entheogenic plants and fungi, she cautioned, "I don't think they should ever be taken lightly, and I don't think they're for everyone. Anyone who takes them will have a hard time now and then, and will most likely have some scary inner encounters. These are tricky teachers. I encourage those who are certain they want to experience these visionary states to turn to indigenous practice and guidance."[6]

One further testimonial may serve to strengthen the case against casual use and in favor of the recommendation for careful, reverent approaches to working with sacraments like this. The following comment comes from Frederick Swain, a Vedantist monk who participated in a mushroom velada with Maria Sabina in 1961: "I don't recommend the mushroom to anyone. Even though they are physically harmless, each person responds differently, according to temperament and psychological makeup. For those who seek the hidden depths of the unconscious mind, the possibilities of exploration are unlimited. The variations are endless...If one gives spiritual meaning to these experiences, as the Indians do, the results are far more significant."[7]

Creating Effective Rituals

You might well wonder at this point how one could wisely approach this powerful plant Spirit. Unlike some of the other plant entheogens, ayahuasca and peyote for example, precious little knowledge remains of ancient traditional practices that could provide a general model. There's no readily accessible body of traditional mushroom songs and prayers, and no known "churches" available currently that work with psilocybe mushrooms as their sacrament. Dr. Ralph Metzner, in his 2005 book *Sacred Mushroom of Visions*, described what appears to be a nascent movement, for lack of a better term, among non-Native people to create what he calls "neo-shamanic hybrid rituals." As Metzner noted, one could relatively easily list a number of elements commonly employed in traditional rituals that could be used respectfully in these new formats: "The tendency to hold ceremonies at night, the use of moderate dosages of psychedelics, the ritual format of circles, the presence of a ceremonial leader, and the prolonged use of rhythmic drumming, singing, or dancing."[8] Referring to rituals fitting this description that he himself had participated in, Metzner wrote: "Participants confirm that entheogenic mushroom or plant medicines combined with meditative or therapeutic insight processes amplify awareness and sensitize perception, particularly somatic, emotional, instinctual, and spiritual awareness."[9]

In the discussion of ancient indigenous prophecies which speak about this time, I briefly described the prophecy of the Eagle and the Condor—the vision of the joining of the four directions and the "four races" into a powerful intention and energy. I mentioned earlier how I'd recently heard from an elder of the NAC that there is a vision arising through these connections that ayahuasca, peyote, and iboga are to play an important role in the realization of this vision. I was curious about the exclusion of the psilocybes from this triumvirate, suspecting it may have to do with the lack of a vibrant, living tradition of practice. My hunch was confirmed when I asked the elder about that. His answer was quick and to the point, "There's no container for it."

My personal opinion is that these developing "neo" rituals are tricky waters to negotiate and should be approached with great care, respect, humility, and willingness to listen and learn. Without the foundation of a solid tradition and the guidance of shamans—healers and elders with a long history of experience who themselves were once rigorously trained by someone similar—one should probably be keenly alert to the level of knowledge, experience, maturity, groundedness, and humility of people who would set themselves up as leaders or guides of such rituals. There's a tendency in the brash, impatient modes of modern Westerners, to grab onto isolated chunks of knowledge removed from their traditional cultural and ritual contexts, and quickly declare themselves authorities. Back in the early 1970s—when I was living in the mountains of British Columbia with the countercultural back-to-the-land community trying to learn old survival and homesteading skills from scratch without teachers—there was a saying floating around: "If you've done it once you're an expert." There is clearly reason to question that approach in working with the plants.

Apart from the potential for charlatanism and commodification, there are a couple of problems with attempting to ape or co-opt practices from other cultures. There is usually in these traditional communities a deep understanding of those rituals that is totally unknown to outsiders and neophytes, sometimes reflecting radical differences in worldview. As Wade Davis has pointed out, there is a huge difference in outlook between someone who grew up seeing a mountain as a big rock and someone who grew up seeing a mountain as a living spirit. The use of instruments in rituals is a good example of this difference. I've been told some remarkable stories about the living spirits of drums in native American ritual practice, incredible to the minds of us who were raised in worlds where nature was believed to be "mute"—as the philosopher Jean-Paul Sartre once famously described it.

One Native elder—the wife of an NAC roadman who carries the ancient wisdom lineage of her people and who is unusually attuned to what we would consider non-material energies—told us she had been to a conference in California attended mainly by non-Native women working in healing modalities. Many of the women had brought drums with them, which were placed around the room where discussions were being held. This elder began to hear and feel something unsettling coming from the area of the drums. When she went over to check it out she was drawn to one very large, double-sided ceremonial drum from which a presence was attempting to communicate to her that it was feeling brokenhearted—that no one knew what it was, what it could do, or what kinds of songs were needed to connect with it. This elder later told the assembled group about this and sang a Native spirit song while playing the drum. Many of the women present broke down and wept and at the end of the conference the drum was gifted to this Native woman. An important point about that gift was that she didn't see it in the way we typically see gifts. She felt it as though she was entering a relationship with a powerful responsibility, and she subsequently went to a good deal of trouble to arrange long distance transportation for this large drum and to create a suitable home for it, including a ceremony to welcome it into her community and her home.

The point, of course, is that often people will pick up ideas, practices, and even sacred "power" objects, and use them with barely an inkling of what they're doing. This same elder has spoken to me about how difficult it is for her to sit through NAC ceremonies attended mainly by non-Natives. There are intangible powers being worked with in that environment that can become confused and entangled when people only know the surfaces of the forms. Other Native American people have said that they actually find it insulting and hurtful to see this casual and uninformed co-optation of their ancient sacred practices. I was told a joke by an older Native man after one meeting I attended, about the white fellow who, after sharing a meal with an old Native, said: "Wow, I wish I had your appetite." The old man slowly looked up from his meal and fixed the guy with a steely stare. "Right then, your people have taken everything precious to us . . . and now you want my appetite?"

On the other hand, we're in a very odd time—a transition period between eras—a time when so many of the customs and traditions inherited by modern societies have run out of gas and have broken down; a time of upheaval, confusion, ground-lessness; a time when new forms are being born or are struggling to be born. It may be that for many of us, boldly creative rituals, hopefully guided by Spirit, are the necessary path forward. I hear and read often from masters of the plant relationship that for those able to listen and act, the Spirit of the plant itself will often be the guide. Again, Kanucas has told me a number of times that many of his decisions are a direct response to communication from Grandfather Peyote.

The example of my beloved old Tibetan master Trungpa Rinpoché may also be instructive in regard to an enlightened attitude and approach to creating new ritual forms. In his childhood, Rinpoché was given a thorough grounding in the traditional teachings of the Kagyu lineage of Tibetan Buddhism—under the tutelage of extremely wise and learned elders. He was on a path to become the Supreme Abbott of a group of seven monasteries in Eastern Tibet when the invasion of the Chinese forced many of the lineage holders out of the country. Several years later he was called by Spirit to come to the United States to help develop Buddhism there. In a very short period of time he established a vibrant infrastructure for the practice and study of these teachings.

In the midst of this explosion of activity, he stunned his

students with the announcement that he would be taking a year-long retreat. On his return, Rinpoché told his senior students that he had received instructions during his retreat to set up a new program of teachings. With no direct precedent, he created a body of teachings inspired by the understanding that many people would be interested in the essence of the Buddhist path but not in the larger and sometimes elaborate ritual context of a religion, especially one as complex as Tibetan Vajrayana Buddhism. The basic practice of meditation he had already taught his students remained the same, but he created a small, succinct group of teachings with a less overtly religious tone to them, a different shrine with symbols borrowed from his own and Japanese Buddhist traditions, and a few specific practices that were new though similar in flavor and intent to existing practices. The point of this story is that here was someone who in the first place had a powerful understanding of an authentic tradition, was humble and respectful toward that tradition, was in contact with Spirit and with the Muses, and who was highly creative and not afraid to trust this guidance and his own mind as he created new forms to meet the needs of a new situation.

> Mushrooms are natural teachers. When one is open to them, they will teach the spiritual seeker the lessons that need to be learned.[10]
> *Martin W. Ball, Ph.D.*

For people seeking to explore these pathways to wisdom, Martin Ball has written a very thoughtful, insightful, responsible, and informative handbook called *Mushroom Wisdom*. As is common with experienced explorers of these realms, Ball points out that the many traditional cultures who used these entheogenic plants have almost universally engaged them in ritual contexts that set the intention and provided a safety net and an environment of skill and knowledge about how to negotiate the deep waters that call the supplicant out of the cocoon of the known, out of the territory of the controlling and limiting ego. Ball describes the mushroom as a clear spiritual mirror. In his own words, "I saw how my patterns and illusions affected others, as well as myself, and I saw how I treated others was simply a mirror for how I treated myself. I looked into my heart and I cleaned it out, and when I did, Spirit flowed openly and freely through me."[11]

Throughout the book, Ball comes back to this notion of "cleaning out the heart" so that Spirit can flow freely through. He talks about how there's a direct correlation between the degree of constriction in our hearts and the degree to which we are living in our illusions and not in the light of reality. If we approach them properly—with an open mind, with humility, respect, careful preparation of mental and physical space, and with intention but not expectation—the mushrooms will reliably show us what we need to see and learn in order to dissolve outer, inner, and secret obstacles and open ourselves to connection with the universal source of being.

Seekers are reminded to pay close attention, stay fully present, not judge or resist whatever material arises. Those attitudes again are perfectly in line with the teachings of Buddhism and other deep wisdom lineages. Meditators are admonished to examine—without praise or blame, without pride or disgust—everything that arises in the mind during meditation as well as in the "post-meditation" experience. As Thaddeus Golas put it, "When you learn to love hell you'll be in heaven." At the very end of *The Lazy Man's Guide to Enlightenment*, Golas reminds readers that if they forget everything else they've read in the book, to simply remember these two words when things get intense: "No resistance." Similarly, the advanced work of the Vajrayana path of Tibetan Buddhism involves a process of learning to face, handle, and relax into increasingly powerful energies, thereby transmuting them into wisdom energy.

Martin Ball talks about "the Witness": the importance of

maintaining contact with the part of our awareness that observes the fluctuations, the stormy seas of our minds and the sometimes frightening thoughts and visions that present themselves. In my experience, the concept of the Witness is not about being detached in the conventional sense, removed from experience, but is more about the courage and clarity of attention to enter completely while fully present and awake to all that occurs as it rises into consciousness, endeavoring to keep breathing, keep paying attention, and not to get caught in fear, in "going solid."

There's a classic story about the Buddha immediately before his final, complete enlightenment. There are several versions of this story, sometimes referred to as *The Attack of Mara*, or *The Temptations of Mara*. Mara is the Lord of Death, the personification of evil and temptation. In one standard version, Mara threw everything he had at Gautama as he sat under the Bodhi Tree meditating. He hurled his ferocious armies forward, tried to terrify the Buddha with various demons, threatened him, and presented him with great temptations. When Gautama was able to stare all this down with equanimity, Mara slinked away in despondency and the Buddha's awakening was complete.

It's not hard to understand how important a carefully designed ritual context can be for improving the chances of a beneficial experience in powerful realms like those invoked when we ingest a plant sacrament. Any good help we can get is worth considering. If people are going to engage with mushrooms where there isn't a readily available environment or community of experienced journeyers—and you know a lot of folks are likely to do just that—they would be wise to make sincere attempts to create as much support and protection as possible: studying the literature, coming in with intention, supplicating the spirit of the plant, avoiding food for several hours prior to ingesting, preparing mentally beforehand, meditating, praying, blessing and clearing the physical space, having, at the very least, a sitter, and preferably the guidance of one or more experienced "psilonauts," especially when taking larger doses that can flatten the ego altogether. The feeling of dying, as I've mentioned before, is not at all uncommon as one approaches the threshold, and without some knowledge of that and some way to move through any fear that arises, can provoke panic reactions that sometimes manifest in very distressing ways, leading on occasion even to dangerous behavior and consequences with unwanted repercussions.

The problem, again, with our relationship to the ego—to this separate self that we've created and maintained for our survival in the world as we know it—is that most of us, to a greater or lesser degree, have identified ourselves with this "self"' exclusively and continuously throughout our lives. It can be quite a shock to suddenly come face to face with the fact that there's something else going on, that things are not as we had so vigorously imagined them to be and counted on them to be, that we are not who we thought we were, and that we're in a living environment much vaster and stranger than we've ever conceived of.

Here's a story I heard recently. I'm relating it because it's a variation on a story heard again and again. Fortunately, in this case disaster was averted, but I've certainly heard of situations where it wasn't—where police, hospital, and other authorities became involved. A friend of mine had a collection of Psilocybe cyanescens he'd picked himself. This friend had a little experience with the mushrooms but no real knowledge of these processes under discussion. He invited a small group of his friends over for a mushroom session in a pleasant, casual setting with no ritual context. The doses were apparently moderate, but—at least in the case of one member of the group—definitely strong enough to pull him toward the threshold of ego dissolution. He panicked, thought he was dying, and wanted to be taken to the hospital. My friend had to intervene, making concerted efforts to calm this fellow, even to the point of telling him he would use physical force to restrain him and prevent him from leaving or calling an ambulance. In this case the situation was defused, but it's not always possible to contain someone who's heart is wildly racing and thumping in fear, perhaps convinced he's actually dying.

With these cautions and admonitions in mind, it's also been suggested by Ball and others that people new to the experience begin with small amounts. Though stronger doses can invoke clearer, deeper experiences, a small amount can also be very beneficial for spiritual work. As an ongoing learning and developing process one might then gradually work up to larger amounts. For inexperienced seekers, large doses can be very confusing and overwhelming.

To be more specific about dosage levels, Paul Stamets has recommended one to two grams of dried mushrooms for first timers. He then suggested that once you know yourself better in these situations, as well as the potency of the mushrooms you're using, you might raise that level in subsequent sessions by increments of one gram of dried weight. Each person has to figure that out. Dan and I concluded at the end of our challenging and remarkable day that we would be very cautious about increasing doses. I think we both felt the need to learn more about grounding and opening into the power we encountered at 2.5 to three grams before jumping up the dosage significantly. Around five dried grams is usually considered a dose capable of unleashing the full spectrum of psychoactive effects. According to Stamets, doses much larger than that are approaching amounts too high even for most veterans. He wouldn't recommend to even the most experienced to exceed seven dried grams.

Stamets also points out that there are important variations to consider as well. A person's body size makes a difference, as does one's sensitivity to the effects. He gives an example of one person who can take one to two dried grams and experience effects generally commensurate with three or four times that amount. In another case, a woman ingested five dried grams of reliable material and experienced nothing. A number of factors can affect the potency of mushrooms as well. Potencies range wildly between specific species of Psilocybe. Different growing conditions, the contents of the soil, exposure to sunlight, the maturity of each mushroom, etc. can all have an impact. The main point, of course, being to know yourself and the mushrooms you're dealing with.

I've talked elsewhere about the use of music in association with spiritual practice and in particular accompanying the use of entheogenic sacraments. Repetitive rhythms, droning sounds, and beautiful, heartfelt singing can ground an experience, function as invocations of spirit allies, and, as Martin Ball says, act to "carry messages between the worlds...catapult visionaries into other realms, or help them commune with transpersonal forces and dimensions."[12]

Although, as I pointed out above, precious little knowledge remains of the once widespread ritual use of the sacred mushroom Teonanácatl, there is some ethnographic information available that demonstrates the continuing though often carefully guarded existence of traditional approaches to petitioning the mushroom spirits for healing and awakening work. Perhaps we can learn something useful from the work done by a number of researchers in the twentieth century, possibly triggered by the explorations of Dr. Schultes and Robert J. Weitlaner in the 1930s, and further developed in the 1950s by R. Gordon Wasson and his wife Dr. Valentina Pavlova Wasson, along with others who followed their lead.

As with other sacraments like this, the mushroom was regarded in these traditional contexts as a sacred being. The pervasiveness of the Christian church influenced the language of the indigenous healers and in their veladas they often spoke of the mushrooms as the spirit of Jesus Christ. Typically, a member of the community would petition the local curandera or curandero and request a healing ceremony. It was believed that the mushrooms could only be eaten successfully by a "clean" person and so certain preparations were required, such as sexual abstinence for several days before and after the ceremony. There were also careful practices associated with the gathering of the mushrooms. The ceremonies were often conducted with rituals similar to those employed with other plant sacraments. These might include a shrine with sacred objects, the purification of the space and the sacraments with incenses like copal, and impassioned praying and singing to invoke and direct praise to the mushroom spirit. The veladas sometimes then proceeded in complete darkness or with candlelight. The curandera might continue to pray and sing as the effects of the mushroom come on. If the circumstances and intentions are right, the mushroom spirit may provide information on the problem—indicating required medicines, revealing the sources and causes of social problems, and pointing to the future so that the petitioners may be able to correct behavior.

At our best, we remember to remember that the whole enterprise is about going out from the ego, not about what we can get from the experience but what we can learn, so that we can become more clear, more compassionate, more able to participate intelligently and effectively—at whatever level is available to us—in the healing and uplifting of others and the reclamation of the sacred planet. As the Maya say: much of good living is about giving back to that which gives us life—thanking the air, the earth, and the water that keep us alive day by day, thanking the Spirit or spirits that create and maintain life, and in this case thanking the medicine plant spirit that shared its teachings with us. As the elders say, without this gratitude everything is in danger of withering and dying.

The universe moves in harmony. My spirit moves with it. I feel as though I have become a thread in the fabric of nature and have returned home.[13]

Paul Stamets

24

Other Healing and Awakening Medicines

Although ayahuasca, peyote, and psilocybe mushrooms are among the most powerful and widely-used entheogenic plant medicines available, there are a great many others in the vast pharmacy of the natural world. In writing this book, I considered devoting full chapters to several more of these, but in the end decided against doing this. There are specific reasons for drawing this somewhat arbitrary line on one side or the other of each substance I considered: my own lack of direct experience with some of them; certain dangers and controversies surrounding particular substances which suggest they may not remain or become significant players; a lack of healthy cultural and ritual contexts in some cases; and questions regarding the issue of plants vs. laboratory-generated compounds.

Nonetheless, some of these other substances have too much potential to be ignored completely in a time when it seems we need all the help we can get. What follows is shorter summaries of a few carefully chosen plants and compounds—summaries that will, I hope, stimulate fresh perspectives and provide jumping-off points for those interested in exploring these avenues more deeply.

Iboga and Ibogaine

Iboga is the name given to a shrub that grows in equatorial West

Africa. Though not well-known outside of that region, this plant medicine has a long history of human use, particularly as a tool for psychological and spiritual healing. Ibogaine, its primary psychoactive alkaloid, was isolated in 1889 and has in recent decades been shown to have remarkable benefits of its own, especially in the treatment of addiction.

In West Africa, iboga is most often used as a sacrament of initiation in the Bwiti religion. Bwiti is a widely accepted and officially recognized religion in Gabon and in recent decades has spread to several neighboring countries. Like the ayahuasca using churches and the NAC, Bwiti is also described as a syncretic religion, combining elements of traditional indigenous beliefs and rituals with those of Christianity. It's interesting to note that Bwiti is considered a universal religion by its members, open to anyone of sincere intention.

In most cases, Bwiti initiates only ingest a significant quantity of the medicine once in their lives. People experienced both with other entheogens and with iboga have said that there are some significant differences. First, the direct psychoactive effects may last several days in the Bwiti initiation and thirty hours or more with ibogaine in a clinical setting. It's been described as a rough ride, both physically and mentally. Second, iboga is said to focus the journeyer very definitely and powerfully toward a direct encounter with her own unconscious—toward the specific, unresolved contents of her own library of memories.

In a properly prepared and guided ritual environment, the spirit of the plant has been described as ruthlessly compassionate in showing you what you need to see. Numerous people have said that at a certain point in the journey, it's as though a movie screen was erected in front of them and they were shown where they were wounded and went wrong in their lives as well as what they needed to do to correct the problems. In the Bwiti religion, they speak of iboga as a living spirit whose intention is to clean you out and remake you as a real person—an initiated person.

There are now plentiful sources of good information about iboga and ibogaine, both online and in books, such as *Iboga: The Visionary Root of African Shamanism* (2007) by Ravalec, Paicheler, and Mallendi. Issue 76, from 2008, of *Shaman's Drum* magazine also has several very informative articles on iboga. If you do a little research, a name you're likely to encounter is that of Howard Lotsof, who is credited by many as having introduced the Western world to ibogaine's uncanny ability to break patterns of addiction and who has long advocated for its legal use. In fact, Lotsof holds the worldwide patent for ibogaine. According to Lotsof: "The suffering that could be eliminated by ibogaine availability would be staggering, both to the individual and to society."[1]

A significant and growing body of evidence indicates that there is simply no other treatment for addiction in the canon of Western medicine that comes remotely close to the effectiveness of properly administered ibogaine therapy. Ibogaine has been called the "anti-drug drug" because of its demonstrated ability to completely knock out the craving for addictive substances like heroin, methadone, cocaine, crack, methedrine (crystal meth), alcohol—and in some studies—even nicotine.

Just as with the iboga plant itself in the Bwiti rituals, ibogaine then leads "patients" through a powerful self-examination process. They're shown the root causes and the destructiveness of their drug use and are granted an unprecedented opportunity to make radical changes in their lives. In almost all cases, ibogaine eliminates the drug craving for a period of several weeks. This is said to be the window of opportunity for addicts to engage in a process of reclaiming the will to live—of relearning the art of living. For this reason, it's more or less universally agreed that careful follow-up and counseling are necessary, especially in those first few weeks. For those interested, an internet search will uncover quite a few clinics that legally offer programs of ibogaine therapy (though unfortunately— and unsurprisingly—not in the U.S.)

Given this bold claim for the efficacy of ibogaine, you might wonder why it hasn't already been recognized and accepted as a pharmaceutical medicine in the West. In the specific case of ibogaine, that story would be much too long to relate here. I suspect you could make a few educated guesses however—such as the scientific and political establishments' superstitious resistance to anything that hints of mind-manifesting powers, as well as the lack of financial motivation to approve a drug that has been shown to heal patients with as little as a single dosage.

I mentioned earlier how Kanucas told me one morning after a meeting that he and others have received a vision in which ayahuasca, peyote, and iboga are to play lead roles in the awakening journey on Earth. One aspect of the vision for the central role to be played by these three sacred plants is that their growing influence will come out of the sharing of the knowledge of their traditional practitioners, and that in this way the hidebound, exceedingly slow-moving world of medical/scientific officialdom may be largely bypassed. Visions reported by Bwiti elders seem to confirm this and according to ethnobotanist Giorgio Samorini, there is among Bwitists "widespread hope that the white man will become more familiar with Bwiti."[2]

One way or another, I think it's safe to say that iboga is an extremely useful plant—truly one of the "Master Plants." We're likely to be hearing much more about it in the coming years.

Salvia Divinorum

She will take who you are and run away with it faster than any plant I know.
Dale Pendell

Out of body experiences, time travel, voices, contact with

entities, transforming into other beings and objects, complete loss of contact with consensual reality—you would be forgiven for thinking we're closer to the realm of science fiction here than to the effects of a plant. I have two reasons for drawing attention to this highly unusual plant however. The first is that since it's available and legal in many places, people considering using it should know how powerful and unpredictable it can be. Kathleen Harrison has passed on a concern from the people she knows in Mexico who have used it traditionally. They told her that some people don't completely come back from the extreme experiences that Salvia divinorum can carry one into. I hope that that little piece of information in itself will cause you to think very seriously before casually taking this plant

The second reason for briefly addressing Salvia is that if used skillfully by people capable of handling it, it is—according to people like Ms. Harrison and others experienced with its use—a true healing plant, ready to help sincere petitioners. Though the modern cultures have much to learn about the safe and effective use of this and other healing and awakening plant medicines, Salvia may be able to play a beneficial role in the years ahead. Because of its availability, a respectful learning process may also act as a link to worldviews addressed throughout this book which may be able to help us turn back toward natural wisdom.

Salvia divinorum—sage of the diviners—is indeed an extraordinary and unique plant. A member of the mint family, it's unique among entheogens in that it contains no alkaloids. Salvinoran A, the primary active substance, is a diterpene and is not chemically related to any other psychoactive plant or drug. Its natural habitat is in the mountains of the Mexican state of Oaxaca, where it has a long and carefully guarded history as a sacred medicine, primarily among the Mazatec Indians of the mountainous Sierra Madre Oriental in the northeast corner of the state. It's said that the healers of the region consulted the "leaves of the shepherdess" when it was necessary to travel to the realms of the spirits to discover the cause of and obtain assistance for a patient's problem.

Also unlike other powerful entheogens, Salvia divinorum is legal in most countries. At this time, however, it's being scrutinized much more carefully, and there is every possibility that it may soon be made illegal in countries such as the U.S., where it may even be dumped into Schedule One of the Controlled Substances Act. If that happens, we can thank both the usual ill-informed fear and control machinations of lawmakers and opinion leaders as well as some irresponsible behavior on the part of people who have attempted to treat Salvia as a thrill drug. For example, some have posted YouTube videos of themselves driving while under its influence. Anyone familiar with Salvia's effects knows that is an extremely dangerous thing to do.

In traditional contexts, the usual method of intake is by chewing relatively large quantities of the fresh leaf. The active substances enter the bloodstream through the oral mucosa so easily accessed in the front of the mouth. The two most common methods of intake in the non-indigenous world are either through smoking the dried leaf—usually fortified with the addition of Salvinoran A—or by using the tincture method, where an eye dropper is used to place a concentrated liquid form of the plant in the front of the mouth.

With smoked Salvia, the onset of effects is almost immediate and the peak of the experience may be over within five minutes or so. With the tincture method, onset may take ten to fifteen minutes and the peak period may last upwards of an hour. In both methods, the effects can range from subtle and gentle to the kinds of astonishing experiences listed above. At the very least, an experienced guide or sitter is recommended. At the upper end of effects, journeyers can experience complete loss of body consciousness—driving is definitely not on the list of recommended activities.

My own limited experiences with the smoked leaf and the

tincture have clearly confirmed both the concerns about safety and the stunning power of the plant. When the full effects kick in—quite suddenly with the smoked leaf—I'm quickly reminded how real the experience feels. At that point the thought "This is not to be trifled with" comes immediately to mind. The following story is not at all untypical. It was recounted to me one day by a young man who said he had smoked Salvia at night with some friends at a campground on the edge of the forest. This fellow suddenly found himself staring, eyes open, at a completely realistic scene. He described it as the "Gates of Death" and said that he was being pulled toward them. At that point, he shrieked in terror, jumped up, and began to run into the pitch-black forest, where, fortunately, he was tackled by his friends before he could hurt himself.

As with most, if not all, other entheogenic, visionary plants, the best circumstances for encountering the spirit of Salvia divinorum include a quiet, protected environment, knowledge, respect, prayer, intention-setting—and ideally—the guidance of an experienced healer with an open conduit to the spirit of the plant. As Kathleen Harrison described it: "The plant spirit is a persona, to be honored, solicited, and thanked for its gifts."[4] Many now understand that plants like this can invoke the direct assistance of powerful, compassionate spirits who are more than willing to help us heal and wake up.

We don't know what the future holds for Salvia. One possible limitation, as is the case with a number of other entheogens, is the current lack of a living tradition to which "moderns" have easy access. If Salvia divinorum is to be an ally in the emerging sacred reality on our planet, the plea must go out—especially to the young, to those on the wave of the future—to treat this plant with the utmost respect, to gain as much knowledge as possible, to engage it responsibly so that the blessings of the leaves can spread wisely and elegantly and the danger of criminalization can be minimized. There's no shortage of information available through numerous discussion groups and excellent websites like The Salvia divinorum Research and Information Center (sagewisdom.org), The Vaults of Erowid (erowid.org), and The Lycaeum (lycaeum.org.) I'll close with these words from Dale Pendell:

> We are not different from the plant.
> It is we who must save the gods.
> It is we who must be diviners.[5]

Cannabis

You might well question the inclusion of cannabis in this section. It certainly has a stained reputation in the current cultural environment. Much of that reputation, of course, comes from its ready availability and the careless recreational use we so often see. Unfortunately, the trivialization of cannabis as a recreational commodity has obscured for most people the fact that this plant has an ancient history in many parts of the planet as a valuable medicinal and spiritual ally.

Archaeological evidence of cannabis' relationship with humans extends back to the Neolithic Era. Pipes, hemp seeds, and other related paraphernalia have been found buried with shamans—one find in Germany estimated at 5500 BCE. Ancient Chinese texts make clear and frequent reference to cannabis, as do writings from Japan, India, Tibet, Mesopotamia, ancient Greece, Scythia, Assyria, and Egypt, as well as the religious traditions of Hinduism, Buddhism, Zoroastrianism, and Sufism—to name only a few. Solid scholarship supports these assertions. For much greater detail on that history take a look, for example, at Dr. Christian Rätsch's book *Marijuana Medicine*, or Rowan Robinson's *The Great Book of Hemp*.

It is simply not possible to evaluate the potential of cannabis as a spiritual medicine based on the casual use with which most people are familiar. As with several other entheogens, the experiential difference between this kind of use and a conducive ritual set and setting is like night and day. If you can silence the noise in your head and bring your total attention to bear in a meditative environment—admittedly not an easy thing to do for many—cannabis has the ability to draw you deeply into the moment in a process of ego dissolution. As Terence McKenna put it: "There is no doubt that when used occasionally in a context of ritual and culturally reinforced expectation of a transformation of consciousness, cannabis is capable of nearly the full spectrum of psychedelic effects associated with hallucinogens."[6]

There still exist numerous historical records of the spiritual use of cannabis. Here are a few particularly interesting examples. The word "tantra" means "that which is woven together" and has multiple and complex practices associated with its name. Tantric practices involving cannabis appeared around the seventh century CE, in what Michael R. Aldrich describes as "an explosive mingling of the doctrines and practices of Shaivite Hinduism and Tibetan Buddhism."[7] The Mahanirvana Tantra— the most important text available in English on these practices— was composed in the eleventh century and is apparently still consulted today.

In an article titled *Tantric Cannabis Use in India*, Aldrich devotes several pages to describing the elaborate sequence of fasting, meditation, prayer, offerings, purifications and other ritual preparations that led to the drinking of "bhang" by a male *sadhaka* and a female *sadhaki*, both expected to be well-trained in meditation and yogic practices. The purpose of this ritual was to create the ideal set and setting for a highly energized commingling of male and female energies in a process of total release from the bounds of the self into mahanirvana—"great liberation."

As with India and Hinduism, the cannabis plant is deeply entwined with the history of Arabic cultures. The Sufis, considered the inner—or esoteric—tradition within Islam, are credited with knowledge of a number of sacred plants. The Sufis have been with us for over a thousand years, and though they are not known today for their use of cannabis, evidence indicates that it has in the past played an important role in their spiritual practices. A famous Sufi poet, Fuzuli (1498-1556) proclaimed that "hashish is the Sufi master himself."[8]

The most visible and unambiguous example of the spiritual use of cannabis in what could be called a religious context today must be the Rastafarians of Jamaica. The plant is central to Rasta culture and is widely used nutritionally, medicinally, and spiritually. Rastafarianism was founded in the 1930s, with roots going back to Africa and even influences from India. Indentured laborers were brought to Jamaica in the mid-nineteenth century and at least two of the Rasta words for cannabis—*ganga* and *kali*—have distinct Indian etymology. "Herb" is the central sacrament for Rastas. In Rowan Robinson's words, "They believe that smoking cannabis in a ritual manner cleanses both body and mind, preparing the user for meditation, prayer, the reception of wisdom, reasoning, and communal harmony with others, a central value for Rastas."[9]

I recently met Leonore, a Oaxacan Indian shaman—or curandera—from Mexico, who told me that in her tradition, cannabis is one of a number of plants that are used occasionally as part of the healing work. One of Leonore's patients, Rosaria, recounted that during the five years of her work with Leonore, cannabis was used once, about two years into the work. Rosaria told me that she had never smoked cannabis herself prior to that day and that the experience was extremely powerful and beneficial. In a description that reminded me of encounters with entheogens such as ayahuasca, peyote, and iboga, Rosaria said that the plant spirit showed her visions of her life, shone a light on the problems she had been working through with Leonore, and instructed her on where to go from there.

There's one final reference I'd like to share with you. The

Indian Hemp Drugs Commission Report of 1893-1894 is considered, in the words of Abel Zug, "the most authentic government sponsored search for the truth about Cannabis ever. It has never been equaled or surpassed in its accuracy, equanimity and honesty."[10] This extensive and outstanding document of ethnobotanical and cultural research made unequivocally clear both the harmlessness of cannabis and its numerous therapeutic benefits. A quote from J.M. Campbell in the report serves to put an exclamation point on this—and almost as an aside cautions us again on the folly of careless use:

> God has granted you the privilege of knowing the secret of these leaves. Thus when you eat it, your dense worries may disappear and your exalted minds may become polished.... In the ecstasy of bhang the spark of the eternal in man turns into light the murkiness of matter or illusion and the self is lost in the central soul fire. The devotee who drinks bhang partakes of the god Shiva. We drank bhang and the mystery I am he, grew plain.... He who drinks bhang wisely and according to rule, be he ever so low, is Shiva. He who drinks bhang foolishly or for pleasure without religious rites is as guilty as the sinner of lakhs (100,000's) of sins.

Honorable Mention

Although they are very controversial to many, there are two other healing allies I feel obligated to acknowledge. The first is LSD. This substance is so strongly associated, in the minds of many, with illegal, irresponsible and even dangerous behavior, that it's easy to ignore the fact that until 1966 it was a legal drug which had been subjected to many hundreds of studies and employed with stunning successes in sanctioned clinical therapeutic environments.

Again, similar to other entheogens, in ideal conditions of set and setting LSD has the potential to usher people through the gateway of ego's dissolution into realms of direct, powerful healing information and astonishing noetic realities. Stanislav Grof, a Czech psychiatrist who immigrated to the U.S. in the 1960s and is still a leading spokesman for the power of entheogens, employed LSD in over a thousand therapeutic interventions before it was made illegal. Many professionals were discovering that it uncovered material which was otherwise very difficult to access, and which, in the right hands, could lead to resolution of apparently intractable psychological problems.

Although, as Terence McKenna pointed out, the Sixties were to a large degree "misplayed"—millions used LSD and other entheogens sloppily and in some cases damage was done—we can't ignore the fact that a great many people encountered information that was buried in the dominant cultures and which provoked radical alterations in their worldviews.

And although it may seem to be of the past, there is actually still advocacy work being done on behalf of LSD by serious, responsible professionals. I bring it up in this context for that reason. There is a case to be made that, given the opportunity for further study, LSD may again be allowed a careful re-entry into the dialogue on healing medicines and modalities.

There is one further substance that deserves to at least be honored for what it has done for people in the best conditions, as well as in the hope that it be granted further sanctioned research and perhaps added into the healing canon. That is MDMA, popularly known as Ecstasy. With all the bad press it's received over the years, I don't know how many people are aware that for several years—from about 1976 until 1985, when it was first placed into Schedule One— MDMA was legal and was rapidly developing a reputation as a remarkable tool in therapy. Over four hundred therapists in California alone were using it safely and effectively with their patients.

I can't possibly do MDMA justice in this short essay. For those interested, I recommend Dr. Julie M. Holland's excellent and thorough book *Ecstasy: The Complete Guide*. There are, however, a few points I could mention that might bring new information to some readers and may stimulate curiosity. First, MDMA is not a hallucinogen. It's been called an "empathogen," meaning "to create an empathetic state." When administered in carefully controlled therapeutic environments, MDMA can elicit experiences ranging from the level of "a gentle invitation to insight"— as Dr. Lester Grinspoon termed it— to, with stronger doses, feelings of strengthened self-image and acceptance, intense love for oneself and others, and even blissful feelings of unity with the whole of life.

Post-Traumatic Stress Disorder (PTSD) provides an excellent example of how MDMA can be of great therapeutic benefit. PTSD has proven to be a particularly difficult condition to resolve in therapy. A respected theory states that the emotional and physical impact of the original trauma becomes locked away in the lower brain centers such as the limbic system, from where— because of the intense pain and fear connected to the memories— the material is inaccessible through most therapeutic techniques. To be resolved, the memories need to be released, seen, and verbalized. MDMA does exactly this. It triggers the release of the memories while simultaneously knocking aside the powerful fear that could otherwise re-traumatize the person or cause her to push any threatening material back into the unconscious. Based on several reports of success with PTSD during that brief period of legal therapeutic work, a number of medical professionals are currently working toward getting approval for further studies using MDMA with patients suffering from PTSD.

There's no doubt that MDMA can be harmful and even dangerous if abused. Because it's illegal, there is, of course, no control over the quality/purity of product, the mental and physical condition of those ingesting it, or the environments in which people are experiencing it. The record shows that, despite the harm that can result from this kind of uncontrolled use, MDMA holds enough promise that it should be given the chance to prove itself through a very careful reintroduction into legitimate scientific investigation.

I have ingested MDMA twice, using material that came to me from a trusted, experienced source. I took it alone, in a quiet, protected environment. Based on that minimal experience, my opinion is that it does indeed open the heart and promote clear thinking and insight. In some respects though, it struck me as a kind of less organic version of peyote. It felt rougher, and where the effects of peyote usually leave a very positive and gentle resonance for several days after a ceremony, MDMA left me feeling somewhat physically depleted for a couple of days. That kind of effect has been reported elsewhere as well, despite the fact that powerful heart opening experiences with MDMA have sometimes left users with a euphoric afterglow for weeks. Much evidence suggests that MDMA should be taken very infrequently. Peyote, on the other hand, can be eaten with great frequency and only seems to enhance one's spiritual and physical health.

Although there very well may be a place for substances like LSD and MDMA in the work ahead, I think it's for reasons like the above that I was motivated to limit my discussion of laboratory synthesized chemical compounds in the overall context of the goals of this book. Many of those experienced with entheogens—and this is the school of thought I lean toward—have suggested that nature is a far better chemist than we are; that there are spirits that can be contacted through the ingestion of plants; and that, in general, this is where we should place greater focus, rather than toward the laboratory.

As a final point on MDMA—and at the risk of appearing to contradict myself on the issue of laboratory vs. natural—I want to draw attention to the work of Rick Doblin and MAPS

(Multidisciplinary Association for Psychedelic Studies at www.maps.org.) Dr. Doblin has made it his life's work to gain legitimacy for the use of some highly beneficial healing and awakening substances. He too is aware of the limits of a compound like MDMA, but has wisely chosen to use it as the advance guard. As I understand it, there are a couple of key reasons for this. It's reliably reproducible in the laboratory and so not subject to unpredictable fluctuations in potency and quality. Perhaps more importantly, MDMA has shown remarkable promise in addressing some very particular problems that have been recognized by many in the professional medical community. In this case I'm referring to the above mentioned PTSD.

Dr. Doblin's approach seems to be working and holds great promise for the future of entheogens and empathogens. As of this writing, MAPS has received government approval in several countries to proceed with real-world clinical trials using MDMA in conjunction with psychotherapy to help people overcome PTSD. I believe this work deserves much support.

To summarize this whole section on the use of plants in healing and awakening work, I'll reiterate the point that—as increasing numbers of people in all walks of life now realize—we are indeed in rapidly changing and difficult times and it behooves us to consider all avenues of awakening. When used wisely, plants like the ones discussed here have the potential to radically reconnect many of us to ourselves and to the Gaian mind.

Dennis McKenna's statement, "we work for the plants" keeps coming back to me. We're being called. As Dr. McKenna put it, the blunt message coming through the plants to those open and courageous enough to listen clearly and enter the dialogue is: "Wake up monkeys, you're really screwing things up."[12]

True as it is, that might be a hard-edged way of expressing the point in the final section of a book whose author proclaimed on the very first page in the introduction that we need hope, we need a vision, and we need to believe in "the possibility of possibility." Perhaps the information could also be translated along the lines of: "The time remaining to clean up the mess and redirect the impetus of human activity is extremely short dear monkeys. We know who you are and what your potential is, so do it now while you still can." And here I want to emphasize again: the stark reminders of the crisis at hand and the exhortations to be bold and open in our explorations of the means to awaken come from the visions of those with a deep love for the Earth and for creation altogether. Despite abundant evidence of monkey madness on this planet, the guides, teachers, and midwives—in all their guises—continue to remind us that the awakened state forever remains the primordial, unconditioned, indestructible, and accessible reality at the core of every human being.

In Conclusion

I want to stress one last time these two powerful words, "hope" and "vision." As I write these final lines it's still too soon to tell what events are staring down at us from the near future. Thinkers and experts from numerous disciplines, and this is my own intuition as well, have suggested that what we're seeing now is a build-up of forces—environmental, political, economic, social— which may burst forth with unexpected speed and impact in the next several years. So many facets of our existence on the planet feel fragile and ominous right now. Without an enlightened vision and the hope that the vision is achievable, I fear that many will fall into despair and hopelessness. It appears that life on Earth is about to become very different, and if that is so, we're going to need all the inspiration and encouragement we can get.

In my own "audacity of hope," I'm unilaterally volunteering myself here to speak on behalf of all of us who are on paths to awakening, on behalf of the ancestors, on behalf of the guides and protectors, and on behalf of the living Gaian mind. And what I first wish to express from that audacity is a simple thank you to readers who have come this far. Thank you for following me and all my mentors and co-conspirators down this little garden path for awhile. I hope from my heart that you've found information in this book that helps clarify your understanding and that encourages you, energizes you, provokes you to look further, to deepen your practice, and to strengthen your commitment to waking up for the benefit of all.

As I've attempted, with sincere intention, to shine some light

on what could be the central concern of our time, my understanding may in places have been incomplete or imbalanced in
emphasis—and really, does anybody down here on the ground
truly know what's going to happen to Mother Earth and her
children?

Even so, it's a good vision. There is such a thing as the real
way—the unconditioned way, the Dharma, the Tao, the Kingdom
of the awakened heart. Despite the shocking misunderstanding
that has cast a thick blanket of illusion and suffering across so
much of the historical experience, we are still awake by nature,
Buddha by nature, sparks of the eternal Creator. And maybe,
having run out of all other options, having run the materialist
illusion into the ground, enough of us will turn our heads, turn
our hearts, turn our inner ears, toward the whispering voices on
the wind—and in the uniting of the four directions, rouse
enough clarity, energy, and compassion so that the prayer and
the vision proclaimed in the ancient prophecies and nurtured in
the hearts of the seekers, the initiates, and "those who care for
us" will finally take its rightful and long-awaited seat on this
beloved planet. Aho.

Notes

Chapter 1: In the Time of Crisis and Transformation

1. Bernadette Rebienot, *Grandmothers Tell Us Your Wisdom*, worldpulsemagazine.com.
2. Terence McKenna, The Archaic Revival, 160.
3. Shunryu Suzuki, *Zen Mind, Beginner's Mind*, 21.
4. Dhyani Ywahoo, *Voices of Our Ancestors: Cherokee Teachings from the Wisdom Fire*, 134.
5. Padmasambhava, *Words for Reflection*, globalsourcenetwork.org/tibet_reflections.
6. Hopi Prophecy, *Which is the One True Religion* by Greg M. Schwartz, kentnewsnet.com/media/storage/paper867/news/2005/04/07/Opinion/Which.Is.The.One.True.Religion-1516746.
7. Carl Johan Calleman, *The Mayan Calendar and the Transformation of Consciousness*, p.xix.
8. Barbara Tedlock, *The Woman in the Shaman's Body*, 6.
9. Edward Benton-Banai, *The Mishomis Book: the Voice of the Ojibway*, the7thfire.com/7thfire.
10. Willaru Huaytu, labyrinthia.com/prophecy.
11. Frank Waters, *Book of the Hopi*, welcomehome.org.
12. Calleman, 140.
13. Ibid., 218.
14. Ken Carey, Vision, p. viii.
15. Ibid., 8.
16. Carey, *The Moment of Quantum Awakening*, awakening-healing.com.
17. Eckhart Tolle, *A New Earth*, 127.

18. Willaru Huaytu, labyrinthia.com.
19. William Blake,
    geocities.com/Athens/Acropolis/2216/clsctexts/
    Intro_Articles/Blake— Painter_Poet_and_Mystic
20. Terence McKenna, *Food of the Gods*, 254.
21. Ella Deloria, quoted in The Spirit of Indian Women, Judith Fitzgerald and Michael Oren Fitzgerald, ed., 114.
22. Martín Prechtel, *Secrets of the Talking Jaguar*, 212-213.
23. Ibid., 97-98.
24. Wallace Black Elk, *The Sacred Ways of a Lakota*, 17.

Chapter 2: When the Grandmothers Speak . . .

1. Ani DiFranco, interviewed by David Swick, *Shambhala Sun*, Nov. 2006.
2. Dalia Herminia Yanes, *Mothers of Our Nations* (DVD), directed by Dr. Dawn Martin-Hill.
3. James Mellaart, *Catal Hyuk: A Neolithic Town in Anatolia*, 181.
4. Charles Eastman (Ohiyesa), *Light on the Indian World*, 13.
5. Edward Edinger, from *2012: The Return of Quetzalcoatl*, by Daniel Pinchbeck, 143.
6. Prechtel, *Long Life, Honey in the Heart*, 363.
7. Steven T. Katz, *The Holocaust in Historical Context Vol. 1*, 438-439.
8. Megisi, *The Spirit of Indian Women*, 113.
9. Julietta Casimiro, *Global Women's Gathering* (cd) 2004.
10. Bernadette Rebienot, sacredstudies.org.
11. Flordemayo, *Global Women's Gathering*.
12. forthenext7generations.com.
13. Flordemayo, *Global Women's Gathering*.
14. *Global Women's Gathering*.

Chapter 3: We Speak on the Basis of Our Visions

1. Wallace Black Elk. 14.
2. Katsi Cook, *Mothers of Our Nations* (DVD).

3. Akushti Butuna Karijuna, *Intelligence in Nature,* by Jeremy Narby, 33.
4. Ronald Wright, *Stolen Continents* 322.
5. Bernadette Rebienot, *Global Women's Gathering.*
6. Grandmother Sarah Smith, *Fire on the Mountain* DVD.

Chapter 4: Come Together

1. Ani DiFranco, *Shambhala Sun,* Nov. 2006.
2. Sam Harris, *The End of Faith: Religion, Terror, and the Future of Reason,* 214.
3. Calleman, 87.
4. David R. Loy, *The Great Awakening,* 29.
5. *Wikipedia.*
6. Thaddeus Golas, *The Lazy Man's Guide to Enlightenment,* 109.
7. Chief Seattle, from *Hallucinogens,* ed. by Charles S. Grob.
8. Carl Jung, *Memories, Dreams, Reflections,* 303.
9. Richard Tarnas, *Cosmos and Psyche: Intimations of a New World View,* 50.
10. McKenna, *Food of the Gods,* 251.
11. Christopher M. Bache, *Dark Night, Early Dawn,* 20.
12. Neil Young, *Don't Let it Bring You Down* (a song on the album *After the Goldrush*).

Chapter 5: Putting the Art Pedal to the Metal

1. Daniel Ladinsky, *The Gift,* 3.
2. Sister Veronica Brady, *Art and Spirituality,* ru.org/brady.
3. Rickie Lee Jones, *Songwriters on Songwriting,* by Paul Zollo, 479,480.
4. Martin Buber, *Art and Spirituality,* ru.org/brady.
5. Bob Dylan, *Songwriters on Songwriting,* 72.
6. David Crosby, *Ibid.,* 377.
7. Louis Perez, *Ibid.,* 562.
8. Chögyam Trungpa, *The Art of Calligraphy: Joining Heaven & Earth,* 17, 18.

9. William Blake, *The Poetry and Prose of William Blake*, p.144.

10. Freddy Silva, lovely.clara.net/education.

11. Walter Pater, allgreatquotes.com/art_quotes11.

12. Lawrence Ferlinghetti, poem "I Am Waiting" from *A Coney Island of the Mind*.

13. Terence McKenna, *The Archaic Revival*, 66.

14. William Blake, David V. Erdman, Harold Bloom, *The Complete Poetry and Prose of William Blake*, 273.

15. Chögyam Trungpa, *Ibid.*, p. 19.

Chapter 7: The Universe is Alive

1. Richard Tarnas, *Cosmos and Psyche*, 41.

2. Terence McKenna, deoxy.org/t_quotes. (no original Terence source given).

3. Thaddeus Golas, 101.

4. Prechtel, *Secrets of the Talking Jaguar*, 282.

5. Ralph Metzner, *Shaman's Drum*, #51, 1999.

6. Tarnas, 486.

7. Bache, 4.

Chapter 9: Slipping Out of the Chains of Fear

1. Ken Carey, *Vision*, 17.

2. Golas, 94.

Chapter 10: Worry>Boredom>Silence

1. Chögyam Trungpa, *The Art of Calligraphy*, 17.

2. Loy, 164.

3. Jelaluddin Rumi, *Masnavi Book 1* (rumi.org.uk/poems).

4. Suzuki, 47.

Chapter 11: Without Goal

1. Roshi Bernie Glassman, *Shambhala Sun*, July 2006.

2. Loy, 177.

Chapter 12: The Worst Horse
1. Suzuki, 38.
2. Suzuki, 36.

Chapter 13: Humble Accomplishment
1. Leonard Cohen, *The Future*, from the album *The Future*.

Chapter 14: Time and the Eternal Now
1. Suzuki, 29.
2. McKenna, *The Archaic Revival*, 94.
3. Prechtel, *Secrets of the Talking Jaguar*, 211.
4. Carl Jung, *Memories, Dreams, Reflections*, 296.
5. Calleman, 217.
6. Eckhart Tolle, *A New Earth*, 207
7. Richard Wagner, *Parsifal*.
8. Bob Dylan, *Buckets of Rain*, from the album *Blood on the Tracks*, 1975.
9. McKenna, 64.

Chapter 15: If You Meet the Buddha on the Road
1. Prechtel, 85.
2. Charles Eastman (Ohiyesa), *Light on the Indian World*, 28.
3. Wright, 101.
4. Golas, 110
5. McKenna, 12.
6. Walt Whitman, *Song of the Open Road*.
7. Eduardo Caldéron Palomino, *Shaman's Drum*, #69, 2005.
8. Wright, 94.
9. Carey, 12.
10. Ywahoo, 88.

Chapter 16: You Came Here to Get Strong
1. en.wikipedia.org/wiki/Tummo.
2. en.wikipedia.org/wiki/Tummo.

3. Wallace Black Elk, 47-48.
4. Black Elk, 49.

Introduction to Part 3

1. Susan Littlehawk, in conversation with the author
2. Calleman, 217.

Chapter 18: Nothing Happens Next

1. Ywahoo, 68.
2. James Joyce, *Finnegan's Wake*, (quoted in McKenna, 93).
3. Chögyam Trungpa, *The Collected Works of Chögyam Trungpa*, Vol.2, 317
4. Leonard Cohen, *Anthem*, from the album *The Future*.
5. Suzuki, 47.

Chapter 19: A Channel Between Voice and Presence

1. Agnes Pilgrim, worldpulsemagazine.com/issues/2/ grand-mothers_tell_us_your_wisdom.
2. Prechtel, 117.
3. Philip K. Dick, *Valis*, 41.
4. Jelaluddin Rumi, *Unseen Rain: Quatrains of Rumi*, translations by John Moyne and Coleman Barks, 25.
5. McKenna, 60.
6. Stephen Harold Buhner, *Shaman's Drum*, #75, 2007.
7. High Hollow Horn, a prayer in *The Sacred Pipe*, ed. Joseph Epes Brown, 12.
8. *geocities.com/redroadcollective/SacredTobacco.*
9. Betty Stockbauer, *lightinfo.org*.
10. Black Elk, Brown, 6.

Chapter 20: Through the Looking Glass

1. Claudio Naranjo, *1993 Psychedelic Summit*, San Francisco.
2. Ralph Metzner, *The Archaic Revival* (McKenna), 56.
3. Ralph Metzner, in Grob. 181.

4. Tom Robbins, *Fierce Invalids Home from Hot Climates*, 33
5. Jeremby Narby, *Intelligence in Nature*, 34
6. Harpignies, 45.
7. Kathleen Harrison, Ibid., 103.
8. Vincent Ravalec, *Iboga: The Visionary Root of African Shamanism*, 49.
9. Kathleen Harrison, *Roads Where There Have Long Been Trails*, terrain.org
10. *The Peyote Cult*, by Weston La Barre, 95.
11. Ravalec, 48
12. Guy Mount, *The Peyote Book: A Study of Native Medicine*, 15.

Chapter 21: Vine of the Soul

1. Alex Polari de Alverga, *Forest of Visions*, p. xxxi.
2. Grob, 190.
3. Benny Shanon, *The Antipodes of the Mind*, 61.
4. Ibid., 309.
5. de Alverga, p.xxxi.
6. de Alverga, 156.

Chapter 22: Heart of the Great Spirit

1. Albert Hensley, *Cleansing the Doors of Perception: The Religious Significance of Entheogenic Plants and Chemicals,*by Huston Smith, 117.
2. Nancy Littlefish, NAC elder, in conversation with the author.
3. Weston La Barre, *The Peyote Cult*, 110
4. Ibid, 110,111
5. Huston Smith, *One Nation Under God: The Triumph of the Native American Church*, 128.
6. La Barre, 71.
7. Aurelio Diaz Tekpankalli, *Fire on the Mountain* DVD.
8. Reuben Snake, *One Nation Under God*, 20.
9. Patricia Mousetail Russell, *One Nation Under God*, 39.
10. Virginia C. Trenholm, *One Nation Under God*, 40.

11. Sun Bear, *The Peyote Book*, by Guy Mount, 62.

Chapter 23: Teonanácatl

1. R. Gordon Wasson, *Entheogens and the Future of Religion*, (ed. Robert Forte), 97.
2. Wade Davis, Harpignies, 51.
3. Paul Stamets, Ibid, 138.
4. Terence McKenna, Ibid, 60.
5. Paul Stamets, Ibid, 139.
6. Kathleen Harrison, Ibid, 128
7. Frederick Swain, in *Sacred Mushroom of Visions*, Ralph Metzner ed., 207.
8. Ralph Metzner, Ritual Approaches to Working with Sacred Medicine Plants, Shaman's Drum #51, 1999, 15-21.
9. Ralph Metzner, *Sacred Mushrooms of Vision*, 45.
10. Martin W. Ball, *Mushroom Wisdom*, 11.
11. Ibid., 114.
12. Ibid., 140.
13. Paul Stamets, *Psilocybin Mushrooms of the World*, 44.

Chapter 24: Other Healing and Awakening Medicines

1. Howard Lotsof, *Howard Lotsof speaks about ibogaine*, video, found at *youtube.com*.
2. Giorgio Samorini, *The Bwiti Religion and the psychoactive plant Tabernanthe iboga* (Equatorial Africa), originally published in *Integration*, 5: 105-114.
3. Dale Pendell, *Pharmako/poeia: The Salvia divinorum chapter*, sagewisdom.org/pharmakopoeia.
4. Kathleen Harrison, *The Leaves of the Shepherdess*, sagewisdom.org/shepherdess.
5. Dale Pendell, Ibid.
6. McKenna, *Food of the Gods*, 163
7. Michael R. Aldrich, in Bey and Zug, *Orgies of the Hemp Eaters*, 114.

8. in Rowan Robinson, *The Great Book of Hemp*, 87.
9. Ibid, 92.
10. Bey and Zug, 47.
11. *Ibid.*, 15.
12. Dr. Dennis McKenna, speaking at the *Fourth Annual Amazonian Shamanism Conference*, Iquitos, Peru, July 19-29, 2008.

Bibliography

Adamson, Sophia. *Through the Gateway of the Heart*. San Francisco: Four Trees Publications. 1985.

Badiner, Allan Hunt, and Alex Grey. *Zig Zag Zen: Buddhism and Psychedelics*. San Francisco: Chronicle Books. 2002.

Bache, Christopher M. *Dark Night Early Dawn : steps to a deep ecology of mind*. Albany NY: State University of New York Press, 2000.

Ball, Martin W.. *Mushroom Wisdom*. Oakland CA: Ronin Publishing, 2006.

— — —. *Sage Spirit: Salvia Divinorum and the Entheogenic Experience*. Goleta CA: Kyandara Publishing, 2007.

Bello, Joan. *The Benefits of Marijuana: Physical, Spiritual, and Psychological*. Cottonwood CA: Sweetlight Books, 1996.

Bey, Hakim, and Abel Zug. *Orgies of the Hemp Eaters*. Brooklyn: Autonomedia. 2004

Brown, Joseph Epes. *The Sacred Pipe*. Norman OK: University of Oklahoma Press, 1953.

Black Elk, Wallace, and William S. Lyon. *The Sacred Way of a Lakota*. New York: HarperCollins, 1990.

Calleman, Carl Johan. *The Mayan Calendar and the Transformation of Consciousness*. Rochester VT: Bear and Company, 2004.

Carey, Ken. *The Third Millennium: Living in the Posthistoric World*. New York: HarperCollins, 1996.

— — —. *Vision*. New York: HarperCollins, 1992

de Alverga, Alex P. *Forest of Visions*. Rochester VT: Park Street Press, 1999

Dick, Philip K. *Valis*. New York: Bantam, 1981.

Eisler, Riane. *The Chalice and the Blade: Our History, Our Future*. New York: HarperCollins, 1988.

Fitzgerald, Michael Oren, ed. *Light on the Indian World: The Essential Writings of Charles Eastman (Ohiyesa)*. Bloomington IN: World Wisdom, 2002.

Fitzgerald, Judith, and Michael Oren Fitzgerald, ed. *The Spirit of Indian Women*. Bloomington IN: World Wisdom, 2005.

Fernandez, James W. *Bwiti: an Ethnography of the Religious Imagination in Africa*. Princeton University Press, 1982. (online version at ibogain.org/fernandez).

Forte, Robert ed. *Entheogens and the Future of Religion*. San Francisco: Council on Spiritual Practices, 1997.

Golas, Thaddeus. *The Lazy Man's Guide to Enlightenment*, Layton Utah: Gibbs Smith, 1995. (originally published by the author in 1972, Seeds 1972, and Bantam 1980 with a much different introduction)

Grob, Charles S., ed. *Hallucinogens*. New York: Tarcher/Putnam, 2002.

Harpignies, J.P. (ed.). *Visionary Plant Consciousness*. Rochester VT: Park Street Press. 2007

Holland, Julie. *Ecstasy: The Complete Guide*. Rochester VT: Park Street Press, 2001.

Jung, Carl. *Memories, Dreams, Reflections*. New York: Random House, 1961.

La Barre, Weston. *The Peyote Cult*. New Haven CT: The Shoe String Press, 1976, (first published in 1938).

Ladinsky, Daniel. *The Gift*. New York: Penguin Group, 1999.

Loy, David R. *The Great Awakening: A Buddhist Social Theory*. Boston: Wisdom Publications, 2003.

Lyttle, Thomas, ed. *Psychedelics Reimagined*. Brooklyn NY: Autonomedia, 1999.

McKenna, Terence. *Food of the Gods: The Search for the Original Tree of Knowledge - A Radical History of Plants, Drugs, and Human*

Evolution. New York: Bantam, 1992

— — —. *The Archaic Revival,* New York, HarperCollins, 1992.

Metzner, Ralph, ed. *Ayahuasca: Hallucinogens, Consciousness, and the Spirit of Nature.* New York: Thunder's Mouth Press. 1999

— — —. *Sacred Mushroom of Visions: Teonanácatl.* Rochester VT: Park Street Press, 2005.

Mount, Guy, ed. *The Peyote Book: A Study of Native Medicine.* 3rd edition, Cottonwood CA: Sweetlight Books, 1993.

Moyne, John, and Coleman Barks. *Unseen Rain: Quatrains of Rumi.* Putney VT: Threshold Books, 1986.

Narby, Jeremy. *Intelligence in Nature.* New York: Penguin Group, 2005.

Pinchbeck, Daniel. *Breaking Open the Head.* New York: Broadway Books, 2002.

— — —. *2012: The Return of Quetzalcoatl.* New York: Penguin Group, 2006

Prechtel, Martín. *Long Life, Honey in the Heart.* New York: Tarcher, 2001.

— — —. *Secrets of the Talking Jaguar.* New York: Tarcher/Putnam, 1998.

Rätsch, Christian. *Marijuana Medicine.* Rochester VT: Healing Arts Press. 2001.

Ravalec, Vincent, Mallendi, and Agnès Paicheler. *Iboga: The Visionary Root of African Shamanism.* Rochester VT: Park Street Press, translated by Jack Cain, English translation copyright © 2007 by Inner Traditions International. Originally published in French under the title *Bois Sacré: Initiation à l'iboga,* 2004.

Shanon, Benny. *The Antipodes of the Mind: Charting the Phenomenology of the Ayahuasca Experience.* New York: Oxford University Press, 2002.

Smith, Huston. *Cleansing the Doors of Perception: The Religious Significance of Entheogenic Plants and Chemicals.* New York: Tarcher/Penguin Putnam, 2000.

Smith, Huston, and Reuben Snake (ed.). *One Nation Under God: The Triumph of the Native American Church.* Santa Fe NM: Clear Light Publishers, 1996.

Stamets, Paul. *Psilocybin Mushrooms of the World: An Identification Guide.* Berkeley CA: Ten Speed Press, 1996.

Stevens, Jay. *Storming Heaven: LSD and the American Dream.* New York: Grove Press, 1978.

Suzuki, Shunryu. *Zen Mind, Beginner's MInd.* New York: Weatherhill, 1970.

Tarnas, Richard. *Cosmos and Psyche: Intimations of a New World View.* New York: Viking/Penguin Group, 2006.

Tedlock, Barbara. *The Woman in the Shaman's Body.* New York: BantamDell, 2005.

Tolle, Eckhart. *A New Earth: Awakening to Your Life's Purpose.* New York: Penguin Group, 2005.

Trungpa, Chögyam. *The Art of Calligraphy: Joining Heaven & Earth.* Boston: Shambhala Publications, 1994.

———. *The Collected Works of Chögyam Trungpa, Volume Two.* Boston: Shambhala Publications Inc., 2003.

———. *Shambhala: The Sacred Path of the Warrior.* Boston: Shambhala Publications,1984.

Walsh, Roger, and Charles S. Grob, ed. *Higher Wisdom: Eminent Elders Explore the Continuing Impact of Psychedelics.* Albany: State University of New York Press, 2005.

Wright, Ronald. *Cut Stones and Crossroads: A Journey in the Two Worlds of Peru.* New York: Penguin Books, 1984.

———. *Stolen Continents: 500 Years of Conquest and Resistance in the Americas.* New York: Penguin Group, 1992.

Ywahoo, Dhyani. *Voices of Our Ancestors: Cherokee Teaching from the Wisdom Fire.* Berkeley: Shambhala Publications, 1987.

Zollo, Paul. *Songwriters on Songwriting,* 4th ed. New York: Da Capo Press, 2003.

BOOKS

O is a symbol of the world, of oneness and unity. In different cultures it also means the "eye," symbolizing knowledge and insight. We aim to publish books that are accessible, constructive and that challenge accepted opinion, both that of academia and the "moral majority."

Our books are available in all good English language bookstores worldwide. If you don't see the book on the shelves ask the bookstore to order it for you, quoting the ISBN number and title. Alternatively you can order online (all major online retail sites carry our titles) or contact the distributor in the relevant country, listed on the copyright page.

See our website www.o-books.net for a full list of over 500 titles, growing by 100 a year.

And tune in to myspiritradio.com for our book review radio show, hosted by June-Elleni Laine, where you can listen to the authors discussing their books.